Janet C. E. Watson

Ṣbaḥtū! A Course in Ṣanʿānī Arabic

Semitica Viva · Series Didactica

Herausgegeben von Otto Jastrow

Band 3

1996
Harrassowitz Verlag · Wiesbaden

Janet C. E. Watson

Ṣbaḥtū! A Course in Ṣanʿānī Arabic

1996
Harrassowitz Verlag · Wiesbaden

Publication of this book was supported by a grant from
the Publications Committee of the University of Durham

Die Deutsche Bibliothek – CIP-Einheitsaufnahme

Watson, Janet C. E.:
Ṣbaḥtū! A Course in Ṣanʿānī Arabic. / Janet C. E. Watson. –
Wiesbaden : Harrassowitz, 1996
(Semitica viva : Series didactica ; Bd. 3)
ISBN 3-447-03755-5
NE: Semitica viva / Series didactica

Printing and binding by MZ-Verlagsdruckerei GmbH, Memmingen
Printed in Germany

ISSN 0935-7556
ISBN 3-447-03755-5

To my Godparents, Margaret Ficken,
Chris Knight, and Rita Serjeant

PREFACE

This book is intended primarily for students of Yemeni Arabic. It will also be of interest to Arabic dialectologists and to linguists with a general interest in Arabic. For readers who wish to consider aspects of Ṣan^{c}ānī syntax in more detail frequent reference is made to my *Syntax of Ṣan^{c}ānī Arabic* published in 1993 by Otto Harrassowitz (Semitica Viva).

The book is a complete course in Ṣan^{c}ānī Arabic and can reasonably be used either for self study or in the classroom. It comprises an introduction, twenty lessons with graded exercises, a glossary and an index. The introduction provides the inventory of consonants and vowels in Ṣan^{c}ānī Arabic. The lessons consist of three major sections: dialogue(s) and vocabulary, grammar (and thematic vocabulary), and exercises. The dialogues in lessons 1-7 and 12 are constructed from real text; at least one of the dialogues in each of lessons 8-11 is taken directly from transcriptions of real text; and all the dialogues in lessons 13-20 come directly from real text (though personal names have been changed in some cases). As a result of this the dialogues exhibit typical features of everyday speech: principally repetition, emphasis and elaboration; though, on the whole, hesitations and speech errors have been removed or corrected. The dialogues are largely organised according to cultural themes: for example, in the market; food in Yemen; learning in Yemen; Yemeni houses; Ṣan^{c}ānī games; marriage in Yemen; birth and wedding parties; *gāt* cultivation and *gāt* chewing; the old city; and death and mourning in Yemen. The grammar section takes a semantically orientated view of the syntax, and discusses aspects of pronunciation, set phrases (such as greetings), word structure and word order which are thrown up by the dialogues in any one particular lesson. The thematic vocabulary section provides lists of practical and culturally relevant vocabulary: for example, major towns in Yemen; areas of the market; food and drink; parts of the body; traditional dress in Ṣan^{c}ā'; weddings and births; travel; buildings and places; communications; the house; Yemeni games. The exercises are designed to practice the grammar and the vocabulary of the lesson at hand, and to revise aspects of the grammar and vocabulary from previous lessons. The glossary at the end of the book draws together the 1400 vocabulary items from the dialogues and the thematic vocabulary sections; additional vocabulary used to illustrate grammatical points in the grammar section are only included in the glossary if they are required for the exercises. By the end of the course the reader should have a good grasp of both Ṣan^{c}ānī Arabic and crucial aspects of the culture and cultural norms and expectations.

ACKNOWLEDGEMENTS

This book could not have been produced without the help and cooperation of many people. Firstly, thanks are due to Otto Jastrow for first suggesting that I produce this book to parallel my *Syntax of Ṣan^{c}ānī Arabic*, and for critical, encouraging comments on early and later drafts of the book. Tim Mackintosh-Smith, arguably the best non-Yemeni speaker of Ṣan^{c}ānī Arabic, read and made critical comments on early drafts of the book, and answered my faxes at a later stage; he introduced me to Abd al-Salam al-Amri, the best informant I could have had; with enviable good humour, he also gave myself, my husband, Alistair (5 years) and Sarah (1 year) the run of his house for four weeks over Christmas in 1994 (it could not have been easy!). I owe a debt of gratitude to my Durham students, Matthew Barrett, Patrick Brittenden, Polly Buchanan, Ayesha Garrett, Kirsty Growcott, and Francesca Walton; in 1994-5 they followed this course as it came, often hot off the printer, as an optional part of their degree in Arabic with Middle Eastern Studies. Their enthusiasm, cheerfulness, and, most of all, their apt criticism of my English have greatly improved the readability of the book. Access to informants can make or break a book of this type, so most of all I thank my informants in Yemen and in Britain: the family of Abd al-Rahman al-Kibsi and Ibrahim al-Kibsi, the family and relations of Abd al-Wahhab Muhammad al-Sayrafi, the family of Abd al-Salam Muhammad Tagi, Abd al-Ila al-Haymi, and Khalid al-Thawr. Most particularly I thank Abd al-Salam al-Amri who produced several hours of excellent recordings, and spoke, with only the very barest of prompting, with interest and animation on topics such as death, weddings, the market, Turkish baths, *gāt* production and consumption, and Ramadan. Almost all of the dialogues in lessons 15, 16, 18, 19 and 20 have been taken directly from recordings made by Abd al-Salam in Ṣan^{c}ā' in December 1994 - January 1995. His acute awareness of his own dialect, his linguistic sensitivity, and his knowledge and interest in Yemeni culture have provided this book with some wonderful texts.

For practical help and encouragement at various times in the course of writing this book I also thank Dick Hayward, Tim Niblock, and Mr and Mrs Anthony Lewis (now Director of the British Council in Riyadh). Thanks in particular to the publications committee at Durham University for providing a publication subvention for the book.

Finally, many thanks to my husband, James Dickins, for discussing aspects of the book, and for accompanying me to Yemen in 1994 and helping me to collect data.

CONTENTS

LESSON 2 *B-ismiš?* What is your f.s. name?

LESSON 3 *Man hū hāḏā?* Who is that?

LESSON 5 *Fi s-sūg* In the market

LESSON 6 *Fi l-maṭ^{c}am* In the restaurant

Grammar

Thematic Vocabulary

Exercises

LESSON 7 *Mā tsawway ġudwuh?* What are you f.s. doing tomorrow?

Grammar

LESSON 18 *Al-gāt fī l-yaman*

LESSON 19 *Al-madīni l-gadīmih*

LESSON 20 *Al-mawt wa-l-ᶜazzā*

INTRODUCTION

Sounds of Ṣanᶜānī Arabic

1.1. Consonants

There are twenty-eight consonant sounds in Ṣanᶜānī Arabic. These are given in the left-hand column below. Of these sounds, five do not correspond to sounds in any dialects of English. The description of the pronunciation of the sounds is provided in the right-hand column:

'	glottal stop,[1] as in Cockney *t* in *bottle*.
b	voiced bilabial stop, as in *b* in *bat*.
t	voiceless alveolar stop, as in *t* in *tap*.
ṯ	voiceless interdental fricative,[2] as in *th* in *thin*.
j	voiced alveo-palatal affricate,[3] as in *J* in *Jane*.
ḥ	voiceless pharyngeal fricative, no English equivalent, but resembles the sound made when you clean glasses.
x	voiceless velar fricative, as in Scottish *ch* in *loch*.
d	voiced alveolar stop, as in *d* in *deed*.
ḏ	voiced interdental fricative, as in *th* in *these*.
r	voiced alveolar tap, as in *r* in rhotic dialects of English.
z	voiced alveolar fricative, as in *z* in *zoo*.
s	voiceless alveolar fricative, as in *s* in *seam*.
š	voiceless alveo-palatal fricative, as in *sh* in *shame*.
ṣ	voiceless pharyngealised alveolar fricative (emphatic); no equivalent in English. The tip of the tongue makes loose contact with the alveolar ridge, while the body of the tongue hollows and the back of the tongue retracts towards the pharynx.
ḍ	voiced pharyngealised interdental fricative (emphatic);[4] no equivalent in English. The tip of the tongue is placed between the teeth, while the body of the tongue hollows and the back of the tongue retracts towards the pharynx.

---

[1] The pronunciation of Arabic *hamza* is ['], as in standard Arabic and most dialects of Arabic. Ṣanᶜānī ['] contrasts with the voiced pharyngeal pronunciation [ᶜ] found in many dialects spoken in the South-East of North Yemen.

[2] The voiceless and voiced interdental fricatives *ṯ* and *ḏ* are maintained as fricatives as in standard Arabic and as in other dialects of the Peninsula, but in contrast to Cairene and Levantine Arabic.

[3] The voiced alveo-palatal affricate *j* is pronounced as [j] as in standard Arabic, Bedouin dialects of the Peninsula and Central Sudanese Arabic, but in contrast to the voiced velar stop [g] of Cairene, the Hugariyyah (southern North Yemen) and parts of South Yemen.

[4] As in most other modern dialects of Arabic, the Arabic sounds *ḍād* and *ḍā'* are pronounced identically. Since fricatives are maintained in Ṣanᶜānī, the sound is pronounced as both emphatic and fricative - [ḏ̣].

ṭ voiceless pharyngealised alveolar stop (emphatic); no equivalent in English. The tip of the tongue makes firm contact with the alveolar ridge, while the body of the tongue hollows and the back of the tongue retracts towards the pharynx.

ᶜ voiced pharyngeal approximant;[5] no equivalent in English. In pronouncing this sound, the mouth is open, and the back of the tongue retracts towards the pharynx. It is similar to the sound made in retching.

ġ voiced velar fricative,[6] similar to Parisian *r* in *Paris,* and as in Northumbrian *r* in *great*; there is no equivalent in most dialects of English.

f voiceless labio-dental fricative, as in *f* in *fish*.

g voiced velar stop,[7] as in *g* in *gold*.

k voiceless velar stop, as in *k* in *kick*, and *c* in *cot*.

l voiced lateral, as in *l* in *lady*.

m voiced bilabial nasal, as in *m* in *mother*.

n voiced alveolar nasal, as in *n* in *nose*.

h voiceless laryngeal fricative, as in *h* in *here*.

w voiced labio-velar approximant, as in *w* in *weather*.

y voiced palatal approximant, as in *y* in *yes*.

1.2. Vowels

There are three short vowels in Ṣanᶜānī. These are given in the left-hand column below:

a open vowel, as in *a* in *bad* and occasionally as in *e* in *bed*.

u close, back, rounded vowel, as in *oo* in *good*, and *u* in *put*.

i close, palatal vowel, as in *i* in *bin*.

Note, however, that when they are unstressed all of these vowels can be pronounced as a shwa as in *a* in English *against* or *about*.

[5] The pronunciation of *ᶜayn* is [ᶜ], as in standard Arabic and most modern dialects of Arabic. Ṣanᶜānī [ᶜ] contrasts with ['] of dialects spoken in the Tihāmah (the coastal region of North Yemen). In these latter dialects, there is no contrast between the sounds *ᶜayn* and *hamza*.

[6] The pronunciation of Arabic *ġayn* is [ġ], as in standard Arabic and most modern dialects of Arabic. Ṣanᶜānī [ġ] does, however, contrast with ['] and [ᶜ] of dialects spoken on the eastern edge of the Tihāmah . In these latter dialects, there is no distinction between *ᶜayn* and *ġayn*, nor, in many cases, between *ᶜayn, ġayn* and *hamza*.

[7] The pronunciation of the Arabic sound *qāf* is [g], which makes it the voiced counterpart of *k*. The [j]-[g] pair for Arabic *jīm* and *qāf* is a typical feature of Bedouin dialects. [g] contrasts with standard Arabic [q], with [q] of many mountain dialects of Yemen and of southern Yemen, with [ġ] of some western dialects of Yemen and with ['] of Cairene Arabic and urban Levantine dialects.

There are three long vowels in Ṣanᶜānī Arabic; these are:

ā open vowel with two possible pronunciations or allophones: an open back sound, as in *ea* in *heart*, and an open front sound, as in *ea* in *bear*.
ū close, back, rounded vowel, as in *u* in *rude*.
ī close, palatal vowel, as in *ee* in *been*.

There are two closing diphthongs in Ṣanᶜānī Arabic; these are:

aw pronunciation varies between *ow* in *how*, and *oh* in *oh!*
ay pronunciation varies between *igh* in *high*, and *ay* in *say*.

1.3. Pronunciation practice: consonants

This section provides pronunciation practice of the consonantal sounds given in section 1.1. above. In order to highlight the similarities and differences sounds in Ṣanᶜānī Arabic have with English, the consonants are grouped into six categories: 1.3.1. sounds which resemble English sounds; 1.3.2. emphatics; 1.3.3. emphatics in contrast with non-emphatics; 1.3.4. other sounds; 1.3.5. other sounds in contrast with sounds similar to English sounds, and 1.3.6. semi-vowels. Sections 1.3.1., 1.3.2. 1.3.4. and 1.3.6. consider the sounds in three positions within the word: initial, medial (between vowels) and final.

1.3.1. *Sounds which resemble English sounds*

Most of the consonantal sounds in Ṣanᶜānī Arabic are similar to sounds found in mainstream dialects of English. Read the following words and produce the sounds given in initial, medial and final position in the word. Most of the words given in these sections are words currently found in Ṣanᶜānī Arabic.

sound	initial	meaning	medial	meaning	final	meaning
ʾ	*'ayn*	where	*ra's*	head	*bā'*	[letter *b*]
b	*bayt*	house	*šibiḥ*	to seize	*bāb*	door
t	*tār*	to be crumbled	*fataḥ*	to open	*bāt*	to spend the night
ṯ	*ṯār*	to rise up	*ᶜaṯar*	to trip	*lāṯ*	to cause havoc
j	*jār*	neighbour	*sajjal*	to record	*rāj*	to undulate
d	*dār*	house	*badal*	instead of	*zād*	to do more

ḏ	*ḏall*	to fear	*šaḏab*	rue	*laḏīḏ*	delicious
r	*rāḥ*	to go	*ḍarab*	to hit	*sār*	to go
z	*zār*	to visit	*ᶜazzam*	to invite	*bayz*	lie
s	*sār*	to go	*yisīr*	he goes	*nās*	men; people
š	*šār*	to advise	*bašar*	to tell good news	*bahš*	type of fruit
f	*fār*	mouse	*lafat*	to turn	*šāf*	to see
g	*gatal*	to kill	*fagar*	to be poor	*rāg*	to exude liquid
k	*kān*	to be	*fakkar*	to think	*sakk*	to lock
l	*lisān*	tongue	*falax*	to open o.'s arms	*gāl*	to say
m	*māt*	to die	*yimūt*	he dies	*summ*	poison
n	*nār*	fire; hell	*banā*	to build	*bayn*	between
h	*hāt*	give!	*bahal*	to welcome	*šabīh*	resembling

1.3.2. *Emphatics*

There are three emphatic sounds in Ṣanᶜānī Arabic. These three sounds involve two points of articulation, one of which is the pharynx, and they are often described as *pharyngealised* consonants. In this section I also include the voiceless pharyngeal fricative *ḥ* because it is felt to be the emphatic counterpart of *h*. Notice that when an emphatic sound comes before or after long *ā*, the *ā* sound is pronounced like *ea* in *heart* and not like *ea* in *bear* as is the case before or after non-emphatic sounds. Emphatic consonants are often said to 'darken' the sound of surrounding vowels.

sound	initial	meaning	medial	meaning	final	meaning
ḥ	*ḥāmī*	hot	*baḥaš*	rough	*šibiḥ*	to seize
ṣ	*ṣām*	to fast	*ᶜaṣam*	to immunise	*bāṣ*	bus
ḍ	*ḍayf*	guest	*ḥaḍar*	to come to s.o.	*bayḍ*	eggs
ṭ	*ṭāᶜ*	to accept	*ᶜaṭaš*	thirst	*fallaṭ*	to leave

1.3.3. *Pronunciation contrasts: emphatics versus non-emphatics*

It is very important to be able to produce and recognise the difference between an emphatic sound and its non-emphatic counterpart, since in any one context an emphatic sound may produce a word with a different meaning to a non-emphatic sound. In this section four emphatic - non-emphatic minimal pairs are given:

emphatic	meaning	non-emphatic	meaning
ḥawā	Eve	*hawā*	air
ṣār	to become	*sār*	to go
ḍalīl	shady	*ḏalīl*	despicable
ṭīn	mud	*tīn*	figs

1.3.4. *Other sounds*

There are three consonantal sounds which are neither strictly emphatic, nor similar to sounds found in mainstream English dialects. These sounds are given in initial, medial and final position.

sound	initial	meaning	medial	meaning	final	meaning
x	*xarr*	to get out of the way	*bi-xayr*	well	*māx*	to cool down
c	*cār*	shame	*ṭacam*	taste	*sāc*	like
ġ	*ġārih*	attack, raid	*ṭaġā*	to seduce	*muṣāġ*	alloyed silver

1.3.5. *Pronunciation contrasts: other sounds versus sounds similar to English sounds*

The three sounds given above can be mistaken by English speakers for sounds which are similar to sounds in English. It is important to make a clear distinction between, for example, *x* and *k*, *x* and *h*, *ġ* and *g*, and *g* and *r*, since the first of these pairs will often produce a word with a different meaning to the second of the pair. In this section five (near) minimal pairs are given.

word	meaning	word	meaning
xāl	maternal uncle	*kāl*	to measure out
xilāl	during	*hilāl*	crescent
cayn	eye	*'ayn*	where
ġayl	river	*gayl*	talk
ġāb	to be absent	*rāb*	to curdle (milk)

It is also important to produce a clear difference between the voiced and the voiceless velar fricatives, *x* and *ġ*. Consider the following minimal pairs:

word	meaning	word	meaning
ġālī	expensive	*xālī*	my maternal uncle
ġarr	only	*xarr*	to get out of the way

1.3.6. *Semi-vowels*

There are two semi-vowels in Ṣanᶜānī Arabic: *w* and *y*. The pronunciation of Ṣanᶜānī *w* and *y* is similar to English *w* and *y*. In this section, *w* and *y* are given in initial, medial and final position in the word:

sound	initial	meaning	medial	meaning	final	meaning
w	*wār*	yard	*ᶜawal*	to bring forth children	*ḏ̣aww*	light
y	*yā*	oh!	*bahāyih*	brightness	*zayy*	shape

1.3.7. *Long consonants*

All consonants in Ṣanᶜānī Arabic can be either short or long. The length of long consonants is approximately twice the length of short consonants. Long consonants are transcribed as double consonants, as in the letters in **bold** in the following words:

*a**s**-**s**altih*	fenugreek broth	*muwa**ḏ̣ḏ̣**af*	employee
*ḏ̣a**ww***	light	*ᶜi**yy**āl*	children
*muṭa**ll**ib*	beggar		

Doubled *voiced* stops (i.e. *d, g, b*) and *j* are often *devoiced*, that is to say they are pronounced as something approaching *t, k, p,* and *č* respectively (*Syntax* p. 10) to give:

*ḥa**kk*** or *ḥa**gg*** for *ḥa**gg***	right, possession; of
*ḏu**pp**ī* or *ḏu**bb**ī* for *ḏu**bb**ī*	fly
*ba**tt**al* or *ba**dd**al* for *ba**dd**al*	he changed (s.th.)

As in *Syntax of Ṣanᶜānī Arabic* (*Syntax* p. 9), the sounds *d, g, b* and *j* are written as *d, g, b* and *j* in this book irrespective of whether their pronunciation in context is nearer to *d, g, b* and *j* or to *t, k, p* and *č*.

1.3.8. *Initial and intervocalic ṭ and t*

For the sake of comprehension, it is particularly important for the learner to note the voiced pronunciation of the sound *ṭ* both at the beginning of a sentence and between vowels. The following words on the left have the pronunciation given on the right (the voiced consonant is given in **bold**):

ṭayyib	***ḍ**ayyib*	good
ṭalī	***ḍ**alī*	sheep

The sound *t* is also pronounced with voice (that is to say, as *d*) in the imperfect prefixes when the word comes at the beginning of a sentence or after a vowel:

tištī	***d**ištī*	you m.s. want
lā tinsāš	*lā **d**insāš*	don't m.s. forget!
bi-tibkay	*bi-**d**ibkay*	you f.s. cry

As in *Syntax of Ṣanᶜānī Arabic* (*Syntax* p. 9), *t* and *ṭ* are written as *t* and *ṭ* in this book, irrespective of whether their pronunciation in context is *t* or *d, ṭ* or *ḍ*.

1.4. Pronunciation practice: vowels

This section provides pronunciation practice of the vocalic sounds given in section 1.2. above. Since the actual pronunciation of the vowels in Ṣanᶜānī Arabic poses no problems for the English speaker, here we are simply concerned with looking at contrasts between the short vowels (1.4.1.), between the long vowels (1.4.2.), and between short and corresponding long vowels (1.4.3.).

1.4.1. *Short vowels*

The three short vowels contrast in the following words:

badd	he mitigated	*yibidd*	he mitigates	*budd*	way out

1.4.2. *Long vowels*

The three long vowels contrast in the following words:

jār	neighbour	*jīrān*	neighbours	*jūrih*	refuge

1.4.3. *Short vowels versus long vowels*

The following (near) minimal pairs illustrate the potential meaning difference between short vowels and their long counterparts:

ḥanaš	snake	*ḥināš*	snakes
dimm	cat	*dīn*	religion
yidugg	he knocks	*yidūg*	he is noisy
ṣuwar	pictures	*ṣūruh*	picture

1.5. **Abbreviations**

The following abbreviations are used in the book:

n.	noun	v.	verb
adv.	adverb	adj.	adjective
adjt.	adjunction	conj.	conjunction
p.	particle	prep.	preposition
def.	definite	indef.	indefinite
f.	feminine	m.	masculine
o.a.	one another	o.s.	oneself
pl.	plural	sg.	singular
s.o.	someone	s.th.	something
1.	first person (I/we)	2.	second person (you)
3.	third person (s/he/they)		

LESSON 1

Kayf al-ḥāl How are you?

Dialogue

A: *ṣbaḥtū*	Good morning.
B: *ṣabbaḥkum allāh bi-l-xayr*	Good morning.
A: *kayf al-ḥāl*	How are you?
B: *al-ḥamdu li-llāh bi-xayr kayf ḥālukum*	Thanks be to God, well. How are you m.s.?
A: *al-ḥamdu li-llāh*	Thanks be to God.
B: *ma^c as-salāmih*	Goodbye.
A: *fī 'aman illāh*	Goodbye.

Vocabulary

al-ḥāl	the state	*al-ḥamd*	thanks; praise
allāh	God	*aman*	security
bi-xayr	well	*fī*	in
ḥālukum	your (m.pl.) state	*kayf*	how
ma^{c}	with	*salāmih*	peace
ṣabbaḥkum	lit: he made you wake up	*ṣbaḥtū*	lit: you (m.pl.) woke up

Grammar

1. *Pronunciation: consonant clusters*

Sequences of two (or even more) initial consonants are common in Ṣan^{c}ānī Arabic, in particular in verbal forms with a consonant-initial pronoun suffix, as in *ṣbaḥ**tū*** above, where the pronoun suffix is ***tū***. Some of these consonant sequences are difficult for English speakers to produce when they involve sequences of sounds which are not found in English. Practice pronouncing the consonant sequences in the following words:

ktabt	'I wrote'
jlastī	'you f.s. sat down'
hribt	'I fled'
tštī	'you m.s. want'

2. *Masculine plural in greetings*

As in other dialects of Yemeni Arabic, there are a large number of *fixed* greetings which are used in a variety of situations in Ṣanᶜānī Arabic. In fixed greetings, the verb is always in the masculine plural form, irrespective of whether one or more people are being addressed, and whether the addressee is female or male. The pronoun suffix is also in the masculine plural form in fixed greetings, such as *as-salām ᶜalay**kum*** 'lit: may peace be upon you m.pl.'. It is often in the masculine plural form in less fixed greetings, such as *kayf ḥālu**kum*** 'lit: how is your m.pl. state' in the dialogue above, and in this case is used as a sign of respect (cf. *Syntax* p. 102, p. 105). Between friends and younger people, however, the pronoun suffix usually inflects for number and gender, as shown in Lesson 2 below.

Exercise

Role Play

With a partner, take the role of first speaker A, and then speaker B. Take particular care in the pronunciation of the emphatic sounds, long vowels and long (doubled) consonants.

LESSON 2

B-ismiš **What is your f.s. name?**

Dialogue

Khadija: *salām ^{c}alaykum.*	Hello.
Samira: *^{c}alaykum as-salām.*	Hello.
Khadija: *anā smī xadījih, w-antī b-ismiš?*	My name is Khadija. What is your f.s. name?
Samira: *anā smī samīrih.*	My name is Samira.
Khadija: *kayf ḥāliš yā samīrih?*	How are you, Samira?
Samira: *al-ḥamdu li-llāh anā bi-xayr, w-antī yā xadījih kayf al-ḥāl?*	Thanks be to God, I am well. And you f.s., Khadija, how are you?
Khadija: *bi-xayr wa-l-ḥamdu l-illāh.*	Well, thanks to God.
Samira: *ma^{c} as-salāmih.*	Goodbye.
Khadija: *allāh yisallimiš.*	Goodbye.

Vocabulary

^{c}alaykum	lit: on you (m.pl.)	*anā*	I
antī	you (f.s.)	*b-ismiš*	what is your (f.s.) name?
ḥāliš	your (f.s.) state (m.)	*ibn*	son (m.)
(i)smī	my name (m.)	*salām*	peace (m.)
samīrih	Samira [female name]	*w(a)*	and
xadījih	Khadija [female name]	*yā*	[vocative particle]
yisallimiš	lit: may he give you (f.s.) peace		

Grammar

1. *Pronunciation: elision of vowels*

When a word ending in a vowel comes before a word beginning with a vowel the second vowel is not pronounced. Thus *anā ismī* 'I, my name' is pronounced as in the dialogue as *anā smī*, and *antī ismiš* 'you f.s., your name' is pronounced as *anti smiš*.

The word for 'what?' in Ṣanᶜānī Arabic is *mā* (cf. Lesson 3) When this word occurs before *ism*, however, the *m* is pronounced as [*b*] and the vowel of the question word is elided, as shown in the dialogue. This is an isolated, frozen instance of *dissimilation* where the initial *m* becomes dissimilar to the *m* in the following word.

2. *Personal pronouns*

Personal pronouns in Ṣanᶜānī Arabic are either independent or dependent: *independent* pronouns function as independent words, while *dependent* pronouns are suffixed (or annexed) to the noun, preposition or verb. Dependent pronouns function as *possessive* pronouns when suffixed to a noun or preposition, and as *object* pronouns when suffixed to a verb. In this section, I shall deal with possessive pronouns. Dependent pronouns cannot be stressed. Where it is necessary to stress a possessive or object pronoun, the dependent pronoun is followed by the appropriate independent pronoun, as in:

b-ismiš antī	'what is *your f.s.* name?'
b-ismih hū	'what is *his* name?'

The complete set of possessive pronouns is:

	singular	plural
1.	*-ī*	*-nā*
2. m.	*-ak*	*-kum*
2. f.	*-iš*	*-kin*
3. m.	*-ih*	*-hum*
3. f.	*-hā*	*-hin*

When a pronoun with an initial consonant is suffixed to a noun or preposition which ends in two consonants or a long vowel or diphthong and a consonant, an initial vowel is pronounced between the noun and the pronoun to facilitate pronunciation, as in *ḥālukum* 'your m.pl. state' given in the dialogue in Lesson 1. This vowel is often pronounced as *u* when the pronoun has an *u* vowel, as in *kum*, and as *a* or shwa (as in *a* in English *about*) when the pronoun has the vowel *i* or *a*.

The complete set of independent pronouns is:

	singular	plural
1.	*anā*	*iḥna*
2. m.	*ant*	*antū*
2. f.	*antī*	*antayn*
3. m.	*hū*	*hum*
3. f.	*hī*	*hin*

3. *Greetings*

In greetings the initial greeting always takes a different form, however slightly, to the replying greeting. In the greeting in this dialogue the word order changes between the initial greeting and the reply. In the first greeting in Lesson 1, a different verb form is used in the reply, and the word *allāh* 'God' is added. When the speakers take their leave at the end of the dialogue in Lesson 1, the reply uses an entirely different structure to the initial greeting. When the speakers take their leave in the dialogue in this lesson, however, the verb in the reply (*yisallimiš*) is similar to the noun in the initial greeting (*as-salāmih*).

4. *Sentences*

A sentence consists of a *subject* (or predicand) and a *predicate*. The subject is the topic of the sentence while the predicate says something about the subject. In simple sentences of the type in the dialogues in Lessons 1 and 2, the subject and predicate are linked without a word like 'is' or 'are', as in:

	subject		predicate	sentence
	ismī	+	*jamīlih*	*ismī jamīlih*
	'name-my'		'Jamila'	'my name is Jamila'
and				
	hū	+	*bi-xayr*	*hū bi-xayr*
	'he'		'well'	'he is well'

Sentences which begin with a noun subject are called *nominal* sentences (cf. *Syntax* p. 97).

Exercises

1. *Possessive pronouns*

Complete the following table adding the correct possessive pronoun, with a linking vowel where necessary, to the nouns *ism* 'name', *ḥāl* 'state' and *ibn* 'boy; son'. The top left-hand corner of the table is completed by way of example:

	ism	*ḥāl*	*ibn*
anā	*ismī*		
ant			
antī			
antayn			
hum			

2. *Gender change*

Re-read the dialogue at the beginning of this lesson, changing the feminine names Khadija and Samira to the masculine names Muhammad and Najib, making all necessary gender changes to the pronouns.

3. *Number change*

Read the following sentences once out loud, then replace all singular pronouns with the corresponding plural pronoun.

Example: *kayf ḥālak* ————> *kayf ḥālukum*

A.

i. *kayf ḥāliš?*

ii. *kayf ḥālih?*

iii. *kayf ḥālahā?*

iv. *kayf ḥālak?*

B.

i. *b-ismih hū?*

ii. *b-ismahā hī?*

iii. *b-ismiš antī?*

iv. *b-ismak ant?*

LESSON 3

Man hū hāḏā? Who is that?

Dialogue 1 *man hū hāḏā?*

Khadija: *man hū hāḏa l-wald?*

Samira: *hāḏā bnī.*

Khadija: *ibniš b-ismih?*

Samira: *hū smih ṣāluḥ.*

Khadija: *wa-man hī hāḏi l-marih?*

Samira: *hāḏī xālatī jīhān.*

Khadija: *wa-man hī hāḏī?*

Samira: *hāḏī 'ummī.*

Khadija: *wa-man hū l-ax?*

Samira: *hāḏā 'axī mḥammad.*

Dialogue 2 *mā hū hāḏā?*

James: *mā hū hāḏā yā mḥammad?*

Muhammad: *hāḏā saltih.*

James: *wa-kayf as-saltih?*

Muhammad: *as-saltih ḥāliyih.*

James: *mā hū hāḏā?*

Muhammad: *hāḏā mšamma*^{c} *mlawwan.*

James: *wa-mā hū hāḏā?*

Muhammad: *hāḏā jāhil zaġīr.*

Vocabulary

al-	the [definite article]	*al-ax*	(the) brother (m.)
al-marih	the woman; the wife (f.)	*al-wald*	the boy (m.)
axī	my brother (m.)	*hāḏā*	this (m.)

ḥāliyih	nice (f.s.)	*jāhil*	child (m.)
jīhān	Jihan [female name]	*mā*	what
man	who	*mlawwan*	coloured (m.s.)
mšamma^c	plastic sheet (m.)	*ṣāluḥ*	Salih [male name]
saltih	Yemeni broth with meat and fenugreek (f.)	*ummī*	my mother (f.)
xālatī	my (maternal) aunt (f.)	*zaġīr/zġīr*	small; young (m.s.)

Grammar

1. *Pronunciation: elision of vowel of definite article*

When a word ending in a long vowel comes before the definite article *al-*, the *a* of the article is not pronounced, and the long vowel is shortened to ease pronunciation, as in:

hāḏā	+	*al-wald*	*hāḏa l-wald*
'this'		'the-boy'	'this boy'

2. *Demonstrative pronouns: near demonstratives*

There are two sets of near demonstrative pronouns in Ṣan^{c}ānī Arabic: those which take initial *hā-*, and those which do not. In this section I am concerned only with the demonstratives which take initial *hā-*. There are three demonstrative pronouns: singular masculine and feminine, and plural. There is no gender distinction in the plural demonstrative pronoun:

	singular	plural
m.	*hāḏā*	*hāḏawlā / hāwlā*
f.	*hāḏī*	

3. *The definite article*

Nouns are basically indefinite in Arabic (as in English), and become definite in one of three ways: either by suffixing a possessive pronoun, as seen in Lessons 1 and 2:

noun		pronoun	
ism	+	*-ī*	*ismī*
'name'		'my'	'my name'

or by annexing a definite noun *annex* (cf. Lesson 8), as in *al-marih* 'the woman' in:

noun		annex	
bayt	+	*al-marih*	*bayt al-marih*
'house'		'the-woman'	'the woman's house'

or by the definite article *al-*, as in:

article		noun	
al-	+	*bayt*	*al-bayt*
'the'		'house'	'the house'

Note that, unlike English 'the', the definite article *al-* cannot stand alone. It must be attached to a noun. Like dependent pronouns (cf. Lesson 2), it cannot normally be stressed.

3.1. *Assimilation of the definite article*

When the definite article occurs with a noun of which the first consonant is a *coronal* sound - that is to say, a sound made in the region between the teeth and the area of the mouth just in front of the palate: *ṯ, ḏ, t, d, n, ṭ, ḍ, ṣ, s, z, r, l, š* - the *l* of the article assimilates totally to the following consonant to produce a geminate (*doubled*, or *long*) consonant (cf. Introduction), as in:

al	+	*ṯawr*	> *aṯ-ṯawr*	'the bull'
al	+	*daymih*	> *ad-daymih*	'the kitchen'
al	+	*ḍayf*	> *aḍ-ḍayf*	'the guest'
al	+	*nār*	> *an-nār*	'the fire'
al	+	*sayyārih*	> *as-sayyārih*	'the car'
al	+	*zawj*	> *az-zawj*	'the husband'
al	+	*ṭālub*	> *aṭ-ṭālub*	'the student'
al	+	*šams*	> *aš-šams*	'the sun'

When the definite article occurs before a noun which takes an initial vowel the *l*-

of the article is usually doubled, as in:

al	+	*umm*	*al-lumm*	'the mother'
al	+	*ism*	*al-lism*	'the name'

4. *'This house': demonstrative plus noun*

In order to say 'this house' 'this woman', etc. in Ṣanᶜānī Arabic, the demonstrative pronoun usually (but cf. Lesson 5) occurs before the noun (as in English), but differs from English in that the noun retains the definite article:

demonstrative	noun	
hāḏā	*al-bayt*	*hāḏa l-bayt*
'this'	'the-house'	'this house'

When the noun is masculine singular, as in *al-bayt* 'the house' the demonstrative is masculine singular:

demonstrative	noun	
hāḏā	*al-bayt*	*hāḏa l-bayt*
'this m.'	'the-house'	'this house'

When the noun is animate (i.e. human) plural, the demonstrative is plural:

demonstrative	noun	
hāḏawlā	*an-nās*	*hāḏawla n-nās*
'these'	'the-people'	'these people'

When the noun is feminine singular, however, the demonstrative may be either feminine singular or, more commonly, masculine singular:

demonstrative	noun	
hāḏī	*al-marih*	*hāḏi l-marih*
'this f.'	'the-woman'	'this woman'

or

hāḏā	*al-marih*	*hāḏa l-marih*
'this m.'	'the-woman'	'this woman'

Finally, when the noun is a plural inanimate (i.e. non-human) noun, the demonstrative is either feminine singular, when the noun refers to a *collectivity*, or plural when the noun refers to *separate, distinct* entities (cf. Lesson 4):

demonstrative	noun	
hāḏī	*al-liyyām*	*hāḏi l-liyyām*
'this f.'	'the-days'	'these days'

or

hāḏawlā	*aṭ-ṭuyūr*	*hāḏawla ṭ-ṭuyūr*
'these'	'the-birds'	'these birds'

5. *Agreement: gender*

5.1. Nouns

There are two genders in Ṣanᶜānī Arabic: *masculine* and *feminine*. Nouns do not inflect for gender, but are inherently either masculine or feminine, and occasionally both. In this book, feminine nouns are marked in the vocabulary list by f. after the gloss, and masculine nouns by m. after the gloss, as in:

bint	girl f.	*wald*	boy m.
dār	house f.	*bayt*	house m.

Where a noun can be either feminine or masculine the noun is marked by m./f. after the gloss, as in:

sūg	market m./f.	*ṭarīg*	road m./f.

As in most languages, masculine is considered to be the normal, or unmarked, gender. Basic feminine nouns fall into a number of categories including: female humans - *bint* 'girl', *marih* 'woman', female animals - *bagarih* 'cow', *faras* 'mare', parts of the body which occur in pairs - *ᶜayn* 'eye', *rijl* 'leg', and many religious concepts - *dunyā* 'world', *nār* 'hell'. For further examples, see *Syntax* p. 24. Most feminine nouns take the feminine ending *-ih*:

*mar**ih***	woman
*bagar**ih***	cow

The feminine ending has two variant pronunciations: *-ah* and *-uh*. It is pronounced as *-ah* when the ending comes immediately after the sounds ^{c} or *ḥ*:

*sā^{c}**ah***	hour
*jāmi^{c}**ah***	university
*fātiḥ**ah***	opening

And it is pronounced as *-uh* when one of the consonants in the word is an emphatic (*ṣ, ṭ, ḍ*) and the ending does not come immediately after ^{c} or *ḥ*:

*ṭāg**uh***	window
*ṭās**uh***	metal plate

Where the feminine noun is not a basic noun and is derived from a masculine noun it invariably takes the feminine ending:

masculine	feminine	gloss
mudīr	*mudīr**ih***	manager
mudarris	*mudarris**ih***	teacher
ṭālub	*ṭālub**uh***	student

When a noun with the feminine ending takes a possessive pronoun (cf. Lesson 2) or a noun annex (cf. Lesson 8), the ending is no longer pronounced as *-ih*/*-uh*/*-ah*, but rather as *-at-*:

marih	+	*ī*	*mar**at**ī*
'wife'		'my'	'my wife'
madrasih	+	*nā*	*madras**at**nā*
'school'		'our'	'our school'
mudīrih	+	*al-madrasih*	*mudīr**at** al-madrasih*
'manager'		'the-school'	'the manager f. of the school'

5.2. Adjectives

In noun phrases involving a noun and an adjective, the adjective follows the noun. Thus, in order to say 'a big boy' the word *wald* 'boy' is followed by the adjective *kabīr* 'big':

noun	adjective	gloss
wald	*kabīr*	'a big boy'
'boy'	'big'	

Adjectives are basically masculine in Arabic, and take feminine agreement to agree with a feminine noun. For most adjectives[1] feminine agreement involves adding the feminine ending *-ih*, as in:

masculine	feminine	gloss
kabīr	*kabīr**ih***	big; old
zaġīr	*zaġīr**ih***	small; young
awwal	*awwal**ih***	first

When an adjective ends in *-ī*, the feminine ending is often not pronounced:

noun	adjective	gloss
bint	*ḥālī*	'a beautiful girl'

When the feminine ending is pronounced in the case of adjectives which end in *-ī*, *y* is added before the feminine ending for ease of pronunciation:

bint	*ḥāliyih*	'a beautiful girl'

6. *'This is my husband': demonstrative subject*

When the demonstrative is the subject of a nominal sentence, it is masculine before a masculine noun and plural before a plural noun (cf. 4. above), as in:

subject		predicate	
hāḏā	+	*zawjī*	*hāḏā zawjī*
'this m.'		'my-husband'	'this m. is my husband'
hāḏawlā	+	*banātī*	*hāḏawlā banātī*
'these'		'my-daughters'	'these are my daughters'

[1] Feminine colour adjectives usually take a different pattern from the basic masculine form (cf. Lesson 13).

When a demonstrative subject occurs before a feminine noun, however, the demonstrative may be feminine (cf. above), as in:

hāḏī	+	*bintī*	*hāḏī bintī*
'this f.'		'my-daughter'	'this f. is my daughter'

but more frequently the demonstrative is masculine, as in:

hāḏā	+	*bintī*	*hāḏā bintī*
'this m.'		'my-daughter'	'this is my daughter'

7. *Topical questions*

Sentences such as *who is he, this man?* are often found in colloquial English. Similarly in Ṣan^{c}ānī Arabic, sentences such as *man hī hāḏa l-marih* 'who is she, this woman' with a pronoun between the question word and the subject are common. Indeed, questions with the question words *man* and *mā* almost invariably involve the insertion of a pronoun. Other examples in the dialogues given in this lesson include:

mā +	*hū* +	*hāḏā*	*mā hū hāḏā*
'what'	'it m.'	'this'	'what is it m., this?'
man +	*hū* +	*hāḏā*	*man hū hāḏā*
'who'	'he'	'this'	'who is he, this one?'

Thematic Vocabulary

Jobs and places of work

bank pl. *bunūk*	bank m.
bāṣ pl. *bāṣāt*	bus m.
fannān pl. *fannānīn*	artist; singer m.
farrāših pl. *farrāšāt*	cleaner f.
ġassāl pl. *ġassālīn*	washer (of clothes) m.
ġassālih pl. *ġassālāt*	laundry f.
gaššām pl. *gaššāmīn*	*gušmī*-patch worker
gaššār pl. *gaššārīn*	coffee seller m.
jāmi^{c}ah pl. *jawāmi^{c}*	university f.
jazzār pl. *jazzārīn*	butcher m.
kātib pl. *kuttāb*	writer; scribe m.

madrasih pl. *madāris*	school f.
maktab pl. *makātib*	office m.
maṭbax pl. *maṭābux*	kitchen m.
miġsālih pl. *maġāsil*	laundry f.
migšāmih pl. *magāšim*	*gušmī* patch f.
mi^c*lāmih* pl. *ma*^{c}*ālim*	traditional school f.
mixbāzih pl. *maxābiz*	bakery f.
mudarris pl. *mudarrisīn*	teacher m.
muġannī pl. *muġanniyīn*	singer m.
mugawwit pl. *mugawwitīn*	*gāt* trader m.
mustašfā pl. *mustašfayāt*	hospital m.
mustawṣaf pl. *mustawṣafāt*	clinic m.
muwaḏḏaf pl. *muwaḏḏafīn*	employee m.
safīr pl. *sufarā*	ambassador m.
ṣarrāf pl. *ṣarrāfīn*	money changer m.
ṣarrāfuh pl. *ṣarrāfāt*	money changers f.
sawwāg pl. *sawwāgīn*	driver m.
sifārih pl. *sifārāt*	embassy f.
ṭabbāx pl. *ṭabbāxīn*	cook m.
ṭālub pl. *ṭullāb*	student m.
ustāḏ pl. *asātiḏih*	professor m.
wazīr pl. *wuzarā*	minister m.
wizārih pl. *wizārāt*	ministry f.
xabbāz pl. *xabbāzīn*	baker m.
xaṭṭāṭ pl. *xaṭṭāṭīn*	sign maker m.
xaṭṭāṭuh pl. *xaṭṭāṭāt*	sign maker's shop f.

Exercises

1. *Indefinite > definite*

Make the following nouns definite by adding the definite article. Where the *l* of the article should assimilate to the initial consonant of the noun, pronounce the resulting geminate (doubled) consonant twice as long as the single consonant. Geminate *rr* should be pronounced as a trill *r*. Geminate voiced stops should be pronounced without voice (cf. Introduction).

	indefinite	*gloss*	*definite*
Example:	*zalaṭ*	money	*az-zalaṭ*
	jāhil	child	
	ab	father	
	riyāl	Riyal (unit of currency)	
	marih	woman; wife	
	ṭāguh	window	
	galam	pen	
	daymih	kitchen	

2. *Gender change*

Change the gender from masculine to feminine. Make any necessary changes to the noun.

Example: *man hū hāḏā?* ————> *man hī hāḏī?*

i. *hāḏā wald kabīr* ______________________________

ii. *hāḏā mdarris* ______________________________

iii. *hāḏā mudīr* ______________________________

iv. *hāḏā ṭālub zaġīr* ______________________________

v. *hāḏā zawjī* ______________________________

3. *Demonstrative pronouns*

Complete the following sentences using the correct demonstrative, then translate the sentences into English.

Example: ________ *ibnī mḥammad* ————> *hāḏā bnī mḥammad*

i. _______ *maratī*

ii. *man hū* _______?

iii. *man hum* _______ *n-nas?*

iv. _______ *jāhil zaġīr*

v. _______ *l-marih xālatī*

4. *Possessive pronouns*

Complete the table by adding the correct possessive pronoun to the words *umm, xālih, madrasih, ibn* making necessary changes to the noun. The top left-hand corner is completed by way of example:

	bint	*xālih*	*madrasih*	*ibn*
anā	*bintī*			
hī				
ant				
antī				
hin				

5. *Adjective-noun agreement*

Complete the table below by providing the correct form of the adjective with the nouns *bagarih, marih, bayt, mšammaᶜ*:

	bagarih	*marih*	*bayt*	*mšammaᶜ*
ḥālī				
kabīr				
zaġīr				
awwal				

6. *Translation*

Taking account of the grammatical points given above, translate the following groups of sentences into Ṣanᶜānī Arabic:

A.

i. What is your m.s. name?

ii. What is your f.s. name?

iii. What is his name?

iv. What is her name?

B.

i. Who is this child?

ii. Who is this girl?

iii. Who is this woman?

iv. Who are these girls?

v. Who are these people?

C.

i. This is my son, Khalid.

ii. This is my daughter, Mariam.

iii. This is my husband, James.

iv. This is my wife, Sophie.

v. These are my daughters.

vi. This is our school.

LESSON 4

Ant min ayn? Where are you m.s. from?

Dialogue 1

Samira: *ṣbaḥtū!*

Ahmad: *ṣabbaḥkum allāh bi-l-xayr!*

Samira: *ant min ayn yā 'aḥmad?*

Ahmad: *anā min al-yaman.*

Samira: *s^{c}am ant yamanī.*

Ahmad: *aywih anā yamanī, w-antī min ayn yā samīrih.*

Samira: *anā min maṣr, anā maṣrīyuh.*

Dialogue 2

Ahmad: *al-marih aṣlahā yamanī yā xadījih?*

Khadija: *māšī, al-marih hāḏā 'aṣlan min al-yūnān.*

Ahmad: *yā s^{c}am hī yūnānīyih.*

Khadija: *ṣaḥḥ hī yūnānīyih, wa-hāḏawl al-^{c}iyyāl min ayn hum yā 'aḥmad.*

Ahmad: *al-^{c}iyyāl min ṣan^{c}ā, hum ṣan^{c}ānīyin.*

Dialogue 3

Khadija: *al-jāhil az-zġīr min al-bayḏ̣ā, mā?*

Muhammad: *aywih hū bayḏ̣ānī.*

Khadija: *wa-zamīlak hāḏā min al-yaman awlā māšī?*

Muhammad: *māšī, zamīlī James miš min al-yaman, hū min brīṭāniyā.*

Khadija: *yā s^{c}am hū brīṭānī, wa-yitḥāka ṣ-ṣan^{c}ānī bulbul!*

Muhammad: *aywih yitḥākā sā^{c}-mā 'iḥna.*

Dialogue 4

Muhammad: *antū min ayn, ant wa-zamīlak yā Jean?*

Jean: *anā min faransā.*

Muhammad: *ya^{c}nī 'antū faransāwīyīn.*

Jean: *māšī 'anā faransāwī wa-zamīlī Klaus aṣlan min almāniyā, hū 'almānī.*

Muhammad: *wa-l-lawlād hāḏawlā min ayn?*

Jean: *hum min ^{c}adan, hum ^{c}adanīyīn.*

Vocabulary

^{c}adan	Aden f.	*^{c}adanī*	Adeni m.
al-bayḏ̣ā	al-Bayḏ̣ā [place in Yemen] f.	*almānī*	German m.
almāniyā	Germany f.	*al-yaman*	Yemen m./f.
al-yūnān	Greece f.	*aṣl* pl. *uṣūl*	origin m.
aṣlan	originally	*awlā*	or
ayn	where	*aywih*	yes
bayḏ̣ānī	of/from al-Bayḏ̣ā m.	*briṭānī*	British m.
briṭāniyā	Britain f.	*bulbul*	fluently [lit: nightingale]
fa-	so conj.	*faransā*	France f.
faransāwī	French m.	*^{c}iyyāl*	children
jāhil pl. *jahhāl*	child m.	*marih* pl. *niswān*	woman f.
māšī	no	*maṣr*	Egypt f.
maṣrī	Egyptian m.	*min*	from
miš	not	*ṣaḥḥ*	true; that's right
s^{c}am	i.e., that is to say	*sā^c-mā*	like
ṣan^{c}ā	Ṣan^{c}ā' f.	*ṣan^{c}ānī*	San^{c}ānī m.
ṣan^{c}ānī	Ṣan^{c}ānī [dialect] f.	*wald* pl. *awlād*	boy m.
yamanī	Yemeni m.	*yamanī*	Yemeni [dialect] f.
ya^{c}nī	i.e., that is to say	*yā s^{c}am*	i.e., that is to say
yitḥākā	he speaks	*yūnānī*	Greek m.
zamīl pl. *zumalā*	colleague; friend m.		

Grammar

1. *Adjective formation*

Adjectives can be formed from the names of countries and from certain other nouns (e.g. *burtugālī* 'orange [in colour]' from *burtugāl* 'orange [fruit]', *yawmī* 'daily' from *yawm* 'day') by adding *-ī*, as in *yamanī* 'Yemeni' from *al-yaman* 'Yemen' and *ᶜadanī* 'Adeni' from *ᶜadan* 'Aden'. This type of adjective is called a *relational* (or, in Arabic, *nisbih*) adjective. The feminine is produced by adding *-yih*. Note the addition of *-y-* before the feminine suffix to ease pronunciation (cf. Lesson 3, 5.2.).

When the place noun ends in *-īyih*, as in *as-saᶜūdīyih* 'Saudi'[1], the *-īyih* ending is not pronounced when the adjective suffix *-ī* is added, as in *saᶜūdī* 'Saudi'. Similarly, when a noun ends in *-iyā*, the ending *-iyā* is not pronounced before the adjective suffix *-ī* is added, as in:

briṭān-iyā	'Britain'	*briṭān-ī*	'British'
almān-iyā	'Germany'	*almān-ī*	'German'

When a place noun ends in *-ā*, but not in *-iyā*, either *-w-* is added before the *-ī* suffix to ease pronunciation, as in *faransāwī* 'French' from *faransā* 'France', or *-ā* is not pronounced when *-ī* is added, as in *faransī* 'French'. Exceptions to this are adjectives derived from *ṣanᶜā* 'Ṣanᶜā' and *al-bayḍā* 'Bayḍā'. Here, *n* is added before the suffix *ī* to give *ṣanᶜ**ānī*** and *bayḍ**ānī***.

When a place noun takes the definite article, as in *al-jazāyir* 'Algeria', the relational adjective does not take the definite article unless it itself is definite.

2. *Plural formation*

In Sanᶜānī Arabic, as in other dialects of Arabic, a noun or adjective plural is formed in one of two ways: either by the addition of a suffix (the sound plural) - *-īn* for the masculine plural and *-āt* for the feminine plural - or by putting the *root* consonants of the singular into a different vocalic *pattern* (the broken plural).

2.1. Sound plural

The sound masculine plural *-īn* is used exclusively for male humans or for groups of male and female humans, as in: *antū faransāwīyīn, hum ᶜadanīyīn, iḥna*

[1] This is because *as-saᶜūdīyih* is shorthand for *al-mamlaki l-ᶜarabīyi s-saᶜūdīyih* 'the Kingdom of Saudi Arabia'.

sa^cūdīyīn, etc. When the ending *-īn* is added to a noun or adjective ending in *-ī*, then *-y-* is added before the *-īn* suffix to ease pronunciation, as in the examples given here (cf. 1. above). Examples of adjectives which take the sound plural include:

singular	plural	gloss
galīl	*galīlīn*	little; few m.
ᶜīs	*ᶜīsīn*	good m.
ḥālī	*ḥālīyīn*	sweet; nice m.
bāhir[2]	*bāhirīn*	good; excellent m.

Most basic nouns which refer to male humans take the broken plural (cf. 2.2. below). A number of nouns which refer to professions take the sound plural ending (cf. Lesson 2, Thematic Vocabulary), as in:

singular	plural	gloss
gaššām	*gaššāmīn*	*gušmī*-patch worker
lāᶜib	*lāᶜibīn*	player m.
mudarris	*mudarrisīn*	teacher m.
muhandis	*muhandisīn*	engineer m.
xabbāz	*xabbāzīn*	baker m.

The sound feminine plural *-āt* is used for nouns and adjectives which refer to female humans, and for a large other nouns where the singular ends in *-ih*. The singular suffix *-ih* is not pronounced when the plural ending *-āt* is added. Consider the following examples of nouns which take the sound feminine plural:

singular	plural	gloss
farrāših	*farrāšāt*	cleaner f.
lāᶜibih	*lāᶜibāt*	player f.
marrih	*marrāt*	time f.
mudarrisih	*mudarrisāt*	teacher f.
sifārih	*sifārāt*	embassy f.

[2] The word *bāhir* is usually used by men about men. For example: *klāmak bāhir* 'what you m.s. say is excellent', *hū rajjāl bāhir* 'he is a very good man'. Between women the words *nāhī* 'nice; good' or *ᶜīs* 'very good' would be used, as in: *antī mdarrisih ᶜīsih* 'you f.s. are a very good teacher', *klāmiš nāhī* 'what you f.s. say is good'.

Adjectives which take the sound masculine plural will also take the sound feminine plural when referring to female humans, as in:

singular	plural	gloss
ḥāliyih	*ḥāliyāt*	nice f.
ᶜīsih	*ᶜīsāt*	good f.
yamanīyih	*yamanīyāt*	Yemeni f.

Note also that the sound masculine plural can, however, also be used for adjectives which refer to female humans, as in: *iḥna maftūḥ***īn** *maᶜa baᶜḍ* 'we are open with each other' where the actual referent of 'we' is two women. From this lesson on, nouns which take one of the sound plurals will be listed in their singular form and their plural form will be given in abbreviated form as *-āt* or *-īn*.

2.2. Broken plural

In the broken plural, the *root* consonants of the plural remain the same as in the singular and maintain the same order, but the number or type of vowels (the *pattern*) will differ. It is important to note that the broken plural is more common than the sound plural and has a large number of patterns. From this lesson on, all nouns will be listed in the vocabulary section in their singular and plural forms when they take one of the broken plural patterns. Nouns which take broken plurals have both human and non-human referents. Some common broken plural patterns with examples of nouns for which they occur are given below. To illustrate the pattern, I use the consonants **KTB** highlighted in **bold**:

pattern	plural	singular	gloss
Ki**T**ū**B**	*biyūt*	*bayt*	house
Ku**T**u**B**	*kutub*	*kitāb*	book
Ki**T**i**B**	*likim*	*lakamih*	hill
	jibih	*jabhih*	forehead
Ki**T**a**B**	*jirab*	*jirbih*	plot of land; terrace
Ku**T**a**B**	*nuwab*	*nūbih*	round defence tower
Ki**T**ā**B**	*jibāl*	*jabal*	mountain
	rijāl	*rajjāl*	man
a**KT**ā**B**	*awlād*	*walad*	boy
	amrāḍ	*marīḍ*	sick person
	aḥrāz	*ḥirz*	amulet
	asmā	*ism*	name

KiTTāB/	*ᶜiyyāl*	*ᶜāyil*[3]	child
KaTTāB	*jahhāl*	*jāhil*	child
KiTBān	*niswān*	*marih*	woman
KiTwaB/	*širwaṭ*	*šarīṭ*	cassette
KuTwaB	*ṭurwag*	*ṭarīg*	road; way
KawāTiB	*šawāriᶜ*	*šāriᶜ*	street; road
	gawārī	*gārī*	small wooden cart
KaTāyiB	*balāyid*	*bilād*	village; country
aKāTiB	*asāmī*	*ism*	name

For more examples of broken plurals of nouns see Appendix I of *Syntax of Ṣanᶜānī Arabic*.

Most adjectives take the sound plural, but some more basic adjectives take a broken plural. Here are two examples of the most common broken plurals of adjectives:

pattern	plural	singular	gloss
KiTāB/	*kibār*	*kabīr*	big; old
KuTāB	*ṭuwāl*	*ṭawīl*	tall
KuTB	*ṣufr*	*aṣfar*	yellow
KuTaBā	*fugarā*	*fagīr*	poor
	kuramā	*karīm*	generous

3. *Adjective predicates*

In constructing noun phrases in Arabic we have seen that the adjective agrees in number and gender with an animate (human) noun. Similarly in sentences, an adjective predicate agrees in number and gender with an animate subject, as in:

subject	predicate	gloss
al-wald	*ṭawīl*	*al-wald ṭawīl*
'the-boy m.s.'	'tall m.s.'	'the boy is tall'
al-bint	*ṭawīluh*	*al-bint ṭawīluh*
'the-girl f.s.'	'tall f.s.'	'the girl is tall'

[3] *ᶜāyil* is not used in the singular.

an-nās	*ṭuwāl*	*an-nās ṭuwāl*
'the-people pl.'	'tall pl.'	'the people are tall'
an-niswān	*ṭawīlāt*	*an-niswān ṭawīlāt*
'the-women f.pl.'	'tall f.pl.'	'the women are tall'

or

an-niswān	*ṭuwāl*	*an-niswān ṭuwāl*
'the-women f.pl.'	'tall pl.'	'the women are tall'

When the subject is inanimate (non-human), the predicate adjective agrees in number and gender with a singular subject, as in:

subject	predicate	
aṯ-ṯawr	*kabīr*	*aṯ-ṯawr kabīr*
'the-bull'	'big m.s.'	'the bull is big'
al-bagarih	*kabīrih*	*al-bagarih kabīrih*
'the-cow'	'big f.s.'	'the cow is big'

However with a plural inanimate subject, the predicate adjective is either feminine singular, when subject referents are viewed as a *collectivity* (cf. Lesson 3), as in:

al-iyyām	*galīlih*	*al-iyyām galīlih*
'the-days'	'few f.s.'	'the days are few/there are few days'

or sound feminine plural or broken plural, when the subject referents are viewed as *separate, particular* entities (*ibid*), as in:

al-jibāl	*ᶜāliyāt*	*al-jibāl ᶜāliyāt*
'the-mountains'	'high f.pl.'	'the mountains are high'
aṭ-ṭurwag	*ṭuwāl*	*aṭ-ṭurwag ṭuwāl*
'the-roads'	'long pl.'	'the roads are long'

4. *Prepositional predicates*

When the predicate of a sentence is a prepositional phrase, no inflection takes place because prepositions (words such as *in, on, from, to*), are invariant and do not inflect for number or gender. The predicate 'in the market' remains the same, therefore, irrespective of whether the subject is feminine or masculine, singular or plural:

gender/number	subject	predicate	gloss
masc./sing.	*ant*	*fī s-sūg*	'you m.s. are in the market'
fem./sing.	*antī*	*fī s-sūg*	'you f.s. are in the market'
masc./plural	*hum*	*fī s-sūg*	'they m. are in the market'
	ar-rijāl	*fī s-sūg*	'the men are in the market'
fem./plural	*antayn*	*fī s-sūg*	'you f.pl. are in the market'
	an-niswān	*fī s-sūg*	'the women are in the market'
inanimate plural	*al-bagar*	*fī s-sūg*	'the cows are in the market'

5. *Topical sentences*

Sentences like 'your mother, where is she from?' where the *topic* (here 'your mother') is followed by a complete clause with a pronoun which refers back to the topic (here 'she') are very common in colloquial English. They are not common, however, in standard written English. This type of sentence, known as a *topical* sentence, is very common in Arabic. In the following examples, the topic and the *referential* pronoun are highlighted in **bold**:

***ummiš**, aṣla**hā** yamanī*	'your f.s. mother, her origin is Yemeni?' i.e. 'your f.s. mother, is she from Yemen?'
bintiš**, b-isma**hā	'your f.s. daughter, what is her name?'
***al-jahhāl, hum** fī l-yaman*	'the children, they are in Yemen'

6. *Negation: 'no' and 'not'*

The word for 'no' in Ṣanᶜānī is *māšī* or, less commonly, *lā*, or *mā* The word for 'not', which negates independent pronouns, nouns, adjectives and prepositional phrases is *miš* or *māš*, occasionally *muš*. The negator comes before the negated word (cf. *Syntax* p. 4), as in:

negator	negated word	gloss
miš	*anā*	'not me!'
miš	*muḥammad*	'not Muhammad'
miš	*yamanī*	'not Yemeni'

miš	*fi s-sūg*	'not in the market'

7. *Definiteness*

When a noun takes an adjective to form a noun phrase, the adjective agrees not only in number and gender with the noun (cf. Lesson 3), but also in *definiteness* (cf. Lesson 2):

	noun	adjective	gloss
	bayt 'house'	*kabīr* 'big'	*bayt kabīr* 'a big house'
versus			
	al-bayt 'the-house'	*al-kabīr* 'the-big'	*al-bayt al-kabīr* 'the big house'

While some nouns are definite by virtue of being proper nouns (names of places and people), and others can be made definite by adding the definite article *al-* or by adding a definite noun annex or possessive pronoun (cf. Lesson 3), adjectives can only be made definite by adding the definite article *al-*.

noun	adjective	gloss
al-bayt	*al-kabīr*	'the big house'
bayt al-marih	*al-kabīr*	'the woman's big house'
baytiš	*al-kabīr*	'your f.s. big house'
aḥmad	*al-kabīr*	'big Ahmad'

When a word which takes the feminine ending *-ih* is followed by a word beginning with the definite article, neither *h* of the feminine ending nor *a* of the definite article are pronounced:

al-marih +	*al-kabīrih*	> *al-mari l-kabīrih*
'the-woman'	'the-big/old'	> 'the big/old woman'

8. *Verbs: the imperfect aspect*

The verb has two *aspects*: the *perfect* and the *imperfect*. In general, the imperfect is used to talk about the present and future tense, while the perfect is used to talk about the past tense. The imperfect is formed from a *stem* and a prefix for all persons, and from a stem and a prefix and a suffix for second and third person plurals and second feminine singular, as illustrated below:

Here is the paradigm of the verb *tḥākā* 'to speak' in the imperfect aspect:

singular		plural	
a-tḥākā	I speak	*ni-tḥākā*	we speak
ti-tḥākā	you m. speak	*ti-tḥāk-aw*	you m. speak
ti-tḥāk-ay	you f. speak	*ti-tḥāk-ayn*	you f. speak
yi-tḥākā	he speaks	*yi-tḥāk-aw*	they m. speak
ti-tḥākā	she speaks	*yi-tḥāk-ayn*	they f. speak

Thematic Vocabulary

Arab countries

al-baḥrayn	Bahrein f.	*al-jazāyir*	Algeria f.
al-kuwayt	Kuwait f.	*al-maġrib*	Morocco m.
al-urdunn	Jordan m.	*lībiyā*	Libya f.
lubnān	Lebanon m.	*sūriyā*	Syria f.
ᶜumān	Oman f.		

Major towns in Yemen

ᶜadan	Aden f.	*ᶜamrān*	Amran f.
al-ḥudaydih	Hudayda f.	*al-muxā*	Mokha f.
ibb	Ibb f.	*kawkabān*	Kawkaban f.
manāxih	Manakha f.	*mārib*	Marib f.
radāᶜ	Rada f.	*ṣaᶜduh*	Ṣaᶜda f.
ṣanᶜā	Ṣanᶜā' f.	*šibām*	Shibam f.
tiᶜizz	Taizz f.		

Terms for administrative areas

The terms for administrative areas in Yemen are listed here according to their size from largest to smallest:

muḥāfaḏuh	pl. *-āt*	governorate f.
nāḥiyih	pl. *nawāḥī*	district f.
gaḏā	pl. *agḏiyuh*	sub-governorate; province m.
markaz	pl. *marākiz*	centre (e.g. of a *nāḥiyih*) m.
gariyih	pl. *gurā*	village f.
bilād	pl. *balāyid*	village; home town f.

Exercises

1. *Substitution*

Replace the prepositional phrase in **bold**, ***min* ___**, in the sentences below by the appropriate adjective. Inflect the adjective for gender and number.

Example: *anā smī xadījih, anā* ***min*** ^{c}***umān****.* —> *anā* ^{c}***umānīyih****.*

i. *anā smī mḥammad, anā* ***min al-yaman****.* ______________

ii. *hū* ***min al-kuwayt****.* ______________

iii. *hī* ***min as-sa***^{c}***ūdī****.* ______________

iv. *ar-rijāl hāḏawlā* ***min al-baḥrayn****.* ______________

v. *al-banāt az-zuġār* ***min ṣan***^{c}***ā****.* ______________

vi. *iḥna* ***min al-jazāyir****.* ______________

2. *Question and answer*

Ask each other where you are from, following the format below:

Q: *ant(ī) min ayn yā* ______________

A: *anā min* ______________

Q: *yā sa*^{c}*am, ant(ī)* ______________

A: *aywih, anā* ______________

3. *Singular > Plural*

Review section 2. above and change the number of nouns, pronouns and adjectives in the following sentences from singular to plural.

Example: *antī min al-yūnān, antī yūnānīyih* ———> *antayn min al-yūnān, antayn yūnānīyāt*

i. *anā min al-yaman, anā yamanī.* ______________________

ii. *al-mudarris rajjāl kabīr.* ______________________

iii. *al-kitāb fī l-bayt.* ______________________

iv. *hū rajjāl bāhir.* ______________________

v. *al-muhandisih lubnāniyih.* ______________________

4. *Negation*

a. Negate the predicate in the following sentences.

Example: *hāḏa r-rajjāl min al-kuwayt* ———> *hāḏa r-rajjāl* ***miš*** *min al-kuwayt.*

i. *al-bint hāḏī yamanīyih.* ______________________

ii. *al-mudarris rajjāl bāhir.* ______________________

iii. *al-marih mudarrisih ᶜīsih.* ______________________

iv. *hāḏī 'ummī.* ______________________

v. *al-ᶜiyyāl fī s-sūg.* ______________________

vi. *aṭ-ṭurwag ṭuwāl.* ______________________

b. Answer the following questions negatively.

Example: *ant min ayn, min al-yaman?*———> ***māšī****, 'anā* ***miš*** *min al-yaman.*

i. *antī yamanīyih?* ______________________

ii. *al-banāt kibār?* ______________________

iii. *ant ismak mḥammad?* ______________________

iv. *al-mudarrisāt faransāwīyāt?* ______________________

v. *hum ᶜadanīyīn?* ______________________

5. *Gender change*

In the following sentences, change the gender of pronouns, nouns, adjectives and verbs from masculine to feminine:

Example: *ant aṣlan yamanī* ————> *antī aṣlan yamanīyih*

i. *ant titḥākā ṣanᶜānī bulbul.* ______________________

ii. *al-wald az-zaġīr miš fī l-bayt.* ______________________

iii. *al-mudarrisīn kuwaytīyīn.* ______________________

iv. *ar-rajjāl ᶜadanī.* ______________________

v. *hū yitḥākā yamanī.* ______________________

6. *Find the plural*

Find the meaning and the plural form(s) for the following nouns and adjectives:

i. *lakamih*	ii. *jabal*	iii. *ḥirz*	iv. *kitāb*
v. *ᶜīs*	vi. *šarīṭ*	vi. *jāhil*	vii. *jirbih*

LESSON 5

Fi s-sūg In the market

Dialogue 1 *mā tištī tištarī, yā samīr?*

Ahmad: *msaytū.*

Samir: *massākum allāh bi-l-xayr wa-l-ᶜāfiyih.*

Ahmad: *mā tištī tištari l-yawm, yā samīr.*

Samir: *ašti bṭāṭ wa-ruzz. bi-kam al-baṭāṭ?*

Ahmad: *al-kīlū al-baṭāṭ bi-ᶜišrīn .*

Samir: *wa-r-ruzz bi-kam al-kīlū?*

Ahmad: *ar-ruzz bi-xamsīn.*

Samir: *nāhī, ddī lī kīlū baṭāṭ wa-nuṣṣ kīlū ruzz.*

Ahmad: *ṭayyub, ddī l-ᶜallāgīyih.*

Samir: *ḥayyāk allāh.*

Ahmad: *allāh yiḥayyīk.*

Dialogue 2 *mā tištī?*

Muhammad: *y-axī štī murr bi-xamsīn.*

Ahmad: *nāhī, tištī min al-baxūr hāḏā?*

Muhammad: *māšī, ma štīš min ḏayyā n-nawᶜ.*

Ahmad: *mā tištī min baxūr?*

Muhammad: *aštī murr bass yikūn nawᶜ ḥālī.*

Ahmad: *wa-hāḏā miš ḥālī?*

Muhammad: *māšī, miš ḥālī gawī bass ġālī. mā yiᶜjibni n-nawᶜ hāḏā.*

Vocabulary

ᶜallāgīyih pl. *-āt*	bag; box f.	*allāh yiḥayyīk*	*[*reply to *ḥayyāk …]*
al-yawm	today	*aštarī (lī)*	I buy
aštī	I want	*bass*	but; only

baṭāṭ	potatoes coll. m.	*baxūr*	incense m.
ḏayyā	this m.s.	*ddī*	give m.s.!
ġālī	expensive	*gawī*	very
ḥayyāk allāh	thank you!	*ᶜišrīn*	twenty
(bi-)kam	how much/many?	*kīlū*	kilo m.
lī	to me	*murr*	myrhh m.
nāhī	yes, okay; good	*nawᶜ* pl. *anwāᶜ*	type; kind; thing m.
nuṣṣ	half m.	*ruzz*	rice coll. m.
sūg pl. *aswāg*	market m./f.	*ṭayyub*	good
tištī	you m.s. want	*tištarī*	you m.s. buy
yiᶜjib	it m. pleases (s.o.)		

Grammar

1. *Greetings*

The phrase for 'good evening' in Ṣanᶜānī Arabic is *msaytū*. The reply is *massākum allāh bi-l-xayr* or *massākum allāh bi-l-xayr* ***wa-l-ᶜāfiyih***.

There are a number of possible equivalents of 'thank you' in Ṣanᶜānī. These range from nothing at all (and indeed 'thank you' is far more common in English than any of the Ṣanᶜānī equivalents), to *ḥayyāk allāh* (lit: 'may God keep you m.s. alive') with the response *allāh yiḥayyīk* and to *akramak allāh* (lit: 'may God bestow honours on you m.s.') with the response *karāmih sahīlih* for small favours and *kaṯṯar allāh xayrukum* or *kaṯṯar allāh* ***min*** *xayrukum* (lit: may God multiply your goodness) with the response *xayr allāh maᶜak* or *xayr allāh* ***sābig*** for, for example, a sumptuous meal.

2. *Demonstrative pronouns: near demonstratives*

In noun phrases, demonstrative pronouns can come before the noun or after the noun, as in the second dialogue in this lesson. It is slightly more common for the demonstrative to come before the noun (cf. Lesson 3). You will hear both the following word orders:

al-baxūr ***hāḏā*** ***hāḏā*** *l-baxūr* 'this incense'

When the demonstrative follows a feminine singular noun, it does not agree in gender (cf. Lesson 3):

al-marih hāḏā 'this woman'

You have been introduced to the first set of near demonstratives in Lesson 3. The second set (without initial *hā-)* is considered to be older than the first set and is as follows:

	singular	plural
m.	*d̲ayyā*	*d̲awlayya'*
f.	*tayyih*	

As for the first set of demonstratives, there is no gender distinction in the plural demonstrative. You will hear *d̲awlayya n-niswān* 'these women' and *d̲awlayya r-rijāl* 'these men'. In contrast to the first set, when the demonstrative follows a feminine singular noun it always takes the feminine singular form *tayyih*:

al-marih hād̲ā but *al-marih* ***tayyih*** 'this woman'

3. *The vocative phrase*

A vocative phrase consists of the vocative particle *yā* and a person's name, as in the dialogues from Lesson 2, or a noun, or a noun with a possessive pronoun, or a noun with a noun annex. The vocative is very common in Arabic. When the vocative particle is followed by a proper noun (a person's name), the construction is straightforward: *yā* is followed by the name with no change, as in:

yā samīrih (hey) Samira! *yā mḥammad* (hey) Muhammad!

When the vocative particle is followed by a *non*-proper noun, the noun is pronounced (as in English) *without* the definite article, even though a particular person is being addressed at the time:

yā wald (hey) boy! *y-awlād*[1] (hey) boys!

When the vocative particle is followed by a noun with a possessive pronoun suffix, the noun keeps its suffix,[2] as in:

yā bintī (hey) daughter! *y-ummī* (hey) Mother!

[1] When the noun following *yā* begins with a vowel (or a glottal stop and vowel) the *ā* of the vocative is usually not pronounced, as in this example.

[2] Unlike in English, where the pronoun 'my' etc. is omitted.

When the vocative particle is followed by a noun with a noun annex (cf. Lesson 8), the noun keeps its annex, as in:

yā marat aš-šayx (hey) wife of the Shaykh! *yā marat mḥammad* (hey) wife of Muhammad!

4. *Pronoun suffixes: words ending in a vowel*

Some pronoun suffixes take a different form when they are suffixed to words ending in a vowel than when they are suffixed to words which end in a consonant (cf. Lesson 2). The full set of pronoun suffixes which occur after words ending in a vowel are as follows:

	singular	plural
1.	*-ī*	*-nā*
2. m.	*-k*	*-kum*
2. f.	*-š*	*-kin*
3. m.	*-h*	*-hum*
3. f.	*-hā*	*-hin*

When the first person singular pronoun suffix is suffixed to a word ending in a vowel, the vowel is generally not pronounced when it is short, as in:

la + ī	*lī*	'to me'
bi + ī	*bī*	'in/with me'

When first person singular pronoun suffix is annexed to the preposition *fī* 'in', the suffix takes an initial *n-* to give *fīnī* 'in me', and the long vowel *ī* of the preposition is pronounced.

When prepositions end in long *ā* - such as *ᶜalā* 'on; against', *ṣalā* 'towards', and *warā* 'behind' - the first person singular pronoun suffix is pronounced as *-ya* to give *ᶜalayya* 'on, against me', *gafāya* 'behind me', and *ṣalayya* 'towards me'. *Gafā* and *ṣalā* both keep the long vowel *ā* before the other pronoun suffixes, to give, for example:

gafā + kum	*gafākum*	'behind you m.pl.'
gafā + nā	*gafānā*	'behind us'

^{c}*alā* takes a diphthong *-ay-* before all prononimal suffixes, to give for example:

^{c}*alā + k*	^{c}*alayk*	'on you m.s.'
^{c}*alā + š*	^{c}*alayš*	'on you f.s.'
^{c}*alā + h*	^{c}*alayh*	'on him'
^{c}*alā + hum*	^{c}*alayhum*	'on them m.'

ma^{c} 'with' acts like a consonant-final word with the singular suffixes with the exception of third feminine singular, to give:

ma^{c} + *ī*	*ma*^{c}*ī*	'with me'[3]
ma^{c} + *ak*	*ma*^{c}*ak*	'with you m.s.'

With third feminine singular and all plural suffixes it either takes a long *ā* before the suffix, to give for example:

ma^{c} + *hum*	*ma*^{c}*āhum*	'with them m.'
ma^{c} + *kum*	*ma*^{c}*ākum*	'with you m.pl.'

or the suffix is attached directly to the preposition. In this case, *h* of the third person pronouns is often not pronounced:

ma^{c}*um*	or	*ma*^{c}*hum*	'with them m'
ma^{c}*in*	or	*ma*^{c}*hin*	'with them f.'

With the preposition *min* 'from' the *n* is doubled before vowel-initial pronouns:

min + ī	*minnī*	'from me'
min + ak	*minnak*	'from you m.s.'
min + iš	*minniš*	'from you f.s.'
min + ih	*minnih*	'from him'

Before consonant-initial pronouns either the *n* is doubled, to give:

min + hum	*minnahum*	'from them m.'
min + hin	*minnahin*	'from them f.'
min + kum	*minnakum*	'from you m.pl.'
min + kin	*minnakin*	'from you f.pl.'

Or the pronoun is attached directly to the form *min*. In this case, the *h* of the third person pronouns is often not pronounced:

[3] Also *ma*^{c}*iyya* or *mi*^{c}*ī* (cf. *Syntax* p.196).

min + hum	*min(h)um*	'from them m.'
min + hin	*min(h)in*	'from them f.'
min + kum	*minkum*	'from you m.pl.'

(For examples of pronoun suffixes annexed to other prepositions cf. *Syntax* pp.195-196.)

Some words end in a consonant when they do not take a pronoun suffix or a noun annex, but take the vowel *ū* before a pronoun suffix or noun annex. These words include *ab* 'father' and *ax* 'brother'. The vowel *ū* is not pronounced before a first singular pronoun suffix, but is pronounced before all other pronouns:

ab(ū) + ī	*abī*	'my father'
ab(ū) + š	*abūš*	'your f.s. father'
ab(ū) + kum	*abūkum*	'your m.pl. father'
ax(ū) + hin	*axūhin*	'their f. brother'
ax(ū) + kin	*axūkin*	'your f.pl. brother'

5. *Verbs: 'to give'*

'To give' is expressed by the verb *yiddī*. The prefixes for this verb are identical to the prefixes for the verb *yitḥākā* 'to speak' (cf. Lesson 4). For singular persons and first plural the verb ends in *ī*, as in *yiddī* 'he gives'. In the plural, with the exception of first plural, the verb *yiddī* takes the same endings as the verb *yitḥākā*. Here is the full paradigm of the verb *yiddī*:

	singular	plural
1.	*a-ddī*	*ni-ddī*
2. m.	*ti-ddī*	*ti-dd-aw*
2. f.	*ti-dd-ay*	*ti-dd-ayn*
3. m.	*yi-ddī*	*yi-dd-aw*
3. f.	*ti-ddī*	*yi-dd-ayn*

6. *Verbs: 'to want'*

'To want' is expressed by the verb *yištī*. The prefixes and suffixes for this verb are identical to the prefixes and suffixes of *yiddī* 'to give' (5. above). Here is the full paradigm of the verb *yištī*:

	singular	plural
1.	*a-štī*	*ni-štī*
2. m.	*ti-štī*	*ti-št-aw*
2. f.	*ti-št-ay*	*ti-št-ayn*
3. m.	*yi-štī*	*yi-št-aw*
3. f.	*ti-štī*	*yi-št-ayn*

Note imperfect verbs are often pronounced without the vowel of the prefix, particularly in rapid speech, to give, for example:

	singular	plural
1.	*a-štī*	*n-štī*
2. m.	*t-štī*	*t-št-aw*
2. f.	*t-št-ay*	*t-št-ayn*
3. m.	*y-štī*	*y-št-aw*
3. f.	*t-štī*	*y-št-ayn*

7. *Verbs: 'to want to do…'*

'To want to do' something is expressed by the verb *yištī* + a second imperfect verb which takes the same subject. There is no infinitive verb in Arabic. The verb *yištarī* 'to buy' (*yštarī)* inflects in exactly the same way as *yištī*. Consider the following examples:

yištī	+ *yištarī*	*yištī yštarī*
'he-wants'	'he-buys'	'he wants to buy'
tištī	+ *tithākā*	*tištī tithākā*
'she-wants'	'she-speaks'	'she wants to speak'
yištaw	+ *yištaraw*	*yištaw yštaraw*
'they-want'	'they-buy'	'they m. want to buy'

8. *Negation of verbs and prepositional phrases*

In Lesson 4 we saw that the word for negating nouns, adjectives and prepositional phrases is *miš, māš* or *muš*. When verbs are negated, the negative particle is split into two elements: *mā* and *-š* or, less commonly today, *ši*. *Mā* comes before the verb and *-š* or *ši* follows the verb, as in:

mā	+ *tišti*	+ *š/ši*	*mā tištiš*
'not'	'you-want'	[neg]	'you m.s. do not want'

The second element - *-š* or *ši* - can also be left out without affecting the negative meaning, as in:

mā	+ *tištī*	*mā tištī*
'not'	'you-want'	'you m.s. do not want'

When two verbs occur together, as in *yištī yištarī* 'he wants to buy' (cf. 6.), only the first verb is negated, as in:

mā	+ *yišti*	+ *š*	+ *yištarī*	*mā yištiš yištarī*
'not'	'he-wants'	[neg]	'he-buys'	'he does not want to buy'
mā	+ *yištaw*	+ *š*	+ *yitḥākaw*	*mā yištawš yitḥākaw*
'not'	'they-want'	[neg]	'they-speak'	'they m. do not want to speak'

When prepositional phrases take a pronoun suffix, they are also negated by *mā* and *-š*, and not by *miš* etc., as in:

mā	+ *fīhā*	+ *š*	*mā fīhāš*
'not'	'in-it f.'	[neg]	'not in it f.'
mā	+ *maᶜak*	+ *š*	*mā maᶜakš*
'not'	'with-you m.'	[neg]	'not with you m.'
mā	+ *ᶜalayk*	+ *š*	*mā ᶜalaykš*
'not'	'on-you m.'	[neg]	'not on you m.'

9. *Adverbs: al-yawm, gawī, aṣlan, bulbul*

Adverbs in Arabic very rarely have a form which distinguishes them from other word types (cf. *Syntax* pp. 320-323). Adverbs are either nouns, adjectives, prepositional phrases or fixed particles. The two adverbs we encounter in the dialogue in this lesson are the time adverb *al-yawm* 'today' and the degree adverb *gawī* 'very'. The adverbs we encounter in Lesson 4 are the manner adverbs *aṣlan* 'originally' and *bulbul* 'fluently'. In a non-adverbial context *al-yawm* means 'the day', *gawī* means 'strong', *aṣl* means 'origin; root', and *bulbul* means 'nightingale'. Most adverbs tend to follow the verb phrase, noun phrase or adjective which they modify, as in:

aštī štarī lī baxūr al-yawm	'I want to buy incense today'
al-gāt hāḏā ḥālī gawī	'this *gāt* is very nice'
zamīlī yitḥākā ṣanᶜānī bulbul	'my friend m. speaks Sanᶜānī fluently'

Some adverbs, however, including *aṣlan* tend to come before the term they modify, as in:

ummiš aṣlan min ayn	'your f.s. mother is originally from where?'

10. *Questions: 'How much a kilo?'*

To ask how much something is a kilo (or a pound = *raṭl*) in Arabic you say *bi-kam* 'for how much' ***al-kīlū*** '**the** kilo' (or ***ar****-raṭl* 'the pound'):

ad-dagīg [= flour] *bi-kam al-kīlū*	'flour is how much a kilo?'
ar-ruzz bi-kam ar-raṭl	'rice is how much a pound?'

To say that something is 'so much a kilo' the word order is 'the kilo', 'the (e.g. rice)', 'amount (e.g. 20):

al-kīlū ad-dagīg bi-ᶜišrīn	'flour is twenty a kilo'
al-kīlū al-burr bi-ᶜašarih	'wheat is ten a kilo'

11. *'It should be...'*

There is no one word to express the English sense of 'should be', however 'should be' tends to be expressed by the imperfect verb *yikūn* for a masculine subject or *tikūn* for a feminine subject, as in:

aštī murr bass yikūn ḥālī	'I want myrhh, but it should be nice'

al-bint tikūn mi'addabih 'the girl should be well-mannered'

12. *Questions: 'What type of incense do you want?'*

In order to say 'what type of X do you want' the question word *mā* 'what' is followed by the verb *tištī* then the preposition *min* followed by the object (e.g. incense). This gives the literal equivalent of 'what do you want of X?':

mā tištī min baxūr 'what type of incense do you want?'

mā tištī min baṭāṭ 'what type of potatoes do you want?'

Thematic Vocabulary

Areas of the market

sūg al-bagar cattle market
sūg al-bazz cloth market
sūg aḏ-ḏahab gold market
sūg al-gāt *gāt* market
sūg al-gišr coffee market
sūg al-ḥabb grain market
sūg al-ḥadīd iron market
sūg al-ᶜinab grape market
sūg al-ᶜirj donkey market
sūg al-milḥ salt market [general name for whole market area]
sūg al-muxlāṣ silver market
sūg an-naḥḥās copper market
sūg aṭ-ṭīsān market for metal plates
sūg at-titin tobacco market
sūg az-zabīb dried fruit market

Main gates to old city[4]

bāb al-balagih
bāb as-salām
bāb šuᶜūb
bāb al-yaman
bāb ṣabāḥ

[4] Of these gates only *bāb al-yaman* remains standing. Thus it is often described simply as *al-bāb* 'the gate'.

Exercises

1. *Pronoun suffixes*

Complete the following table by suffixing the correct pronoun to the words *ab* 'father', *ax* 'brother', *lā* 'to', *ṣalā* 'towards' and ^{c}*alā* 'on; against'. The top left-hand corner is completed by way of example:

	ab	*ax*	*lā*	*ṣalā*	^{c}*alā*
anā	*abī*				
ant					
antī					
antayn					
hum					

2. *The vocative*

Call the following people using the vocative:

i. Muhammad. ii. Najla. iii. The boys. iv. The teachers m. v. The girls. vi. My son. vii. My wife.

3. *Negation*

Negate the following sentences.

Example: *aštī min hāḏā n-naw*^{c}. ———> *ma štīš min hāḏa n-naw*^{c}

i. *tištī tištarī baxūr.* ____________________

ii. *ništī nitḥākā ṣan*^{c}*ānī.* ____________________

iii. *tištaray baṭāṭ.* ____________________

iv. *tištarī nuṣṣ kīlū ruzz.* ____________________

v. *hū yitḥākā ṣan*^{c}*ānī bulbul.* ____________________

4. *Substitution*

Substitute the correct form of *yitḥākā* for the verb *yištarī,* and substitute the word *yamanī* for *hāḏā* in the following sentences.

Example: *aštī štarī hāḏā.*———> *aštī tḥākā yamanī.*

i. *ništī ništarī hāḏā.* ______________________________

ii. *yištayn yištarayn hāḏā.*__________________________

iii. *yištaw yištaraw hāḏā.*___________________________

iv. *tištī tištarī hāḏā.* ______________________________

v. *tištay tištaray hāḏā.* ____________________________

5. *Gap filling*

Supply the correct demonstrative pronoun from the *hā-* set to the following nouns. Then substitute the initial *hā-* demonstrative with the appropriate demonstrative from the second demonstrative set (*ḏayyā*, etc.).

Example: *al-marih* _____ ——> *al-marih hāḏā* ——> *al-marih tayyih*

i. *al-bint* _______

ii. *ar-rijāl* _______

iii. _________ *n-niswān*

iv. _________ *l-bayt*

v. _________ *s-sūg*

vi. _________ *n-naw*ᶜ

vii. *al-baxūr* _______

6. *Word order*

Re-order the following groups of words to produce meaningful sentences in Ṣanᶜānī Arabic.

Example: *bayt, gawī, kabīr, hāḏā* ——> *hāḏā bayt kabīr gawī*

i. *yištarayn, an-niswān, gawī, baxūr, yištayn, ḥālī*

ii. *hum, ar-rijāl, as-sūg, al-yawm, fī*

iii. *sāᶜ-mā, hum, iḥna*

iv. *hī, al-marih, samīrih, ismahā*

v. *al-yamanī, bulbul, zamīlī, yitḥākā*

vi. *hū, zamīlak, ayn, min, aṣlan*

vii. *bi-, ad-dagīg, ar-raṭl, kam*

viii. *ar-ruzz, bi-, ᶜišrīn, al-kīlū*

LESSON 6

Fi l-maṭ^{c}am In the restaurant

Dialogue 1 *gadanā jāwi^{c}*

Tim: *gadanā jāwi^{c} yā ṣāluḥ, ^{c}ādanī ma ṣṭabaḥtš*

Salih: *mā tštī tākul?*

Tim: *aštī 'ākul fūl, šī bih fūl al-yawm?*

Salih: *aywih, bih.*

Tim: *wa-kayf al-fūl?*

Salih: *gadū ḥālī marrih.*

Tim: *gad baynih bisbās?*

Salih: *aywih, gadū faḥḥ, wa-ma^{c}ānā bayḏ̣, tištī fūl bi-bayḏ̣?*

Tim: *nāhī, ddī lī fūl bi-bayḏ̣ w-iṯnayn xubz wa-šahay yā ṣāluḥ.*

Tim: *allāh yixallīk.*

Dialogue 2 *gadiḥna ^{c}āṭušīn gawī*

Salih: *yā mḥammad, gadiḥna ^{c}āṭušīn gawī.*

Muhammad: *nāhī, 'addī lkum šahay antū l-iṯnayn?*

Salih: *māšī, ana štī šahay wa-zamīlī hāḏā yištī ḥabbat bibs.*

Muhammad: *āsif, bass al-bibs ^{c}ādī mā wuṣulatš al-yawm.*

Salih: *ṭayyub, ddī bass iṯnayn šahay.*

Vocabulary

^{c}ādanī	I (am) still	*^{c}ādī*	it f. (is) still
ākul	I eat	*allāh yixallīk*	may God preserve you [i.e. thank you]
āsif	sorry m.s.	*^{c}āṭuš*	thirsty
bayḏ̣	eggs coll. m.	*baynih*	in it m.
bibs	Pepsi m.	*bih*	there is

bisbās	chilli pepper m.	*faḥḥ*	hot and spicy
fūl	horse beans m.	*gadanā*	I (am)
gadiḥna	we (are)	*gadū*	he (is)
ḥabbih pl. *-āt*	a unit; one f.	*iṯnayn*	two m.
jāwi^{c}	hungry	*kaṯīr*	a lot; many
maṭ^{c}*am* pl. *maṭā*^{c}*um*	restaurant m.	*nišrab*	we drink
šahay	tea m.	*(i)ṣṭabaḥt*	I had breakfast
tākul	you m.s. eat	*xubz*	bread coll. m.

Grammar

1. *Pronunciation*

1.1. Emphasis

The putative origin of the word *(i)ṣṭabaḥt* is *(i)ṣtabaḥt* with a non-emphatic *t*. The sound *t* is pronounced as emphatic *ṭ* when it comes immediately after an emphatic sound - in this case, *ṣ*.

1.2. Diphthongisation

The sounds *ī* and *ū* are often diphthongised and pronounced as *-ey,* as in the sound *ay* in English *bay*, and *-ow,* as in the sound *ow* in English *bow,* at the end of a sentence, or whenever a speaker takes a pause (cf. *Syntax* p. 10):

non-pause	pause	gloss
aštī	*aštey*	'I want'
tākulū	*tākulow*	'you m.pl. eat'

2. *Verbs: 'to eat'*

The paradigm of the verb 'to eat' in the imperfect aspect is as follows:

singular		plural	
ā-kul	I eat	*nā-kul*	we eat
tā-kul	you m. eat	*tā-kul-ū*	you m.pl. eat
tā-kul-ī	you f. eat	*tā-kul-ayn*	you f.pl. eat
yā-kul	he eats	*yā-kul-ū*	they m. eat
tā-kul	she eats	*yā-kul-ayn*	they f. eat

3. *Verbs: the perfect aspect*

The perfect aspect of the verb is generally used to talk about the past tense (cf. Lesson 4, 8.). The inflected verb in the perfect has a stem and a suffix, but, unlike in the imperfect, it has no prefix:

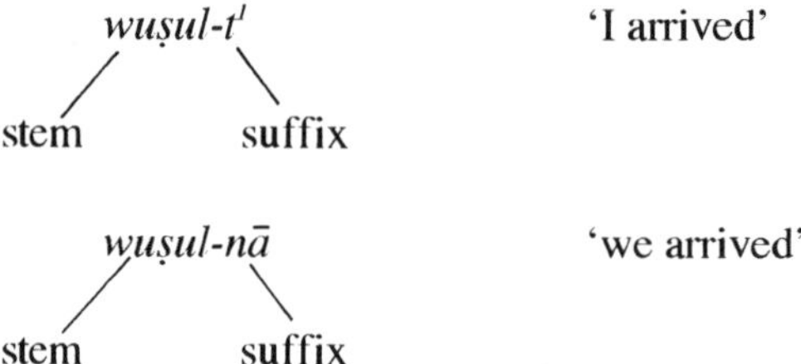

'I arrived'

'we arrived'

When the perfect verb occurs without a preceding adverbial particle (cf. 3. below), it usually refers to a past action without reference to whether the action involved was momentary or continuous (cf. in particular Naim-Sanbar 1993):

wuṣult	'I arrived'
širibnā[2] *bibs*	'we drank Pepsi'

Here is the complete paradigm of the verb *wuṣul* 'to arrive' in the perfect aspect:

singular		plural	
wuṣul-t	I arrived	*wuṣul-nā*	we arrived
wuṣul-t	you m. arrived	*wuṣul-tū*	you m.pl. arrived
wuṣul-tī	you f. arrived	*wuṣul-tayn*	you f.pl. arrived
wuṣul	he arrived	*wuṣul-ū*	they m. arrived
wuṣul-at	she arrived	*wuṣul-ayn*	they f. arrived [3]

From this lesson on, verbs will be listed in the perfect and imperfect in the third masculine singular (i.e. 'he') form, and the English translation will be given in the infinitive. For example:

širib - yišrab to drink *katab - yuktub* to write

[1] Also pronounced *wṣult* 'I arrived', also *wṣulnā* 'we arrived' (cf. Lesson 1).

[2] Also pronounced *šribnā* 'we drank' (*ibid*).

[3] All the verbal forms which take a consonant-initial suffix (i.e. first and second persons) can be pronounced without the first vowel i.e. *wuṣul-t* versus *wṣult*.

4. *Adverbs: ᶜād and gad*

The adverbial particles *ᶜād* and *gad* often take independent pronouns, or, in the case of the second persons and the first person singular, dependent pronouns as suffixes. When *ᶜād* and *gad* are followed by a third person singular, the *h* is not pronounced (cf. Lesson 7):

ᶜād + *hī* 'still' 'she'	*ᶜādī* 'she is still'
gad + *hū* 'still' 'he'	*gadū* 'he is'

ᶜād gives the sense of 'still' in a positive sentence, and the sense of 'yet' in a negative sentence:

ummī ᶜādī fi l-bayt	'my mother, she is still in the house'
ummī ᶜādī mā wuṣulatš	'my mother, she has not yet arrived'

When *ᶜād* + pronoun precedes a verb in the perfect aspect in a positive sentence, it gives the sense of 'just':

ᶜādanī šribt	'I have just drank'
ᶜādī wuṣulat	'she has just arrived'

Here is the full set of *ᶜād* plus pronoun suffixes:

	singular	plural
1.	*ᶜādanī*	*ᶜādiḥna*
2. m.	*ᶜādak* or *ᶜādant*	*ᶜādkum* or *ᶜādakum*
2. f.	*ᶜādiš* or *ᶜādantī*	*ᶜādkin* or *ᶜādakin*
3. m.	*ᶜādū*	*ᶜādum* or *ᶜādahum*
3. m.	*ᶜādī*	*ᶜādin* or *ᶜādahin*

gad is a very common adverbial particle in most dialects of Yemeni Arabic. It often comes before a pronoun when the pronoun is the subject of a sentence, as in:

gadū fi l-bayt	'he is in the house'

gad also comes before a prepositional phrase, as in:

gad lahā sanih fi l-yaman	'she has been in Yemen for one year'
gad baynih bisbās kaṯīr	'it has a lot of chilli in'

Before a pronoun or a prepositional phrase, *gad* gives no particular difference in meaning to the sentence; when *gad* occurs before a verb in the imperfect aspect (with or without an intervening pronoun), however, it does alter the meaning of the sentence and gives the sense of immediate futurity - i.e. 'about to do something' - or 'almost', as in:

gad tisīrī	'are you f.s. about to go?'
gadū yijī	'he is about to come'

The verb following *gad* can also take the future prefix (cf. Lesson 7):

gadiš ᶜa-tsīrī	'are you f.s. about to go?'

Depending on the context, it can also give the sense of 'may' or 'maybe', as in:

gadiḥna nisīr	'we may go'
gad nisīr	'ditto'

When *gad* occurs before a verb in the perfect aspect (with or without a pronoun) it gives the sense of the English present perfect - i.e. 'has done' (cf. in particular Naim-Sanbar 1993):

mḥammad gad jā'	'Muhammad has come'
jamīlih gad wuṣulat	'Jamila has arrived'

In certain contexts it can also convey the sense of 'already':

gad addaythā lak	'I have already given it to you m.s.'

The full set of *gad* plus pronoun suffixes is as follows:

	singular	plural
1.	*gadanī* or *gadanā*	*gadiḥna*
2. m.	*gadak* or *gadant*	*gadkum* or *gadakum*
2. f.	*gadiš* or *gadantī*	*gadkin* or *gadakin*
3. m.	*gadū*	*gadum* or *gadahum*
3. f.	*gadī*	*gadin* or *gadahin*

When *gad* + pronoun or *ᶜād* + pronoun is negated in a sentence without a verb, the negative particle *mā* precedes the particle, and the negative suffix *-š* comes after the suffixed pronoun:

mā gadīš lā ᶜindahum	'she isn't with them ...'
mā ᶜādūš fi l-bayt	'he is not still in the house'

5. *Cardinal numbers 1-10*

The counting form of the numbers from 1 -10 is as follows:

1	*wāḥid*	6	*sittih*
2	*iṯnayn*	7	*sabᶜah*
3	*ṯalāṯih*	8	*ṯamāniyih*
4	*arbaᶜah*	9	*tisᶜah*
5	*xamsih*	10	*ᶜašarih*

When ordering food or drink the numbers are used in this form before a noun in the singular:

iṯnayn bibs	'two pepsis'
ṯalaṯih šay	'three teas'
xamsih līm	'five lime (juices)'

This is also the case with certain measures of weight, money, distance, etc.:

iṯnayn riyāl	'two *riyāl*s [Yemeni currency]'
sabᶜah mitr	'seven metres'
ṯamāniyih wār	'eight yards'
tisᶜah kīlū	'nine kilos'

Numbers are asked about using the question word *kam*:

kam līm	'how many lime juices?'
kam bunn	'how many coffees?'
kam mitr	'how many metres?'

6. *The imperative*

The imperative is formed by removing the *ti-* prefix (which indicates second person) from the imperfect verb:

imperfect	imperative	gloss
tithākaw	*thākaw*	'speak m.pl.!'
tākulī	*kulī*	'eat f.s.!'
tiddī	*ddī*	'give m.s.!'
tišrabayn	*šrabayn*	'drink f.pl.!'

Where removal of the prefix leaves two consonants at the beginning of a sentence, an initial helping vowel *i* may be pronounced:

thākaw	***i**thākaw*	'speak m.pl.!'
ddī	***i**ddī*	'give m.s.!'
šrabayn	***i**šrabayn*	'drink f.pl.!'

7. *'To have'*

There is no verb 'to have' in Arabic. To express the sense of 'having' Ṣan^{c}ānī Arabic uses the preposition *ma^{c}* 'with' with a pronoun before the possessed object. Thus, to say 'I have a car' in Ṣan^{c}ānī Arabic the expression is literally 'with me, a car':

ma^{c}ī	+	*sayyārih*	*ma^{c}ī sayyārih*
'with-me'		'car'	'I have a car'

To say 'the men have a car' where the 'haver' is a noun rather than a pronoun, a topicalised sentence must be used (cf. Lesson 4): in this case, the subject 'the men' comes first, the prepositional phrase 'with them' comes second, and the possessed object 'a car' comes third:

ar-rijāl ma^{c}āhum sayyārih 'the men, they have a car'

To say 'the car is with me' as opposed to 'I have a car' the word order is reversed. 'The car' takes first position, while the prepositional phrase 'with me' takes second position:

as-sayyārih ma^{c}ī 'the car is with me'

8. *'There is' and yes-no questions*

'There is' and 'there are' are expressed by *bih* in Ṣan^{c}ānī Arabic. It is *almost* always followed by an indefinite noun:

bih fūl 'there is *fūl* [horse beans]'
bih niswān 'there are women'

In yes-no questions - questions which ask about the existence of something - *bih* is often preceded by the particle *šī*, as in:

šī bih bisbās 'is there any chilli?'
šī bih niswān 'are there any women?'

bih can also be followed by a more specific prepositional phrase:

šī bih ma^{c}ākum sayyārih 'do you m.pl. have a car?'

šī can also come before another prepositional phrase or on its own in yes-no questions:

šī ma^{c}ak sayyārih 'do you m.s. have a car?'
šī ġadā 'is there any lunch?'

When *^{c}ād* is put at the beginning of a yes-no question it gives the sense of 'another' or 'any other':

^{c}ād šī ma^{c}ak sayyārih 'do you m.s. have another car?'

^{c}ād šī gahwih 'is there any more coffee?'

^{c}ād šī dafātir 'are there any more exercise books?

When a question has been asked once and answered negatively, it may be asked again with initial *gad*; in this case *gad* expresses intensity and a sense of *nowness*:

gad šī bih mā'	'is there any water now?'
gad šī ma^{c}ak aṯ-ṯawrih	'do you m.s. have the Thawra paper now?'

In replying positively to questions the particle *šī* is not pronounced. The following (positive) answers would be correct to the question *šī bih bisbās* 'is there any chilli?':

aywih bih bisbās	'yes, there is chilli'
bih bisbās	'there is chilli'
aywih bih	'yes, there is'
bih	'there is'

bih is negated by *mā* and *-š* in the same way as other prepositional phrases which take a pronominal suffix (cf. Lesson 5). The *h* of *bih* is generally not pronounced when negated by *mā -š*:

mā + bih + -š	*mā biš* or *mā bišš*

Thematic Vocabulary

Food and drink

^{c}asīd	porridge m.
^{c}aṣīr	juice m.
bāmiyih	ladies' fingers f.
baṣal	large spring onions coll. m.
bibs	Pepsi m.
bārid	cold; cold drink m.
bint aṣ-ṣaḥn	sweet dish of layered pastry with honey and black onion seed f.
bisbās	chilli m.
bunn	coffee m.
burtagāl	oranges coll. m.
buṣṣālūh	round onions coll. m.
dijāj	chicken coll. m.
dijājih	a chicken f.
ḍubbuh	pumpkin f.

fasūliyih	French beans f.
fūl	horse beans m.
gaḥš abyaḏ	grey mullet m.
gaḥš aḥmar	red mullet m.
gahwih	spicy coffee husk drink f.
gišr	spicy coffee husk drink known as *gahwih* m.
ḥabbih sawdā	onion seed f.
ḥāmī	hot
ḥilbih	fenugreek f.
jibnih	cheese f.
jibnih bayḏā	white cheese f.
kidmih pl. *kidam*	a roll of soldiers' bread f.
lawz	almonds coll. m.
līm	lime juice m.
mā'	water m.
makarūnih	macaroni m.
malūj	large, flat bread coll. m.
malūjih	a large, flat bread m.
marag	broth m.
maraysī	sugar m.
milḥ	salt m.
mlawwaḥ	large thin flaky bread often eaten with fish m.
mšakkal	drink of mixed fresh fruit juices m.
muṭabbag	thin pastry pocket fried with egg, onion and tomato inside m.
niskafey	Nescafé
raṭab	bread layered with fat and baked in *tannūr* oven m.
ruzz	rice m.
ṣalaṭuh	salad f.
saltih	hot dish of meat broth topped with fenugreek f.
samn	clarified butter m.
samn baladī	local clarified butter m.
ṣanūnuh	tomato, fish, and potato dish f.
šay / šahay	tea m.
širkih	red meat f.
sukkar	sugar m.
ṭabax - yuṭbux	to cook (s.th.)
ṭabīx	mixed vegetables m.
ṭamāṭis	tomatoes coll. m.
tᶜaššā - yitᶜaššā	to have supper
tġaddā - yitġaddā	to have lunch
xubz	flat round bread coll. m.

xubzih	a flat round bread f.
zabīb	raisins coll. m.
zaḥāwug	mixture of pulverised green chilli and tomato m.
zibādī	yoghurt m.
zibdih	butter f.

Meals

ṣubūḥ	breakfast m.
ġadā	lunch m.
ᶜašā	evening meal [often a snack]

Exercises

1. *Translation*

Translate the following groups of sentences into Ṣanᶜānī Arabic:

A. Use *šī* or *šī bih*

i. Is there any *mšakkal*?

ii. Is there any tea?

iii. Is there any lunch?

B. Use a form of *yištī*

i. My friend m. wants two lime juices.

ii. I want a Pepsi.

iii. We want two teas.

C. Use *kam*

i. How many teas?

ii. How many lime juices?

iii. How many Pepsis?

D. Use *^{c}ād* + pronoun

i. He is still in the house.

ii. My mother is still at [trans. as 'in'] the market.

iii. They have just arrived.

E. Use *ma^{c}* + pronoun

i. We have a small house.

ii. They m. have a car.

iii. She has a girl and a boy.

2. *Agreement*

Fill the gaps by providing the correct endings to the nouns and adjectives in the following sentences:

Example: *bintī jāwi^{c}*_____ *bass ibnī miš jāwi^{c}*_____ ——> *bintī jāwi^{c}ah bass ibnī miš jāwi^{c}*

i. *al-^{c}iyyāl ^{c}āṭuš*_____ *gawī.*

ii. *al-fūl ḥālī*_____ *gawī l-yawm.*

iii. *gadiḥna jāwi^{c}*_____.

iv. *al-bint ṣaġīr*_____ *bass axūhā kabīr*_____.

v. *ummī gadī mudīr*_____ *fī ti^{c}izz.*

vi. *hin mudarris*_____.

3. *Verb inflection*

Complete the table below by inflecting the following verbs in the perfect. The top left-hand corner is completed by way of example:

	širib	*libis* [to dress]	*wuṣul*
anā	*širibt*		
hū			
hin			
antayn			

4. *Imperative*

Complete the table below by providing the correct imperative forms. The horizontal line gives the stem of the imperfect verb. The top left-hand corner is completed by way of example:

	šrab	*tḥākā*	*ddī*
ant	*šrab*		
antayn			
antī			
antū			

5. *Word order*

Put the groups of words below into the correct order to produce meaningful sentences:

Example: *anā, gad, al-bayt, fī* ———> *gadanā fī l-bayt*

i. *abī, al-yawm, wuṣul, gad*

ii. *az-zaġīrih, ᶜād, al-bint, hī, as-sūg, fī*

iii. *lī, ddī, xubz, ṯalāṯih*

iv. *nišrab, ništī, bibs, iḥna, gad, ᶜāṭušīn*

v. *bih, šī, al-yawm, xubz*

vi. *saltih, ma^cāhum, al-jahhāl, gad*

6. *Question formation*

Using *šī* (with or without *bih*), ask whether the following things are available.

Example: *ġadā* ——> *šī ġadā? / šī bih ġadā?*

i. *gahwih*. ii. *bunn*. iii. *jibnih*. iv. *ṣubūḥ*. v. *samn baladī*. vi. *gaḥš aḥmar*. vii. *ᶜašā*.

LESSON 7

Mā tsawway ġudwuh What are you f.s. doing tomorrow?

Dialogue 1 *mā tsawway ġudwuh*

Najla: *mā tsawway ġudwuh yā Sally?*

Sally: *šā-sīr at-tafruṭuh.*

Najla: *at-tafruṭuh fī bayt man?*

Sally: *fī bayt ^{c}abd al-karīm.*

Najla: *tisīrī lā waḥdiš?*

Sally: *māšī, 'anā sīr anā wa-zamīlatī hāḏīk.*

Najla: *ayyaḥīn tisīrayn?*

Sally: *ba^{c}d al-ġadā, 'in šā' allāh.*

Dialogue 2 *mā tsawwī yawm al-jum^{c}ah*

Najib: *mā tsawwī yawm al-jum^{c}ah yā tīm?*

Tim: *šā-xazzin.*

Najib: *tixazzin fī bayt man?*

Tim: *fī bayt muḥammad.*

Najib: *aynū sākin muḥammad? mišū sākin fī l-gā^{c}?*

Tim: *māšī, gadū sākin fī l-bāb šigg sūg al-muxlāṣ.*

Najib: *aywih, anā ^{c}ārif ḏalḥīn.*

Tim: *lilmā ma tjīš ma^{c}ānā yā najīb?*

Najib: *āsif bass asāfir ti^{c}izz fī ṣ-ṣubḥ.*

Vocabulary

al-bāb	the gate [of old city]	*^{c}ārif*	knowing m.s.
ayyaḥīn	when	*ba^{c}d*	after
bayt pl. *biyūt*	house m.	*ḏalḥīn*	now
fī	in	*ġadā*	lunch m.
ġudwuh	tomorrow	*in šā' allāh*	God willing;

	hopefully
jā' - yijī	to come
muxlāṣ	silver m.
sāfar - yisāfir	to travel
sār - yisīr	to go
šigg	beside; next to
tafruṭuh / tufruṭuh	women's party f.
yawm al-jum^{c}ah	Friday
zamīlih pl. *-āt*	friend f.
lilmā	why
šā-	[future particle]
sākin	living m.s.
sawwā - yisawwī	to do (s.th.)
ṣubḥ	morning m.
xazzan - yixazzin	to chew (*gāt*)
waḥdiš	your f.s. own

Grammar

1. *Pronunciation*

1.1. Syncope

When the stem of an imperfect verb begins with a single consonant, the vowel of the prefix *yi-*, *ni-* or *ti-* is usually not pronounced when the verb follows a noun or particle which ends in a vowel:

mā	+	*tisawwī*	——>	*mā tsawwī*
'what'		'you are doing'		'what are you m.s. doing?'
^{c}a-	+	*tisawwī*	——>	*^{c}a-tsawwī*
[future]		'you are doing'		'you m.s. will do/will be doing'

1.2. Deletion of *h* in pronouns

When a question word such as *man* 'who', *kayf* 'how', *ayn* 'where' takes a third person singular pronoun as a suffix, or the negative particle *miš*, *h* of the pronoun is not pronounced (cf. Lesson 6, 3.):

kayf	+	*hū*	——>	*kayfū*
'how'		'he'		'how is he?'
man	+	*hī*	——>	*manī*
'who'		'she'		'who is she?'
ayn	+	*hī*	——>	*aynī*
'where'		'she'		'where is she?'

miš	+ *hū*	——> *mišū*
'not'	'he'	'he is not'

1.3. Syllables

In most languages words can be divided into syllables. A syllable is typically a unit of pronunciation larger than a single sound and smaller than a word. In Ṣan^{c}ānī Arabic words can be of one or many syllables. The word *bayt* 'house' has a single syllable, while the word *biyūt* 'houses' has two syllables (*bi* and *yūt*). In Arabic, syllables can be light, heavy or superheavy. Syllables are described as *light* when they consist of a consonant (C) and a short vowel (V), as in:

fa-	'then'	*wa-*	'and'

and as in the first syllable in:

.bi.yūt	'houses'	*.ma.rih*	'woman'

Syllables are described as *heavy* when they consist of CVC or CVV (consonant followed by a long vowel), as in the final syllables in:

bi.yūt	'houses'	*ma.rih.*	'woman'
ṣbaḥ.tū.	'good morning'	*ma.^{c}ī.*	'with me'

and as in both syllables in:

.mak.laf.	'woman'	*.mak.tab.*	'office'

Finally, syllables are described as *superheavy* when they consist of either of the sequences CVVC or CVCC. These syllables only occur in monosyllabic words, as in:

.bayt.	'house'	*.ktabt.*	'I wrote'

or at the end of words:

basā.tīn.	'gardens'	*mudarri.sāt.*	'teachers f.'

Initial consonant clusters do not affect the 'weight' of a syllable. The single syllable in the words *xšab* 'wood' and *tštī* 'you m.s. want' is heavy, even though there are two and three consonants respectively at the beginning of the syllable; the syllable in *kbīr* 'large' or *zġīr* 'small' is superheavy, even though the words have two consonants at the beginning.

1.4. Word stress[1]

In the following description of word stress the asterix * is written before the stressed syllable as in **bayt* 'house' and *bi*yūt* 'houses', and syllables are divided by dots as in the two syllables in the word *.bi.yūt.* 'houses'. When words are pronounced individually, the following stress rules apply:

In words of a single syllable, that syllable is stressed:

**bayt*	'house'	**bank*	'bank'
**bint*	'girl'	**ibn*	'son'

In words of two syllables, the first syllable is stressed if it is heavy and of the shape CVV:

**.ṣā.būn.*	'soap'	**.kā.fir.*	'unbeliever'

If the first syllable is either heavy and of the shape CVC, or light, the second syllable is stressed if it is superheavy:

.ka.ṯīr.*	'many'	*.ba*.ᶜīd.*	'far'
.aḥ.wāḏ̣.*	'troughs'	*.ab*.wār.*	'wells'

If the second syllable is heavy, the first syllable is usually stressed if it is heavy:

**.mak.tab.*	'office'	**.šik.mih.*	'*šikmih* party'[2]

If the first syllable is light, however, either the first or second syllable may be stressed. This is particularly the case where the word ends in *-ih* or has a sibilant sound *s* or *š*:

.ma.rih.*	or	**.ma.rih.*	'woman'
.xa.šab.*	or	**.xa.šab.*	'wood'
.ku.tub.*	or	**.ku.tub.*	'books'

---

[1] For a detailed study of stress in the speech of older women speakers of Ṣanᶜānī Arabic see Naim-Sanbar (1994).

[2] Words which end in *-ih*, or which have the sound *š* or *s* can also be stressed on the final syllable, particularly at the end of a sentence, to give, in this case, *škmih*.

In a word has three or more syllables, the penultimate syllable is stressed if that is heavy:

a.sā.mī.* 'names' *.ma*.kā.tib.* 'offices'

If the penultimate syllable is light, the final syllable is stressed if that is superheavy:

.wu.za.rā.* 'ministers' *.mu.dar.ri*.sīn.* 'teachers'

If the final syllable is only heavy, then the right-most, non-final, heavy syllable is stressed:

**.jā.mi.ᶜah.* 'university' *.mu*.dar.ri.sih.* 'teacher f.'

If a word has no heavy syllables within the word and the final syllable is not superheavy, the first syllable is stressed:

**.ʃa.ᶜi.lih.* 'problem' **.da.ra.sat.* 'she learnt'

Note that the definite article does not count as part of the word for word stress purposes. Therefore *al-marih* 'the woman' takes stress on the first or second syllable of the noun *marih*, and not on the syllable *al-*.

1.5. Glottalisation in pause

Yemeni Arabic has a very glottal sound. This is because the last consonant of stressed syllables is usually pronounced with a glottal stop (for details Naim-Sanbar 1994, cf. also Jastrow 1984, Behnstedt 1985). For example:

non-pause	pause	gloss
kitāb	*kitā'b*	book
bustān	*bustā'n*	garden
basātīn	*basā'tīn*	gardens
xubz	*xubz'*	bread
samn	*sam'n*	clarified butter

2. *Future prefixes*

The future can be expressed in Arabic either by the imperfect verb on its own, or by the imperfect verb with a future prefix. It is important to note that future prefixes are used far less in Arabic than the future tense is in English. In Ṣanᶜānī Arabic the future prefixes are *šā-* or *ᶜad-* for the first person singular, and *ᶜa-* for all other persons (cf. 1.1. above). When the first singular takes the future prefix *šā-*, the imperfect prefix vowel *a-* is not pronounced (cf. 1. above):

šā-	+ *asawwī*	——>	*šā-sawwī*
[future]	'I-do'		'I will do'

When the future prefix *šā-* is used for a verb the stem of which begins with a cluster of two consonants, the long vowel *ā* of the prefix is reduced to *a*:

šā-	+ *ašrab*	——>	*ša-šrab*
[future]	'I-drink'		'I will drink'

The prefix *ᶜad-* differs from *šā-* in that *ᶜad-* gives the sense that the speaker will do something at *some* time, while *šā-* indicates that the speaker will do something at a *definite* time (for example, tomorrow, next week, next month).

3. *Demonstrative pronouns: far demonstratives*

As with the near demonstratives, there are two sets of far demonstratives denoting 'that' and 'those': a set which begins with *hā-* and a set which does not. The far demonstratives are used considerably less than the near demonstratives (and *hāḏā*, for example, is often used where 'that' would be used in English). The two sets of far demonstratives are given as a) and b) below:

		singular	plural
a)			
	m.	*hāḍāk*	*hāḏawlāk*
	f.	*hāḍīk*[3]	
b)			
	m.	*ḏayyāk*	*ḏawlayyak / ḏawlāk / awlāk / awlā'ik*
	f.	*tayyik*	

[3] The singular far demonstratives can also be pronounced without emphatic *ḍ* as *hāḏāk and hāḏīk*.

In the set of non-*hā-* far demonstratives there are four alternants for 'those', all of which can be used for male or female. The singular demonstratives in this set can be reduced to *ḏāk* or *ḏayk* 'that m.' and *tīk* or *tayk* 'that f.', or can take initial *hā-*, as in *hātayyik* 'that f.' (*Syntax* p. 44).

4. *Demonstrative-noun word order*

In a noun phrase a demonstrative can either precede or follow a simple definite noun (cf. Lesson 5). However, when a demonstrative is used with a complex noun: that is to say, a noun which has a possessive pronoun suffix, as in *zamīlatī* 'my friend f.', or a noun annex (cf. Lessons 3 and 8) as in *bayt* ***al-marih*** 'the woman's house', the demonstrative virtually always follows the noun:

zamīlatī hāḏī	'this friend f. of mine'
bayt ar-rajjāl hāḏ̣āk	'that man's house'

Similarly when a demonstrative is used with a proper noun, such as *aḥmad, ibb,* or *jamīlih,* the demonstrative usually follows the noun:

aḥmad hāḏā	'this Ahmad'

5. *Active participles*

Active participles of verbs are often used in place of their related verb to express a state or, in some cases, to express movement. The active particles we have seen in the dialogues in this lesson and in previous lessons are formed on the pattern **KāTiB**[4]. For certain states, such as the state of hunger and thirst, cold or heat (cf. Lesson 6), the active participle is used to the almost total exclusion of the verb. For other states, such as tiredness, knowledge and travelling, use of the active participle is slightly more common than use of the corresponding verb. The active participles considered so far include:

ᶜāṭuš	'thirsty'	*ᶜārif*	'knowing'
jāwiᶜ	'hungry'	*sākin*	'living'

Other common active participles which are used in place of the corresponding verb include:

[4] **KāT*u*B** when **K** or **T** is an emphatic consonant (*ṭ, ṣ,* or *ḍ*), as in ***ṭālub*** 'student m.'.

state:	*tāᶜib*	'tired'	*dārī*	'knowing'
	fāhim	'understanding'	*jālis*	'staying'
	bārid	'cold'	*ḥāmī*	'hot'
	rāgid	'sleeping'	*ṣāyum*	'fasting'
	ḥāfiḍ	'knowing [a language]'	*šāṭur*	'clever'
movement:	*nāzil*	'getting out'	*wāgif*	'stopping; waiting'
	ḍāwī	'going home'		

The active participles take the same endings as ordinary adjectives: that is to say, they take the feminine ending *-ih* to express feminine singular[5], the sound plural ending *-īn* to express masculine plural, and the sound plural *-āt* to express feminine plural:

hū ᶜārif	'he knows'
*hī ᶜārif**ih***	'she knows'
*hum ᶜārif**īn***	'they m. know'
*hin ᶜārif**āt***	'they f. know'
hū ḥāfiḍ al-yamanī	'he knows Yemeni well'
*hī ḥāfiḍ**uh** al-yamani*	'she knows Yemeni well'
*hum ḥāfiḍ**īn** al-yamanī*	'they m. know Yemeni well'
*hin ḥāfiḍ**āt** al-yamanī*	'they f. know Yemeni well'

When an active participle ends in *-ī*, however, as in *dārī* 'knowing', the feminine ending *-yih* is often not pronounced. 'She knows' is translated as *hī dārī* and only exceptionally as *hī dāriyih* (cf. Lesson 4).

6. *Weak verbs: yisīr, yijī, yisawwī, yinsā*

There are a number of different types of verb in Arabic depending on the number and type of consonants in the stem of the verb. *Sound* verbs are verbs like *yišrab* 'to drink' and *yilbas* 'to wear; put on' which have three strong, or sound, consonants in the stem: in the case of *yišrab* these are *š, r* and *b*. *Weak* verbs are verbs which have a weak consonant - either a glottal stop ('), *w* or *y* - in the stem. These consonants are known as *weak* consonants because they change into another sound in the perfect or imperfect aspect of the verb, and in different verbal derivatives. Weak verbs can be hollow - where they take a middle *w* or *y* - or final weak - where they take a final *y* or '.

5 *-uh* after emphatic consonants *ṭ, ṣ*, or *ḍ*, and *-ah* immediately after the pharyngeals ᶜ or *ḥ* (cf. Lesson 3).

6.1. Hollow verbs

The hollow verb encountered in this lesson is the verb *yisīr* 'to go' in which the middle consonant of the verbal stem is *y*. In the imperfect aspect, *y* is not pronounced as a consonant but rather as a long vowel *ī*:

	singular	plural
1.	*a-sīr*	*ni-sīr*
2. m.	*ti-sīr*	*ti-sīr-ū*
2. f.	*ti-sīr-ī*	*ti-sīr-ayn*
3. m.	*yi-sīr*	*yi-sīr-ū*
3. f.	*ti-sīr*	*yi-sīr-ayn*

Note that the vowel *i* of the imperfect prefix is often not pronounced to give forms like *tsīr* 'you m.s. go' and *nsīr* 'we go' beside *tisīr* and *nisīr* (cf. Lesson 5). In the perfect aspect, the middle consonant *y* is not pronounced at all. In its place, a long vowel *ā* is pronounced for the third person inflections 'he', 'she' and 'they':

	singular	plural
3. m.	*sār*	*sār-ū*
3. f.	*sār-at*	*sār-ayn*

For first and second person inflections (which have a consonant-initial pronoun suffix), *y* is replaced by the short vowel *i*:

	singular	plural
1.	*sir-t*	*sir-nā*
2. m.	*sir-t*	*sir-tū*
2. f.	*sir-tī*	*sir-tayn*

6.2. Final weak verbs

The final weak verbs encountered in this lesson are the verbs *yijī* 'to come' and *yisawwī* 'to do'.[6] These verbs have the distinction of being both hollow - the middle consonant of both verbs is *w* - and final weak - the final consonant of *yijī* 'to come' is the glottal stop, while the final consonant of *yisawwī* 'to do' is *y*. The

[6] Other final weak verbs encountered so far include *yištarī* 'to buy', *yištī* 'to want', and *yitḥākā* 'to talk'.

verb *yisawwī* inflects in the same way as the verbs *yištī* 'to want' and *yištarī* 'to buy' (cf. Lesson 5, 5.). The paradigm of the verb *sawwā* - *yisawwī* in the imperfect aspect is:

	singular	plural
1.	*a-sawwī*	*ni-sawwī*
2. m.	*ti-sawwī*	*ti-saww-aw*
2. f.	*ti-saww-ay*	*ti-saww-ayn*
3. m.	*yi-sawwī*	*yi-saww-aw*
3. f.	*ti-sawwī*	*yi-saww-ayn*

In the perfect aspect, the final weak consonant *y* is pronounced in the first and second person inflectional forms:

	singular	plural
1.	*sawway-t*	*sawway-nā*
2. m.	*sawway-t*	*sawway-tū*
2. f.	*sawway-tī*	*sawway-tayn*

In the third person inflectional forms the final consonant *y* is not pronounced. In all but the third masculine singular form *ā* is not pronounced and the pronoun suffix is added directly to the last consonant *w*:

3. m.	*sawwā*	*saww-aw*
3. f.	*saww-at*[7]	*saww-ayn*

The paradigm of the verb *jā'* - *yijī* 'to come' in the imperfect aspect is:

	singular	plural
1.	*a-jī*	*ni-jī*
2. m.	*ti-jī*	*ti-j-aw*
2. f.	*ti-j-ay*	*ti-j-ayn*
3. m.	*yi-jī*	*yi-j-aw*
3. f.	*ti-jī*	*yi-j-ayn*

[7] In a few final weak verbs, the third feminine singular ending in the perfect is pronounced as *-it*, and **not** as *-at* (eg. *imtal-it* or *imtil-it* 'it was filled', *add-it* 'she gave' and *awf-it* or *fit* 'it f. came to an end' cf. also *Syntax* p. 56).

The paradigm of *jā'* in the perfect aspect is:

	singular	plural
1.	*jī-t*	*jī-nā*
2. m.	*jī-t*	*jī-tū*
2. f.	*jī-tī*	*jī-tayn*
3. m.	*jā'*	*j-aw*
3. f.	*jā'-at / ji-t / jī-t*	*j-ayn*

The final weak verb *nisī - yinsā* 'to forget' has a slightly different pattern from *jā' - yijī* and *sawwā - yisawwī* in that the final vowel in the perfect is *ī* and the final vowel in the imperfect is *ā*. The paradigm of *nisī - yinsā* 'to forget' in the imperfect aspect is:

	singular	plural
1.	*a-nsā*	*ni-nsā*
2. m.	*ti-nsā*	*ti-ns-aw*
2. f.	*ti-ns-ay*	*ti-ns-ayn*
3. m.	*yi-nsā*	*yi-ns-aw*
3. f.	*ti-nsā*	*yi-ns-ayn*

The paradigm of *nisī* in the perfect aspect is:

	singular	plural
1.	*nisī-t*	*nisī-nā*
2. m.	*nisī-t*	*nisī-tū*
2. f.	*nisī-tī*	*nisī-tayn*
3. m.	*nisī*	*nisy-aw*
3. f.	*nisy-at*	*nisy-ayn*

7. *Transitive verbs: objects*

Verbs are either transitive, or intransitive. Transitive verbs take objects, and some transitive verbs actually require objects, while intransitive verbs do not take objects. *xazzan - yixazzin* 'to chew (*gāt*)' is a transitive verb which does not require an object. Both the following sentences are grammatical, but the first is far more common:

verb	object	gloss
axazzin		'I chew'
axazzin	*gāt*	'I chew *gāt*'

Similarly, *širib - yišrab* 'to drink' can either take an object or can occur without an object:

verb	object	gloss
ašrab		'I drink'
ašrab	*šahay*	'I drink tea'

Transitive verbs which usually require objects include *sawwā - yisawwī* 'to do' and *yištī* 'to want'.

verb	object	gloss
yištī	*gāt*	'he wants *gāt*'
tisawwī	*l-ġadā*	'she is making lunch'

Active participles from transitive verbs can also take objects, just like their related verb:

	participle	object	gloss
(anā)	*ᶜārif*	*manū*	'I know who he is'
	fāhim	*hāḏā*	'do you m.s. understand this m.?'
(hū)	*ḥāfiḍ*	*al-yamanī*	'he knows Yemeni well'

Thematic Vocabulary

Quadriliteral verbs

In Ṣanᶜānī Arabic, words can have a stem with two or three consonants - as in the words considered so far in this book - or with four consonants. A number of basic words have stems with four consonants (cf. *Syntax* pp. 442-444). These include the following verbs (given in the perfect aspect):

gambar	to sit
laxbaṭ	to mix up

In a number of quadriliteral verbs, the second two consonants are identical to the first two:

dagdag	to knock
gaṣgaṣ	to cut up
maṣmaṣ	to suck
wizwiz (*ᶜalā*)	to make fun (of s.o.)

In other quadriliteral verbs the third and fourth consonant are identical:

daᶜmam	to ignore
baᶜsas	to muck around
tbaxṭaṭ	to write (s.th.)

A number of quadriliteral verbs have an intrusive *w*. These include:

šagwar	to smoke a cigarette
xazwag	to make a hole
gawzab	to sit, squat

A few quadriliteral verb have an intrusive *l*:

ḍalḥak	to laugh
ṣalfā	to clean
xalfaᶜ	to beat, strike, wear down [stone]

Some words which have four main, or *root*, consonants in the stem, have an initial *t*, as in:

tgahwā	to drink coffee
tkarbas	to squat
tgargaš	to wear a bonnet
tšaršaf	to wear the *širšaf*

Parts of the body

al-bunṣar	fourth finger f.
al-kabīsih	index finger f.
al-muhallilih	index finger f.

al-wusṭā	middle finger f.
ᶜayn pl. *ᶜuyūn*	eye f.
az-zġīrih	little finger f.
baṭn pl. *buṭūn*	stomach f.
ḏahr pl. *ḏuhūr*	back m.
ḏars pl. *aḏrās*	molar tooth m.
galb pl. *gulūb*	heart m.
jiḥr	behind m.
lisān pl. *alsinih*	tongue m.
lugf pl. *algāf*	mouth m.
mabsam pl. *mabāsim*	lip m.
nīb pl. *anyāb*	canine tooth m.
ragabih pl. *-āt*	neck f.
rās / *ra'-s* pl. *ru'ūs*	head m.
rijl pl. *arjul*	leg f.
rukbih pl. *rukab*	knee f.
šaᶜr	hair coll. m.
ṣbuᶜ pl. *aṣābuᶜ*	finger m.
sidr pl. *sudūr*	chest m.
sinnih pl. *sinān*	incisor tooth f.
uḏn pl. *āḏān*	ear f.
ᶜurgūb pl. *ᶜarāgīb*	heel m.
yad pl. *aydī*	hand f.

Exercises

1. *Translation*

Translate the following groups of sentences into Ṣanᶜānī Arabic:

A. Use a future prefix.

i. What are you m.s. going to do today?

ii. I will go to the market.

iii. When will she make lunch?

B. Use a topical sentence.

i. Your friend Fayza, where does she live?

ii. My mother(, she) is in the house.

C. Use the perfect aspect.

i. Where [= *ilayn*] has he gone?

ii. Where have they m. gone?

iii. Where have they f. gone?

D. Use an active participle.

i. My sister lives in al-Gā^{c}.

ii. Do you understand this?

iii. They know Yemeni well.

2. *Agreement*

Provide the correct endings in the following sentences.

Example: *al-^{c}iyyāl jāwi^{c}*_____ *gawī* ———> *al-^{c}iyyāl jāwi^{c}īn gawī.*

i. *ant sākin*_____ *fī l-kuwayt.*

ii. *al-banāt ^{c}āṭuš*_____.

iii. *fāhim*_____ *hāḏā yā xadījih?*

iv. *hī miš ^{c}ārif*_____ *šī.*

v. *ummī ^{c}ādī fī l-bayt jālis*_____.

3. *Present > future*

Add the future prefix to the verbs in the following sentences.

Example: *asawwī l-ġadā* ———> *šā-sawwī l-ġadā*

i. *tisawwī ṣ-ṣubūḥ.* ______________________________

ii. *ašrab gahwih.* ______________________________

iii. *nixazzin gāt al-yawm.* ______________________________

iv. *tixazzinayn ma^{c}ānā.* ______________________________

v. *yištaraw xubz min as-sūg.* ______________________________

vi. *yisawwayn al-ġadā.* ________________________________

vii. *ajīkum ba^c^d yawmayn, in šā' allāh.* ____________________

4. *Gap filling*

Complete the following sentences, correctly inflecting the verb given in brackets.

Example: *yištayn________ma^c^ānā (yitḥākā)* ———> *yištayn yitḥākayn ma^c^ānā*

i. *ašti* ________ *gāt min bāb al-yaman (yištarī).*

ii. *ništī* ________ *l-xubz ḏalḥīn (yisawwī).*

iii. *tištayn* ________ *lā ^c^indanā l-yawm, yā banāt (yijī).*

iv. *yištaw* ________ *ma^c^ al-wazīr (yitḥākā).*

v. *tištay* ________ *ḏayyā (yākul).*

5. *Verbs and objects*

Complete the table below by matching the objects on the horizontal line with appropriate verbs on the vertical line. The first line has been completed by way of example. Certain verbs may take more than one object (e.g. *ništī* 'we want' may take as an object *bibs, saltih, libs* [= clothes] *ḥālī* or *ṣubūḥ*):

	bibs	*saltih*	*libs ḥālī*	*ṣubūḥ*	*tafruṭuh*
tisīrī	-	-	-	-	X
yišrabū					
yākulayn					
nisawwī					
tilbasī					
ništī					

6. *Word stress*

Put the word-stress mark * before the stressed syllable in the following words.

Example: *ri*jāl*

i. *makālif* ii. *makātīb* iii. *miškilih* iv. *banāt* v. *maktab* vi. *makātib* vii. *šikmih*

7. *Word order*

Put the groups of words below into the correct order to produce meaningful sentences.

Example: *as-sūg, sākinih, fī, bintī, gadī* ———> *bintī gadī sākinih fī s-sūg*

i. *fāhim, anā, mā, ma^c^nā, hāḏā*
ii. *sayyārih, ġāliyih, ma^c^ih, zawjī, gad*
iii. *šā-, šahay, šrab, anā, gawī, ^c^āṭuš*
iv. *al-kutub, ^c^ād, l-bayt, fī, hin*
v. *yixazzin, yištī, al-yawm, gāt*
vi. *al-jibnih, bi-, al-kīlū, kam*

LESSON 8

Kayf al-xuṭūbuh fī l-yaman?

Dialogue 1 *al-xuṭūbuh*

Sally: *kayf ḥāliš yā salwā, mā liš šī?*

Salwa: *allāh yi^{c}āfīš wa-l-ḥamdu li-llāh ^{c}ala l-^{c}āfīyih.*

Sally: *gulī lī yā salwā, al-xuṭūbuh fī l-yaman, kayfhā?*

Salwa: *kayf sa^{c}am?*

Sally: *yā s^{c}am kayf al-xuṭūbuh bi-nisbih la l-wald?*

Salwa: *bi-nisbih la l-wald al-awlād yijma^{c}ū zalaṭ ḥagg miyat alf, yisīrū lā ^{c}ind bayt al-ḥarīwih yuxṭubū xuṭbuh. yišillū ma^{c}āhum šwayyat zabīb wa-lawz, yišillū ma^{c}āhum badlih ḏahab li-ḥawālī ^{c}ašarih alf, yišillū ma^{c}āhum sā^{c}ah, kulūnīyih ^{c}uṭr wa-ṭab^{c}an awwal šī ad-dublih, yitḥākaw ba^{c}dā ^{c}an al-xuṭūbuh xalāṣ. tintahī. yiwāfigū l-ahl wa-yimšaw.*

Dialogue 2 *al-mahr*

Sally: *yā salwā kam al-mahr fī l-yaman?*

Salwa: *mā biš ^{c}indukum mahr fī bilādkum mā?*

Sally: *māšī, nitzawwij balāš!*

Salwa: *ṭayyub kam šahr ba^{c}d al-xuṭūbuh yisīr al-ḥarīw lā ^{c}ind bayt al-ḥarīwih yišill ma^{c}ih zabīb wa-lawz ^{c}alā sibb al-milkih. yittafigū ^{c}alā l-mahr. lā kān ma^{c}ih maṯalan miyat alf yišillū awwal šī xamsīn alf min al-miyat alf la l-mahr, wa-ba^{c}da š-šarṭ.*

Sally: *wa-l-mahr wa-š-šarṭ mišin šī wāḥid?*

Salwa: *māšī, yā Sally, yišillū ṯalāṯīn alf šarṭ wa-ba^{c}dā xamsih alf la l-umm wa-xamsih alf la l-ḥarīwih ba^{c}d yawm aṣ-ṣabāḥīyih, sa^{c}am yawm aṣ-ṣabāḥ ba^{c}d az-zawāj. xalāṣ gad intahat al-miyat alf!*

Sally: *al-xisārih ḥagg al-^{c}iris kaṯīr!*

Salwa: *nāhī, nixsir ḥawālī miyatayn wa-xamsīn alf fī kull bayt.*

Sally: *mā šā' allāh!*

Vocabulary

ahl pl. *ahālī*	family m.	^{c}*alā sibb*/^{c}*asibb*	for; because (of)
alf pl. *alāf*	one thousand m.	^{c}*an*	about
awwal šī	the first thing	*ba*^{c}*dā*	then; afterwards
badlih d̲ahab	a wide gold collar f.	*balāš*	for nothing
dublih	gold wedding ring f.	*fatrih* pl. *-āt*	while; time span f.
gāl - yigūl / yugūl	to say (s.th.)	*ḥagg*	of, amounting to
ḥarīwih pl. *ḥarāwī*	bride f.	*ḥawālī*	around; about
^{c}*ind*	with; at the house of	^{c}*iris* pl. *a*^{c}*rās*	wedding m.
jama^{c} *- yijma*^{c}	to gather, collect	*kull*	each; every; all
kulūnīyih	cologne f.	*lā*	if
lā / li-	to; for	*lawz*	almonds coll. m.
mā šā' allāh	goodness!	*mahr*	bride price m.
mat̲alan	for example	*milkih*	wedding ceremony f.
mišī - yimšī	to walk; to go	*miyih* pl. *-āt*	hundred f.
nafs	[the] same	*nisbih* pl. *nisab*	relation f.
(*bi-nisbih lā*	in relation to)	*ntahā - yintahī*	to be finished
sā^{c}*ah* pl. *-āt*	watch; hour f.	*ṣabāḥ*	morning m.
šahr pl. *šuhūr*	month m.	*šahrayn*	two months
šall - yišill	to take (s.th.)	*šarṭ*	bridal sum m.
šī / šay pl. *ašyā*	thing m.	*šwayyih*	a little
ṭab^{c}*an*	of course	*t̲alāt̲īn*	thirty
ttafag - yittafig	to agree	*tzawwaj - yitzawwaj*	to get married
^{c}*uṭr*	perfume m.	*wāfag - yiwāfig*	to agree
wald pl. *awlād*	boy m.	*xalāṣ*	that's it!
xamsīn	fifty	*xaṭab - yuxṭub*	to engage (a woman)
xayrāt	a lot	*xisārih*	loss; payment; f.
xisir - yixsir	to spend (s.th.)	*xuṭbuh*	engagement f.
xuṭūbuh	engagement f.	*yawm aṣ-ṣabāḥ(īyih)*	the day after the wedding night m.
zabīb	raisins coll. m.	*zawāj* pl. *-āt*	wedding m.

Grammar

1. *Pronunciation: epenthesis*

When a word ends in a *geminate* (doubled) consonant, such as *ḥagg* 'of, belonging to, amounting to', an additional (*helping* or *epenthetic*) vowel *a* is pronounced before a following word which begins in a consonant:

ḥagg + *miyat alf* ——> *ḥagg**a** miyat alf* 'amounting to a hundred thousand'

šall + *miyat alf* ——> *šall**a** miyat alf* 'he took a hundred thousand'

As in *Syntax of Ṣanᶜānī Arabic* (*Syntax* p. 9), this additional vowel is not written in the texts and exercises used in this book

2. *Greetings*

There are many ways of asking how someone is in Ṣanᶜānī Arabic. One common phrase, particulary between people who already know each other, is *mā lak šī* to a man, *mā liš šī* to a woman or *mā lukum šī* when the masculine plural is used (cf. Lesson 2). This phrase literally means 'is there nothing wrong with you?'. The response can be as in the dialogue in this lesson: *allāh yiᶜāfīk(š) wa-l-ḥamdu li-llāh ᶜala l-ᶜāfiyih* 'may God give you health and thank God for health' or simply *mā lī šī* (or *mā lanā šī* in reply to *mā lukum šī*). Another phrase commonly used between women is *ḥayyā* 'may [God] give you life' with the response *allāh yiḥayyīš*.

3. *Habitual prefixes*

In Ṣanᶜānī Arabic an *habitual* or *continuous* aspect can be expressed by using the prefixes *bayn-* for the first person singular, and *bi-* for all other persons before the appropriate form of the imperfect verb, as in:

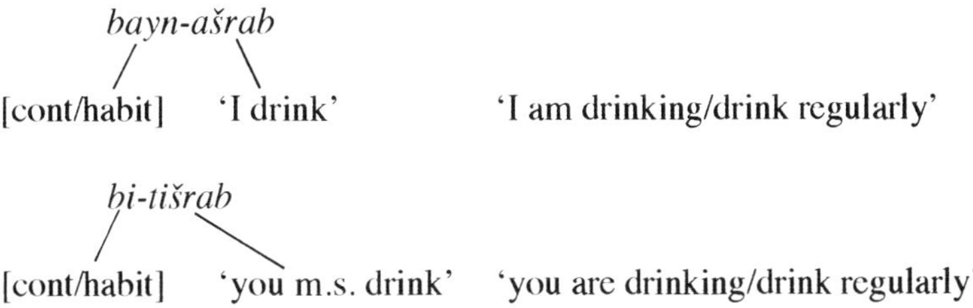

When the stem of the imperfect verb begins with a single consonant, as in *yisawwī* 'he does', the vowel of the imperfect prefix *yi-*, *ni-* or *ti-* is not pronounced when the continuous/habitual prefix *bi-* is used (cf. Lesson 7):

bi- + yisawwī	——>	*bī-sawwī*[1]	'he is doing'
bi- + tisawwī	——>	*bi-tsawwī*	'you m.s. are doing'
bi- + nisāfir	——>	*bi-nsāfir*	'we are travelling'

When *bi-* is pronounced before the imperfect prefix *yi-*, the entire imperfect prefix is not pronounced when the stem of the verb begins with two consonants:

bi- + yišrab	——>	*bi-šrab*	'he is drinking'
bi- + yitḥākaw	——>	*bi-tḥākaw*	'they m. are talking'

4. *'So many days...'*

In order to express phrases such as 'so many days, months, etc.' where 'so many' refers to a small, indefinite number, Ṣanᶜānī Arabic uses the word *kam* followed by a *singular* indefinite noun:

baᶜd kam yawm	'after so many days'
baᶜd kam šahr	'after so many months'
jilis kam sanih	'he stayed for so many years'

5. *Annexion: 'the woman's house'*

In Lesson 3 we saw that one of the three ways in which a noun can be made definite is by *annexing* a definite noun Y (the *annex*) to another noun X (the *annexed*). This produces the equivalent of 'the Y's X':

annexed	annex	gloss
bayt	*al-marih*	*bayt al-marih*
'house'	'the-woman'	'the woman's house'

This type of construction is termed *annexion* and is dealt with in detail in Chapter 6 of *Syntax of Ṣanᶜānī Arabic* . Annexion is used to express a number of semantic relationships between nouns including possession, as in the above

[1] In the case of *bī-sawwī* 'he is doing' the sequence *iy* is pronounced as a long vowel *ī*.

example, and as in:

annexed	annex	gloss
galam	*al-wald*	*galam al-wald*
'pen'	'the-boy'	'the boy's pen'

partition, where the annexed noun describes a *part* of the annex, as in:

annexed	annex	gloss
sublaṭ	*al-ᶜīd*	*sublat al-ᶜīd*
'tail-end'	'the-festival'	'the tail-end of the festival'
ra's	*al-wazīr*	*ra's al-wazīr*
'head	'the-minister'	'the minister's head'

and apposition, as in expressions of places, certain names, and days of the week[2] :

annexed	annex	gloss
madīnat	*ṣanᶜā*	'the town, Sanᶜā'
'town'	'Sanᶜā'	
mustašfā	*ṯ-ṯawrih*	'the hospital, al-Thawra'
'hospital'	'al-Thawra'	
yawm	*al-jumᶜah*	'the day, Friday [i.e. Friday]'
'day'	'Friday'	
jarīdat	*aṯ-ṯawrih*	'the newspaper, al-Thawra'
'newspaper'	'al-Thawra'	

For other semantic relationships cf. *Syntax*, Chapter 6. The annexed noun can never take the definite article, nor can it be a pronoun. The annex can be a noun, as in the above examples, or a pronoun. Therefore, just as the phrase '*the woman's* house' can be expressed as '*her* house' in English - where 'her' has the same referent as 'the woman's' - so in Arabic a pronoun can be used as the annex in place of a noun:

[2] In appositive annexion phrases, the first term of the phrase can be left out with no change in meaning: *yawm ar-rabūᶜ* or *ar-rabūᶜ* 'Wednesday', *mustašfā ṯ-ṯawrih* or *aṯ-ṯawrih* 'al-Thawra (hospital)'.

annexed	annex	gloss
bayt	*al-marih*	*bayt al-marih*
'house'	'the-woman'	'the woman's house'

or

bayt	*-hā*	*baytahā*
'house'	'her'	'her house'

In all cases, when the annexed term is a word which ends in the (normally) feminine ending *-ih*, *-ih* is replaced by the annexion ending *-at* (cf. Lesson 3):

*mar**at** aš-šayx* 'the Sheikh's wife'

or

*mar**at**-ih* 'his wife'

6. *Days of the week*

Days of the week are expressed by an annexion phrase in which *yawm* 'day' is the annexed term, and the number (or name) of the actual day the annex. The annex takes the definite article. In Lesson 7 we saw *yawm al-jum^{c}ah* 'Friday' (also mentioned in 5. above) which means literally 'day of the gathering'. The word *jum^{c}ah* is closely related to the religious word *jāmi^{c}* '(Friday) mosque'. With the exception of this and *yawm as-sabt* 'Saturday', which means literally 'day of the rest' and is etymologically related to the word 'sabbath', the names of the days of the week are closely related to their number, with Sunday counting as Day One (as in English).

number	day	gloss
wāḥid	*yawm al-aḥad*	'Sunday'
iṯnayn	*yawm al-iṯnayn*	'Monday'
ṯalāṯih	*yawm aṯ-ṯalūṯ*	'Tuesday'
arba^{c}ah	*yawm ar-rabū^{c}*	'Wednesday'
xamsih	*yawm al-xamīs*	'Thursday'
sittih	*yawm al-jum^{c}ah**	'Friday'
sab^{c}ah	*yawm as-sabt**	'Saturday'

In all these expressions, the term *yawm* 'day' can be omitted without changing the meaning of the phrase (see 5. above).

7. *Cardinal numbers 10 - 100 and 1000*

In Lesson 6 we considered the cardinal numbers from 1 to 10. The dialogues in this lesson have used the cardinal tens, hundreds and thousands. The tens from 20 to 100 and 1000 are as follows:

20	*^{c}išrīn*	30	*ṯalāṯīn*
40	*arba^{c}īn*	50	*xamsīn*
60	*sittīn*	70	*sab^{c}īn*
80	*ṯamānīn*	90	*tis^{c}īn*
100	*mīyih*	1000	*alf*

The numbers 20 - 90 are formed by adding the sound masculine plural ending *-īn* to the unit number (minus the ending *-ih/-ah*):

xams + *īn* —> *xamsīn*
'five' + [plural] 'fifty'

arba^{c} + *īn* —> *arba^{c}īn*
'four' + [plural] 'forty'

The numbers which have three syllables, such as *arba^{c}īn, ṯalāṯīn, ṯamānīn* are often pronounced with the stress on the *first* syllable, particularly in the middle of a sentence. As a result, the second syllable is pronounced as short *a*:

**ṯalaṯīn* 'thirty'

**arba^{c}īn* 'forty'

**ṯamanīn* 'eighty'

The numbers 20 to 90 and 1000 are followed by a singular noun to express a number of something, for example:

^{c}išrīn yawm 'twenty days'

ṯalāṯīn alf 'thirty thousand'

alf girš 'one thousand riyals'

The number 100, *miyih*, is also followed by a singular noun to express one hundred X, but it differs from the other numbers in that it acts as the first part of an annexion phrase. Thus, the ending *-ih* of *miyih* is replaced by the annexion ending *-at* (cf. 5. above):

miyih	+ *yawm*	——>	*miyat yawm*
'hundred'	'day'		'one hundred days'

8. *Ordinal numbers 1st - 10th*

Ordinal numbers are numbers which denote order, quality or degree within a group. With the exception of the word for 'first' - *awwal*, f. *awwalih*, pl. *awwalīn* - the ordinal numbers in Arabic are formed on the same pattern as the active participle, namely **KāTiB** (cf. Lesson 7). In most cases, the relationship between the cardinal number and its corresponding ordinal number is clear and predictable. The following table gives the masculine ordinals from 'first' to 'tenth' to the right of the corresponding masculine cardinals:

	cardinal	ordinal
1	*wāḥid*	*awwal*
2	*iṯnayn*	*ṯānī*
3	*ṯalāṯih*	*ṯāliṯ*
4	*arba^{c}ah*	*rābi^c*
5	*xamsih*	*xāmis*
6	*sittih*	*sādis*
7	*sab^{c}ah*	*sābi^c*
8	*ṯamāniyih*	*ṯāmin*
9	*tis^{c}ah*	*tāsi^c*
10	*^{c}ašarih*	*^{c}āšir*

Ordinal numbers are often used as the annexed term in an annexion phrase followed by a singular *indefinite* annex to mean '*the* first X', etc. (cf. 5. above). When used in this way the ordinal does not inflect for number or gender:

annexed	annex	gloss
awwal	*yawm*	*awwal yawm*
'first'	'day'	'the first day'
ṯānī	*bint*	*ṯānī bint*
'second'	'girl'	'the second girl'

The word for 'last' *āxir* is formed on the same pattern as the other ordinals:

āxir	*wāḥid*	*āxir wāḥid*
'last'	'one'	'the last one'

Alternatively, the ordinal may be used as an adjective to a noun. In this case, the ordinal *does* inflect for number and gender as well as for definiteness to agree with the noun:

noun	adjective	gloss
yawm	*ṯānī*	*yawm ṯānī*
'day'	'second'	'another day'
al-bint	*aṯ-ṯāliṯih*	*al-bint aṯ-ṯāliṯih*
'the-girl'	'the-third f.s.'	'the third girl'
ar-rijāl	*al-awwalīn*	*ar-rijāl al-awwalīn*
'the-men'	'the-first m.pl.'	'the first men'

9. *Dual formation*

In Lesson 4 we considered types of plural formation. Arabic also has a dual inflection. The dual is formed by adding the suffix *-ayn* to nouns which do not end in the feminine ending *-ih*, and elision of *-ih* and addition of the suffix *-atayn* to nouns which do end in *-ih*:

singular	dual	gloss
yawm	*yawm-ayn*[3]	'two days'
alf	*alf-ayn*	'two thousand'
girš	*girš-ayn*	'two riyals'
riyāl	*riyāl-ayn*	'two riyals'
dagīgih	*dagīg-atayn*	'two minutes'
sā^cah	*sā^c-atayn*	'two hours'

In contrast to many other modern dialects of Arabic, use of the dual in San^cānī is limited to expressions of time or money, as in the examples given above. When talking about two objects other than time, the cardinal number *iṯnayn* for masculine nouns, *ṯintayn* for feminine nouns is put before the plural noun:

[3] Also *yawmatayn* which has a slightly different connotation to *yawmayn*, namely 'next couple of days'.

iṯnayn ᶜiyyāl	'two children/boys'
ṯintayn banāt	'two girls'

Verbs and adjectives do not inflect for the dual, and agree with dual nouns by taking plural endings (cf. *Syntax* p.104).

10. *Doubled verbs*

In Lesson 7 we considered hollow verbs and final weak verbs. In this lesson we encounter an example of the *doubled* verb *šall - yišill* 'to take'. A verb is described as doubled when the second and third consonant of the stem are identical. In the imperfect, the doubled verb takes the same prefixes and suffixes as the sound verb:

	singular	plural
1.	*a-šill*	*ni-šill*
2. m.	*ti-šill*	*ti-šill-ū*
2. f.	*ti-šill-ī*	*ti-šill-ayn*
3. m.	*yi-šill*	*yi-šill-ū*
3. f.	*ti-šill*	*yi-šill-ayn*

In the perfect, however, the doubled verb takes an additional diphthong *-ay-* (like final weak verbs such as *sawwa**y**t* 'I did', *šta**ray**t* 'I bought', cf. Lesson 7) between the stem and all subject pronouns which begin with a consonant:

	singular	plural
1.	*šall-ay-t*	*šall-ay-nā*
2. m.	*šall-ay-t*	*šall-ay-tū*
2. f.	*šall-ay-tī*	*šall-ay-tayn*
3. m.	*šall*	*šall-ū*
3. f.	*šall-at*	*šall-ayn*

11. *Transitive verbs: object pronouns*

At the end of Lesson 7 we saw that some verbs and their active participles take objects while others do not. An object can be an independent noun or clause, as in:

noun	*axazzin* ***gāt***	'I chew *gāt*'
clause	*anā ᶜārif* ***man hū***	'I know who he is'

or a dependent pronoun, as in:

*axazzin-**ih***	'I chew it m.'
*anā ᶜārif-**hā***	'I know her'

Object pronouns are dependent pronouns which are suffixed to a transitive verb. Here is the complete set of object pronouns in Ṣanᶜānī Arabic:

	singular	plural
1.	*-nī/-anī*	*-nā/-anā*
2. m.	*-ak*	*-kum/-akum*
2. f.	*-iš*	*-kin/-akin*
3. m.	*-ih*	*-hum/-ahum*[4]
3. f.	*-hā/-ahā*	*-hin/-ahin*

Where alternants are given, the alternant on the left is used when the verb ends in a single consonant, while the alternant on the right is used when the verb ends in two consonants:

	absar-nī	'he saw me'
but		
	absart-anī	'you m.s. saw me'
	absar-kum	'he saw you m.pl.'
but		
	absart-akum[5]	'I saw you m.pl.'

Note that the object pronouns are identical to the possessive pronouns seen in Lesson 2 with the exception of the object pronoun *-nī* 'me' versus the possessive pronoun *-ī* 'my'.

---

[4] Note, however, that the forms -ahum and -ahin can alternate with *-um* and *-in* and with *-hum* and *-hin*: *absartahum* v. *absartum* v. *absarthum* 'I saw them m.'

[5] The epenthetic vowel between the verb and the object can also be pronounced as [*u*] when the object pronoun has a [*u*] vowel: *absartukum* v. *absartakum* 'I saw you m.pl.'

Thematic Vocabulary

Traditional dress in Ṣan^{c}ā'

Men's dress

^{c}asīb pl. *^{c}uswab*	scabbard m.
fūṭuh pl. *fuwaṭ*	sarong f.
ḥizām pl. *aḥzimih*	belt m.
jambiyih pl. *janābī*	curved silver dagger f.
kūfiyih pl. *kawāfī*	coloured head cloth f.
kūt pl. *akwāt*	jacket m.
šāl pl. *šīlān*	large light-coloured shawl worn over shoulders m.
ṣumāṭuh pl. *ṣamāyuṭ*	men's turban f.
zinnih pl. *zinān*	loose full-length robe worn under *kūt* f.

Women's dress

gamīṣ pl. *gumṣān*	loose dress; dress worn by a bride m.
gargūš pl. *garāgīš*	square bonnet worn by babies and young girls m.
ġimāg	black head covering of the *širšaf* which can be lowered over the face m.
ginā^{c} pl. *-āt*	veil m.
gunṭurih pl. *ganāṭur*	shoe f.
liṯmih pl. *liṯam*	tight black covering to cover mouth and nose f.
magramih pl. *magārim*	large colourful cloth to cover hair and face f.
masār pl. *-āt*	head scarf m.
masār nāzilī	head scarf worn under *masār ṭālu^{c}ī* m.
masār ṭālu^{c}ī	head scarf worn over *masār nāzilī* m.
niks / nuks pl. *-āt*	pants m.
ridā' pl. *-āt*	cape of the *širšaf* m.
ṣarmīyuh pl. *-āt*	head covering f.
ṣarmīyuh abū xaṭṭ	face veil: rectangular black cotton bordered in red f.
šaršaf / širšaf pl. *šarāšif*	long black overall with skirt, cape and veil which covers clothes and hair m.
šāših pl. *-āt*	very thin black cloth to cover head f.
sirwāl pl. *sarāwīl*	loose trousers worn under *zinnih* m.
sitārih pl. *sitāyir*	coloured flat wrap worn outside over indoor clothes f.
^{c}uṣbuh pl. *^{c}uṣab*	brightly-coloured, wide hair band f.
ximār	loose black face veil covering all but the eyes m.
zinnih pl. *zinan*	fitted dress f.

Exercises

1. *Object pronouns*

Complete the table below by suffixing the correct *object* pronoun to the verbs. The top left-hand corner of the table has been completed by way of example:

	absart	*yištī*	*yitzawwaj*	*nuxṭub*	*tištay*
anā	*absartanī*				
ant					
antū					
hū					
hum					

2. *Cardinal > ordinal*

Put the cardinal number given in bold into its corresponding ordinal. Where necessary inflect the ordinal for number and gender:

Examples: ***wāḥid*** *šī* ———> ***awwal*** *šī*
aš-šī ***wāḥid*** ———> *aš-šī* ***l-lawwal***

i. ***wāḥid*** *yawm*. ______________________

ii. ***iṯnayn*** *sayyārih*. ______________________

iii. *al-bint* ***arba^cah***. ______________________

iv. *ibnī* ***wāḥid***. ______________________

v. *zawjih* ***ṯalāṯih***. ______________________

3. *Singular > dual*

Answer the following questions in Arabic putting the noun in brackets into the dual. Provide single word answers, then full sentence answers:

Example: *kam tijiss fi l-bayt yā mḥammad? (sāᶜah)* ———> *ša-jiss sāᶜatayn*

i. *kam tištī bayḍ? (bayḍuh)* ______________________________

ii. *al-bint lahā kam sanih? (sanih)* ______________________________

iii. *bi-kam al-galam? (girš)* ______________________________

iv. *ayyaḥīn tijī l-ḥarīwih? baᶜd (sāᶜah)* ____________________

4. *Agreement*

Provide the correct adjective endings in the following sentences.

Example: *bint ar-rajjāl ṭawīl*______ ——> *bint ar-rajjāl aṭ-ṭawīluh*

i. *ar-rijāl kabīr*____.

ii. *al-ᶜiyyāl ṣāyum*____.

iii. *al-mudarris jāwiᶜ*____ *gawī.*

iv. *zamīlī rajjāl šāṭur*____.

v. *al-jibāl ᶜālī*____.

5. *Continuous/habitual*

Put the appropriate form of the continuous/habitual prefix *bayn-/bi-* before the imperfect verb in the following sentences. Make any necessary changes to the imperfect prefix.

Example: *ašrab šahay al-yawm* ——> *bayn-ašrab šahay al-yawm*

i. *tixazzin gāt fi l-madīnih?* ______________________________

ii. *zawjī yištarī xubz min as-sūg.* ______________________________

iii. *hī tuṭbux w-anā 'ākul.* ______________________________

iv. *mā tākul yā 'aḥmad?* ______________________________

v. *asīr tafruṭuh al-yawm.* ______________________________

6. *Substitution*

Use the appropriate pronoun in place of the noun or noun phrase given in **bold** in the following sentences.

Example: *gad absart* ***al-marih*** *fī l-bayt* ——> *gad absarta****hā*** *fī l-bayt*

i. *yištī yitḥākā ma*^{c} ***ummī***. ______________________________

ii. *ištarayt* ***al-gāt*** *min bāb al-yaman.* ____________________

iii. *b-ism* ***hāḏa l-jāhil****?* ______________________________

iv. *kayf al-*^{c}*iris bi-nisbih la-****l-bint****?* ____________________

v. *yilabbisū* [= dress] ***l-ḥarīwih*** *gamīṣ.* ____________________

7. *Topicalisation*

Suffix the appropriate pronoun to ^{c}*ād* and *gad* in the following sentences.

Example: *abī* ^{c}*ād____mā wuṣulš* ——> *abī* ^{c}*ādū mā wuṣulš*

i. *waynū Tim?* ^{c}*ād____sākin fī l-gā*^{c}*?*

ii. ^{c}*iyyālī gad____*^{c}*āṭušīn jāwi*^{c}*īn.*

iii. *al-mudarrisih gad____ jālisih fī l-bayt.*

iv. *anā wa-zawjī gad____ nsāfir yawm ar-rabū*^{c}.

v. *al-banāt* ^{c}*ād____*^{c}*ind at-tafruṭuh?*

8. *Question and answer formation*

Construct questions and answers using the question word *ayyaḥīn* 'when?' and the days of the week.

Example: Qu. ***ayyaḥīn*** *tisāfir al-yaman?* A. *asāfir al-yaman* ***yawm al-xamīs***.

LESSON 9

Kayf al-^{c}iris?

Dialogue 1 ***kayf al-^{c}iris?***

Sarah: *ḥayyā!*

Khadija: *allāh yiḥayyīš, yā Sarah!*

Sarah: *anā ma^{c}zūmih ^{c}ind nās fi l-gā^{c}, bih ḥaflat ^{c}iris al-yawm, gulī lī kayf al-^{c}iris bi-nisbih la-l-bint.*

Khadija: *nāhī, bi-nisbih la-l-bint tibda' min yawm al-iṯnayn lā hum nās murtāḥīn, yi^{c}malū lahā ḥinnā wa-hāḏā, wa-yawm aṯ-ṯalūṯ al-gamīṣ yilabbisūhā.*

Sarah: *s^{c}am man yilabbishā? al-banāt?*

Khadija: *māšī, al-banāt az-zuġār mā yi^{c}malanš min hāḏā! bass al-makālif, makālif al-bayt yilabbisannahā.*

Sarah: *wa-l-muġannīyīn?*

Khadija: *aywih, yilabbisūha l-gamīṣ wa-yijībū l-muġannīyīn yizaffūhā w-ba^{c}dā yinaggišūhā hāḏā yad wāḥidih fagaṭ.*

Sarah: *yad wāḥidih bass!*

Khadija: *nāhī, wa-yawm ar-rabū^{c} tijī š-šāri^{c}ah min aṣ-ṣabāḥ baḥīn, tijī tinaggišhā ba-l-xaḏab.*

Sarah: *kam tijiss tinaggišhā?*

Khadija: *tijī tijiss ^{c}āliyat sā^{c}ah sā^{c}atayn.*

Sarah: *wa-mā yi^{c}malū yawm al-xamīs?*

Khadija: *yawm al-xamīs hum yi^{c}malū ġadā lā l-ḥarīwih, wa-l-layl yi^{c}malū lahā t-tāj, xalāṣ wa-l-ḥarīwi tsīr lā ^{c}ind al-ḥarīw, wa-yawm al-jum^{c}ah hāḏā nisammīh yawm aṣ-ṣabāḥ.*

Dialogue 2 ***ḥagg an-nās fi ṭ-ṭāguh***

fi l-^{c}iris lāzim nijīb ma^{c}ānā ṭarḥ. miṯl maṯalan jaw fi ^{c}irisī wa-ṭaraḥū lī zinnih aw ṣarmīyuh aw xāṭam, wa-law-mā y^{c}arrisū lā ḥadd min ahlahā 'aw min bint hāḏa *llaḏī ṭaraḥat lī 'aw ibnahā 'aw uxtahā lāzim nisīr wa-njīb lahā nafs allaḏī jābat lanā. fī hāḏā yigūlū ḥagg an-nās fī ṭ-ṭāguh. ya^{c}ni ntī jibtī lī ḥājih axallīhā fī ṭ-ṭāguh law-mā tūga^{c} liš ḥājih ajirrahā w-arijji^{c}hā lā ^{c}indiš.*

Vocabulary

^{c}āliyat sā^{c}ah	at the most an hour	*allaḏī*	that; which
allāh yiḥayyīš	[reply to *ḥayyā*]	*^{c}amal - yi^{c}mal*	to do
^{c}arras - yi^{c}arris (lā)	to marry (s.o.) off	*aw*	or
bida'/bada' - yibda'	to begin	*ḥadd*	someone m.
ḥaflat ^{c}iris	wedding party f.	*ḥājih* pl. *-āt*	thing f.
ḥarīw pl. *ḥarāwī*	bridegroom m.	*ḥayyā*	may [God] give you life!
ḥinnā	henna m.	*insān* pl. *nās*	person m.
jāb - yijīb (lā)	to bring (to s.o.)	*jass - yijiss*	to stay; keep doing (s.th.)
labbas - yilabbis	to dress (s.o., in s.th.)	*law-mā*	when; until adjt.
layl pl. *layālī*	night m.	*maklaf* pl. *makālif*	woman f.
ma^{c}zūm	invited	*miṯl*	like prep.
muġannī pl. *-īn*	singer m.	*murtāḥ*	well off
naggaš - yinaggiš	to tatoo (s.o., with antimony)		
rajja^{c} - yirijji^{c}	to give back (s.th.)	*sammā - yisammī*	to call (s.o., s.th.)
šāri^{c}ah pl. *-āt*	bride's dresser woman f.	*ṭāguh* pl. *ṭīgān*	window f.
tāj pl. *tījān*	wedding tiara m.	*ṭaraḥ - yiṭraḥ (lā)*	to give (s.th., to s.o.)
ṭarḥ	wedding present m.	*uxt* pl. *xawāt*	sister f.
waga^{c} - yūga^{c} (lā)	to happen (to s.o.)	*xaḏab*	antimony m.
xallā - yixallī	to leave (s.th.); let (s.o.)	*xāṭam*	ring m.
zaff - yizaff	to accompany (a bride)		

Grammar

1. *Pronunciation: imperfect prefix vowel*

In Ṣanᶜānī Arabic the imperfect prefix vowel is pronounced as *i* when the vowel of the verbal stem is either *i* or *a*:

yišrab	'he drinks'
yijiss	'he sits; stays'

When the imperative takes an initial vowel it is also pronounced as *i* when the vowel of the verbal stem is either *i* or *a*:

išrab (or *šrab)*	'drink! m.s.'
*ijlis (*or *jlis)*	'sit! m.s.'

When the vowel of the stem is *u*, however, as in the verbs *yuxṭub* 'he engages' and *yugūl* 'he says' seen in Lesson 8 and in the dialogue in this lesson, the imperfect prefix vowel and the initial vowel of the imperative may be pronounced as *u*:

yuxṭub versus *yixṭub*	'he engages'
yugūl versus *yigūl*	'he says'
uskut versus *iskut* (or *skut)*	'shut up!'

2. *Feminine plural*

Although Ṣanᶜānī Arabic has a feminine plural verbal form, it is not very commonly used. It is used when the speaker specifically talks about human females, as in *al-banāt az-zuġār mā yiᶜmalanš min hāḏā* 'young girls don't do that!' in the dialogue in this lesson. In other cases, the masculine plural form is given, even when it is clear that the type of activity referred to could only be undertaken by women. In this dialogue we see the masculine form used in:

hum yiᶜmalū ġadā lā l-ḥarīwih	'they make lunch for the bride'

although we know that it is women, and not men, or men and women, who will be preparing lunch.

3. *Feminine plural + suffix*

When the feminine plural verbal form takes an object pronoun, the ending *-ayn* (-*tayn* 'you f.pl.') is pronounced as *-ann* (cf. *Syntax* p. 8). When the object pronoun begins with a consonant other than *-n, a* is pronounced between the second *-n* of the feminine form and the object pronoun, as in:

absarayn + hā	*absarann**a**hā*	'they f. saw her'
absartayn + hin	*absartann**a**hin*	'you f.pl. saw them f.'
absarayn + kum	*absarann**a**kum*	'they f. saw you m.pl.'

When the object pronoun begins with *-n*, as in *-nī* 'me' and *-nā* 'us' one of the *n*'s is not pronounced to give:

absarayn + nā	*absarannā*	'they f. saw us'
absarayn + nī	*absarannī*	'they f. saw me'

When the object pronoun begins with a vowel the pronoun is simply suffixed onto *-ann* with no change:

absarayn + ih	*absarann**ih***	'they f. saw him'
absarayn + ak	*absarann**ak***	'they f. saw you m.s.'
absarayn + iš	*absarann**iš***	'they f. saw you f.s.'

When the feminine plural form is negated with *mā... -š*, *-ayn* is pronounced as *-an*:

mā + absarayn + š	*ma bsar**anš***	'they f. did not see'
mā + absartayn + š	*ma bsart**anš***	'you f.pl. did not see'
mā + tištayn + š	*mā tišt**anš***	'you f.pl. did not want'

4. *Indefinite annexion: 'a woman's house'*

In Lesson 8 we saw that a definite noun Y could be annexed to an initial noun X to translate phrases of the form '*the* Y's X':

annexed	annex	gloss
bayt	*al-marih*	'the woman's house'

In this lesson, we have examples of an *indefinite* noun being annexed to an initial noun. This structure is used to translate phrases of the type '*a* Y's X':

annexed	annex	gloss
bayt	*marih*	'a woman's house'
ra's	*wazīr*	'a minister's head'

It is also used when the annex, Y, describes the *type* of annexed term, X, as in phrases like 'a wedding party', 'an engagement present' where the nouns 'wedding' and 'engagement' describe the type of 'party' and 'present':

annexed	annex	gloss
ḥaflat	*ᶜiris*	'a wedding party'

An indefinite annexion phrase is commonly used when the initial noun is an ordinal number and the annex is a singular noun (cf. Lesson 8). This translates English phrases of the type '*the* first thing'.

annexed	annex	gloss
awwal	*bayt*	'the first house'
ṯānī	*yawm*	'the second day'

Certain words are very commonly the annexed term in an indefinite annexion phrase. These include words like *ᶜāliyih* 'at the most...', and words which describe a part of, or a unit of, a collective entity such as *ḥabbih* 'unit', *bardag* 'cup', *šwayyih* 'a little' which are used to translate phrases of the type 'a X of Y' (cf. Lesson 18):

annexed	annex	gloss
ᶜāliyat	*sāᶜah*	'at the most an hour'
bardag	*mā'*	'a cup of water'
ḥabbat	*ruzz*	'a bit of rice'
šwayyat	*dagīg*	'a little flour'

5. *Annexion: nafs and kull*

Two of the most common nouns to function as an annexed term in an annexion phrase are *nafs* 'same' and *kull* 'all, the whole, every' (these are dealt with in detail in *Syntax,* Chapter 6). Briefly, *nafs* followed by a *definite* annex means 'the *same* X':

annexed	annex	gloss
nafs	*aš-šī*	'the same thing'
nafs	*al-ašyā*	'the same things'

kull can mean either 'all of', 'the whole', or 'every', depending on whether the annex is definite or indefinite, singular or plural. *kull* plus an *indefinite singular* noun means '*every* Y':

annexed	annex	gloss
kull	*šī*	'everything'
kull	*bayt*	'every household'
kull	*wāḥid*	'everyone'

kull plus a *definite* singular noun means 'the *whole* X':

annexed	annex	gloss
kull	*al-bayt*	'the whole household'
kull	*al-yawm*	'the whole day'

kull plus a definite *plural* noun means '*all* the X':

annexed	annex	gloss
kull	*al-biyūt*	'all the houses'
kull	*al-ᶜiyyāl*	'all the children'

Other nouns which are commonly used as the annexed term in an annexion phrase include *zārat* 'some X' and *ḥagg* 'belonging to, of, amounting to'. *ḥagg* is dealt with below in Lesson 10. For other common annexed terms see *Syntax*, Chapter 6.

6. *Apposition*

A noun can be modified not only by a following adjective but also by a second *noun*. This type of modification is called *apposition*. Examples of apposition in English include phrases like 'Mr Smith, the baker' where 'the baker' provides us with more information about 'Mr Smith', and 'William the Conqueror' where 'the Conqueror' gives us more information about 'William'. Two examples of apposition are encountered in the dialogues in Chapter 8:

noun	noun	gloss
badlih	*ḏahab*	'a wide collar of gold'
kulūnīyih	*ᶜuṭr*	'cologne perfume'

When the first noun does not take the feminine ending *-ih,* there is no obvious distinction between an apposition phrase and an annexion phrase. When the first noun does end in *-ih*, however, the ending will be pronounced as *-ih* in an apposition phrase and as *-at* in an annexion phrase. Different types of apposition are dealt with in detail in *Syntax,* Chapter 7.

7. *Purpose clauses*

Certain verbs regularly take a following imperfect verb to indicate purpose. These verbs include *jalas - yijlis/yijiss* 'to continue, keep on, remain doing', *jā' - yijī* 'to come to', *gām - yugūm* 'to start doing'.[1,2] and *sār - yisīr* 'to go'. The second verb takes the same inflection as the first verb but translates into English as an infinitive (cf. Lesson 5):

first verb	second verb		
tijiss 'she-continues'	*tinaggiš* 'she-tatoos'	*al-ḥarīwih* 'the-bride'	*tijiss tinaggiš al-ḥarīwih* 'she continues to tatoo the bride'
yijaw 'they-get-to'	*yiġannaw* 'they-sing'	*kull al-yawm* 'all the-day'	*yijaw yiġannaw kull al-yawm* 'they get to sing the whole day'
tisīr 'she-goes'	*titfarraṭ* 'she-parties'		*tisīr titfarraṭ* 'she goes to party'

8. *The past tense*

As we have seen, Arabic does not use the verb 'to be' in the present (cf. Lesson 2). The English words 'is', 'am' and 'are' have no correspondence in Arabic:

hū jāwiᶜ 'he (is) hungry'	*as-sayyārih maᶜ abī* 'the-car (is) with my-father'

In order to put verbless nominal sentences (sentences which begin with a noun)

[1] Other verbs which take a following imperfect verb are discussed in detail in *Syntax,* Chapter 5.

[2] These three verbs can also function without a following imperfect verb, but have a different meaning in this cas *jalas - yijlis/yijiss* means 'to sit', *jā' - yijī* means 'to come' and *gām - yugūm* means 'to get up'.

into the past, the verb *kān* 'it was' is used in the appropriate inflectional form:

hū kān jāwi^{c}	*as-sayyārih kānat ma*^{c} *abī*
'he was hungry'	'the-car was with my-father'

In order to put prepositional sentences (sentences which begin with a preposition) into the past, the verb *kān* is used in its unmarked form (i.e. *kān):*

kān bih rajjāl	'there was a man'
kān bih sayyārih kabīrih	'there was a large car'
kān ma^{c}*ānā biyūt kaṯīr*	'we had a lot of houses'

When a sentence begins with *gad, kān* comes between *gad* and the prepositional phrase:

gad kān bih rajjāl	'there was a man'
gad kān ma^{c}*ānā biyūt kaṯīr*	'we had a lot of houses'

Finally, the verb *yištī* 'to want' does not have a perfect form which is used in the sense of 'he wanted'. In order to express 'he wanted' the verb *kān* is used followed by *yištī*:

kān yištī yisāfir ma^{c}*ānā*	'he wanted to travel with us'
kunnā[3] *ništī nirja*^{c}	'we wanted to return'

The verb *kān* is a hollow verb (cf. Lesson 7) with a middle consonant *w*. The full paradigm of *kān* in the perfect aspect is as follows:

	singular	plural
1.	*kun-t*	*kun-nā*
2. m.	*kun-t*	*kun-tū*
2. f.	*kun-tī*	*kun-tayn*
3. m.	*kān*	*kān-ū*
3. f.	*kān-at*	*kān-ayn*

[3] When *kunnā* is followed by a verb in the imperfect aspect it is often contracted to *kun*, as in: *kun ništī nsīr* 'we wanted to go'.

9. *Wāḥid*

The number one, *wāḥid*, is used in a number of ways. Two typical uses of *wāḥid* are:

i. After a noun to emphasize the sense of oneness (as opposed to more than one):

yad wāḥidih fagaṭ	'one hand only'

ii. Before an indefinite adjective to produce an indefinite noun phrase. In English you cannot say 'a big' or 'the big' without adding 'one' after the adjective. In Arabic, the literal equivalent of 'the big' is very common, as in:

al-kabīrih	'the big f. [one]'
az-zaġīr	'the small m. [one]'

The equivalent of indefinite phrases like 'a big', on the other hand, usually require preceding *wāḥid* 'one' in order to function as an noun phrase[4] , as in:

kān bih wāḥid aṣla^c	'there was one bald [a bald one]'
kān bih wāḥid kabīr	'there was one big [a big one]'

10. *Word order: 'they took raisins with them'*

In English, the normal word order in a sentence like 'they took raisins with them' is [subj]-verb-object-prepositional phrase. In Arabic, however, when a prepositional phrase takes an object pronoun, the prepositional phrase comes *before* the object:

yišillū ma^c*āhum zabīb*	'they m. took raisins with them'

and not

* *yišillū zabīb ma*^{c}*āhum*

Also:

yilabbisū laha t-tāj	'they dress her in the tiara'

Similarly, in existential sentences and in sentences which express possession using the preposition *ma*^{c}, the prepositional phrase comes before the subject:

[4] Negative indefinite adjectives can be used as noun phrases, however, particularly in proverbs and proverb-like utterances (cf. *Syntax* pp. 111-112).

bih maraysī[5] 'there is sugar'
ma^{c}ih sayyārih 'he has a car'

When the verb *kān* is used to put a sentence like the two above into the past, the prepositional phrase comes between the verb and the subject (cf. 8. above):

kān bih maraysī 'there was sugar'
kān ma^{c}ih sayyārih 'he had a car'

Thematic Vocabulary

Weddings and births

^{c}ayyāf	morning sickness in pregnancy m.
farḥah pl. *faraḥāt*	present given on birth of a child f.
firiḥ - yifraḥ (lā)	to visit (a new mother)
fustān zifāf	wedding dress m.
ḥāmil	pregnant
^{c}iris pl. *a^{c}rās*	wedding m.
jiddih pl. *-āt*	midwife f.
laylat al-gubūl	wedding night f.
laylat al-ḥilfih	wedding night f.
malak - yimlik (lā)	to conduct the *milkih* (for s.o.)
mawsim pl. *mawāsim*	season m. [the wedding season is after festivals]
m^{c}ayyafih	having morning sickness f.
milkih	wedding contract f.
miṭgilih	heavily pregnant
mizmār pl. *mazāmīr*	pipe m. [played at weddings]
muṭallaguh pl. *-āt*	divorcee f.
mwajjilih pl. *-āt*	widow f.
nifās	childbirth; childbirth sickness m.
nīnī pl. *nawānī*	baby m.
ṭabīnuh pl. *ṭabāyun*	co-wife f.
ṭallag - yiṭallug	to divorce (a woman)
ṭalāg	divorce m.
ṭāluguh pl. *-āt*	recently divorced woman f.
ṭarḥah pl. *taraḥāt*	wedding present m.
waragat al-milkih	wedding contract f.
wāhimih	pregnant
wihim - yawham	to become pregnant

[5] The opposite word order can be used, but in an emphatic sense - perhaps in answer to the question 'is there any sugar'. The answer could be *aywih, maraysī bih* 'yes, there is sugar'.

wilād	time after birth during which women visit the new mother m.
wilādih	birth f.
wulid - yūlad	to give birth; to be born
zaffāfih pl. *-āt*	woman who sings at weddings and makes the bride dance f.
zawāj pl. *-āt*	wedding m.
zawwaj fawgahā	he married [a wife] in addition to her
zifāf	wedding procession to take bride to bridegroom m.

Exercises

1. *Greetings*

Give appropriate replies to the following greetings:

i. *kayf ḥāliš yā salwā?* ______________________

ii. *ḥayyā!* ______________________

iii. *ṣbaḥtū!* ______________________

iv. *mā liš šī?* ______________________

v. *ma^{c} as-salāmih!* ______________________

2. *Object pronouns*

Complete the table below by suffixing the correct *object* pronoun to the verbs below making any necessary changes to the verbal form. The top left-hand corner is completed by way of example:

	absartayn	*tištī*	*šallayn*	*yuxṭub*	*absarū*
anā	*absartannī*				
ant					
antī					
hī					
hin					

3. *Present > past*

Put the following sentences into the past using the appropriate form of *kān*.

Example: *gad ma^{c}ānā sayyārih* ——> *gad* ***kān*** *ma^{c}ānā sayyārih*

i. *kull al-^{c}iyyāl rāgidīn* [= sleeping]. ________________________

ii. *at-tafruṭuh fī bayt aḥmad.*________________________

iii. *anā ^{c}ārif al-lumm.* ________________________

iv. *ništī nisāfir ti^{c}izz al-yawm.*________________________

v. *bih ġadā.* ________________________

vi. *al-gahwih bāridih gawī.*________________________

4. *Noun phrase formation*

Produce two noun phrases from the following adjectives: the first by adding the correct form of *wāḥid*, and the second by adding the definite article.

Example: *zaġīr* ——> i. *wāḥid zaġīr* ii. *az-zaġīr*

i. *rāgid.* ________________________

ii. *jāwi^{c}ah.* ________________________

iii. *tā^{c}ibih* [= tired]. ________________________

iv. *murtāḥ.*________________________

v. *kabīrih.*________________________

vi. *ġanī* [= rich].________________________

vii. *ḥālī.*________________________

5. *Word order*

Put the groups of words below into the correct order to produce meaningful sentences. In some cases there may be more than one possible order:

Example: *wāḥid, yišti, kull, al-bilād, yisāfir* ——> *kull wāḥid yišti ysāfir al-bilād*

i. *bih, līm, šī*

ii. *al-yawm, bih, kabīr, kān, wāḥid*

iii. *bayt, fī, man, tixazzin*

iv. *tištaw, kam, kilū*

v. *al-xamīs, yijaw, yawm, al-ᶜiyyāl, kull*

6. *Word stress*

Put the word-stress mark * before the stressed syllable in the following words:

Example: **māšī*

i. *wāḥid* ii. *tixazzin* iii. *mafraj* iv. *gahwih* v. *miᶜlāmih* vi. *al-xamīs* vii. *murtāḥ* viii. *murtāḥīn*

7. *Translation*

Translate the following groups of sentences into Ṣanᶜānī Arabic:

A. Use *kān*

i. We wanted to take money with us.

ii. He wanted to drink coffee.

iii. They wanted to decorate the bride with antimony.

iv. The *gāt* was very expensive.

B. Use verb + prepositional phrase.

i. The groom's family took raisins and almonds with them.

ii. I gave her a hair band.

iii. They dressed her in a wedding dress.

iv. I shall bring a wedding present with me.

C. Days of the week

i. I will come on Monday.

ii. He will come on Tuesday.

iii. They m. will come on Wednesday.

iv. You f.pl. will come on Thursday.

LESSON 10

Ayyaḥīn jīti l-yaman awwal marrih?

Dialogue 1 *ayyaḥīn jīti l-yaman awwal marrih?*

Salwa: *yā Louise hāḏā 'awwal marrih tuzūri l-yaman?*

Louise: *māšī, ṯānī marrih.*

Salwa: *ayyaḥīn jīti l-yaman awwal marrih?*

Louise: *jīt min sanih wa-jlast šahr fī ṣanᶜā.*

Salwa: *w-awwal-ma wṣultī ṣanᶜā kayf absartī l-bilād?*

Louise: *bilād ḥāliyih fīhā nās ṭayyubīn bass al-jaww ḥārr marrih wa-š-šawāriᶜ fī l-ᶜāṣumuh kullahā ġubār.*

Salwa: *w-allāhi kalāmiš ṣaḥḥ. kull al-ajānib allī gad jaw bī-gūlū hākaḏā. gulī lī, antī mitzawwijih awlā ᶜādiš?*

Louise: *anā mitzawwijih gad lī sanatayn.*

Salwa: *wa-zawjiš gad sāfar al-yaman maᶜiš?*

Louise: *māšī, ᶜala l-asaf. gad jīt li-waḥdī.*

Salwa: *kam liš min zawjiš ḏalḥīn?*

Louise: *gad lī šahrayn wa-nuṣṣ.*

Salwa: *kam maᶜiš ᶜiyyāl?*

Louise: *gad li ṯnayn, wald wa-bint.*

Salwa: *allāh yixallīhum liš.*

Louise: *āmīn.*

Salwa: *w-aynuhum ḏalḥīnih? miš maᶜiš fī ṣanᶜā?*

Louise: *māšī, xallaytuhum ᶜind abūhum fī l-bilād.*

Salwa: *w-ayyaḥīn tirjaᶜī bilādiš?*

Louise: *m-aniš dārī bi-ḏabṭ, bass mumkin asāfir baᶜd usbūᶜayn wallā šahr.*

Dialogue 2 *ḥagg man al-bint tayyih?*

Samira: *ḥagg man al-bint tayyih?*

Janet: *gadī ḥaggī 'anā!*

Samira: *hāḏā miš al-bint allaḏī jibtūhā law-mā jītū hānā 'awwal?*

Janet: *aywih, hāḏā nafs al-bint, hāḏā Sarah.*

Samira: *bass ḍa^{c}īfuh marrih gadī ḏalḥīnih wa-samrā. mā lahā?*

Janet: *gad fīhā 'ishāl min yawm as-sabt u-mā gad akalat kaṯīr.*

Samira: *laggimīhā ruzz wa-zibādī bass.*

Janet: *nāhī. alaggimhā min hāḏā.*

Samira: *wa-lilmā xallaytīhā hākaḏāhā fi š-šams? labbisīhā min al-garāgīš allī yibī^{c}ūhā min hānā.*

Janet: *kalāmiš ṣaḥḥ, ša-ḏwī wa-ġudwuh šā-labbis lahā gargūš min ḥaggukum.*

Vocabulary

absar - yibsir	to see (s.th.)	*^{c}ādiš*	you f.s. are single
ajnabī pl. *ajānib*	foreigner m.	*^{c}ala l-asaf*	unfortunately
allāh yixallīhum liš	may God preserve them for you f.s.	*āmīn*	amen!
ams	yesterday	*^{c}āṣumuh* pl. *^{c}awāṣum*	capital f.
awwal	first; at first	*awwal-mā*	when first adjt.
bā^c - yibī^c	to sell (s.th.)	*bi-ḏabṭ*	exactly
bilād pl. *balāyid*	country; home f.	*ḍa^{c}īf*	weak; thin
ḏawā - yuḏwī	to go home	*gabl-mā*	before adjt.
ġubār	dust m.	*hānā*	here
ḥārr	hot	*ishāl*	diarrheoa m.
jaww	weather m.	*kalām*	speech; s.th. said m.
laggam - yilaggim	to feed (s.o., s.th.)	*marrih* pl. *-āt*	time f.
marrih	very	*mitzawwij*	married
mumkin	[it is] possible	*nisī - yinsā*	to forget (s.th.)
rijī^c - yirja^c	to return	*samrā*	brown f.
sanih pl. *sinīn*	year f.	*wallā*	or
w-allāhi	by God!	*zār - yuzūr*	to visit (s.o.)

zawj pl. *azwāj* husband m.

Grammar

1. *Questions: 'how long?'*

In order to ask 'how long' someone has been somewhere, or has spent away from someone, Ṣanᶜānī Arabic uses *kam* followed by the preposition *li-* plus the appropriate pronoun suffix. Although English uses the near past tense to say, for example, 'how long have you m.s. been in Yemen' and 'my son has been here for a month', Arabic does not use a verb in the perfect: questions about length of time often involve two prepositional phrases, as in:

kam	+ *lak*	+ *fī l-yaman*	*kam lak fī l-yaman*
'how long'	'to you m.s.'	'in Yemen'	'How long have you m.s. been in Yemen?'

kam	+ *liš*	+ *min zawjiš*	*kam liš min zawjiš*
'how long'	'to you f.s.'	'from your husband'	'How long have you f.s. been away from your husband?'

Alternatively, the second prepositional phrase can be replaced by a locative adverb such as *hānā* 'here' or *hnaykā* 'there':

kam	+ *lukum*	+ *hānā*	*kam lak hānā*
'how long'	'to you m.pl.'	'here'	'How long have you been here?'

In order to state how long as opposed to ask how long, Ṣanᶜānī Arabic generally uses *gad* in place of the question word *kam* and puts the length of time between the prepositional phrase *li* + pronoun and the second prepositional phrase or locative adverb:

gad lī sanatayn hānā	'I have been here for two years'
al-ᶜiyyāl gad luhum šahr fī l-ᶜāṣumuh	'the children, they have been in the capital for a month'

2. *Emphasis: kull + pronoun suffix*

In Lesson 9 we considered the use of *kull* 'all, whole of'. A very common emphatic variant of *kull* + definite noun is a phrase involving the definite noun followed by *kull* + pronoun suffix where the pronoun suffix refers to the definite noun and agrees with the noun in number and gender. Thus:

kull + al-bayt	*kull al-bayt*
'all' 'the-house'	'the whole house'

can be realised emphatically as:

al-bayt + kull + ih	*al-bayt kullih*
'the-house' 'all' 'it m.'	'the house, all of it'

Similarly:

kull + aš-šawāri^{c}	*kull aš-šawāri*^{c}
'all' 'the-streets'	'all the streets'

can be realised emphatically as:

aš-šawāri^{c} *+ kull + hā*	*aš-šawāri*^{c} *kullahā*[1]
'the-streets' 'all' 'it f.'	'the streets, all of them'

3. *Emphasis: nafs + pronoun suffix*

As with *kull*, the word *nafs* also has an emphatic and a less emphatic sense; it is less emphatic when followed by a definite noun in the sense of '... itself', 'the same...', 'the actual...' or 'exactly...' (cf. Lesson 9), as in:

aštī + nafs + al-wald	*aštī nafs al-wald*
'I-want' 'same' 'the-boy'	'I want the same boy'
tštī + nafs + al-bāb	*tštī nafs al-bāb*
'you-want' 'same' 'the-gate'	'you want the gate itself'

A more emphatic way of expressing '...itself', etc. is for *nafs* + pronoun suffix to *follow* a definite noun in the same way as *kull* + pronoun suffix may follow a definite noun. Again, the pronoun suffix refers to the definite noun and agrees with the noun in number and gender (cf. 2. above):

tštī + al-bāb + nafsih	*tštī al-bāb nafsih*
'you-want' 'the-gate' 'itself'	'you want the gate itself'

[1] When the noun is an inanimate plural, the referential pronoun is either third feminine singular, as here, or third feminine plural (cf. Lesson 4).

tšti + *al-bint* + *nafsahā* 'you-want' 'the-girl' 'herself'	*tšti al-bint nafsahā* 'you want the same girl'
ašti + *al-wizārih* + *nafsahā* 'I-want' 'the-ministry' 'itself'	*ašti al-wizārih nafsahā* 'you want the actual ministry'

4. *The relative pronoun: definite relative clauses*

The relative pronoun in Ṣan^cānī Arabic is *allaḏī, illī* or *allī*. The relative pronoun links two statements which refer to a common *definite* entity; thus, the two statements below which both refer to *ar-rajjāl* 'the man':

absart ***ar-rajjāl*** / ***ar-rajjāl*** *hānāk*	'I saw the man' / 'the man is there'

can be reduced to a single sentence by inserting *allaḏī* between the statements and by omitting the second mention of *ar-rajjāl*:

absart ar-rajjāl ***allaḏī*** *hānāk*	'I saw the man **who** is there'

Similarly, the following two statements which both refer to *al-bayt* 'the house':

tibsir ***al-bayt*** / ***al-bayt*** *ba*^{c}*īd min hānā*	'see the house' 'the house is far from here'

can be reduced to:

tibsir al-bayt ***allaḏī*** *ba*^{c}*īd min hānā*	'see the house **which** is far from here'

And the two statements below which both refer to *ar-rajjāl*:

absart ar-rajjāl / ***ar-rajjāl*** *tzawwaj ams*	'I saw the man' 'the man married yesterday'

can be reduced to:

absart ar-rajjāl allaḏī ***tzawwaj*** *ams*	'I saw the man who married yesterday'

When the noun in the second statement is *not* the subject of the clause (as it is in the above examples), it is replaced in the relative clause by a referential pronoun which has the same number and gender as the noun. Thus, when the noun in the second statement is the *object* of a verb, as in:

ar-rajjāl hānā / absart ***ar-rajjāl*** *ams*	'the man is here' 'I saw the man yesterday'

The referential pronoun is the *object* of the verb in the relative clause:

*ar-rajjāl hānā alladī absart**ih** ams*	'the man is here who I saw [him] yesterday'

When the noun is the *prepositional object* in the second statement, as in:

tibsir ar-rajjāl / aštī tḥākā ma^c ***ar-rajjāl***	'see the man' 'I want to talk to the man'

The referential pronoun is the *prepositional object* in the relative clause:

*tibsir ar-rajjāl alladī aštī tḥākā ma^c**ih***	'see the man who I want to talk to [him]'

And when the noun is the *annexed* term in the second statement, as in:

absart ar-rajjāl / aštī tḥākā ma^c marat ***ar-rajjāl***	'I saw the man' 'I want to talk to the man's wife'

The referential pronoun is the *annexed* term in the relative clause:

*tibsir ar-rajjāl alladī 'aštī tḥākā ma^c marat**ih***	'I saw the man whose wife I want to talk to'

5. *Possession: ḥagg*

One word which occurs very frequently as the first term of an annexion phrase is the word *ḥagg*. It is often used after[2] a definite noun to express possession and in this context generally means 'of, possession of' (cf. *Syntax* pp. 220-224). This is an alternative, and more emphatic, way of expressing possession to the noun + possessive pronoun and noun + noun annexion phrases considered in earlier lessons (cf. Lesson 3 and Lesson 8). Just as 'her house' can be expressed more emphatically in English as 'the house *belonging* to her', so *baytahā* or *baythā* can

[2] Less commonly *before* a definite noun (see below).

be expressed more emphatically in San^c^ānī as *al-bayt* ***ḥagg****ahā*:[3]

	bayt + *hā* 'house' 'her'	*baytahā* 'her house'
or		
	al-bayt + *ḥagg* + *hā* 'the-house' 'of' 'her'	*al-bayt ḥaggahā* 'the house belonging to/of her'

Similarly, *bayt al-marih* 'the woman's house' can be expressed more emphatically as *al-bayt* ***ḥagg*** *al-marih* 'the house belonging to the woman'. In contrast to many other modern dialects of Arabic, *ḥagg* + noun or pronoun can occasionally be used to describe family relations, as seen in the second dialogue in this lesson:

	ḥagg man al-bint tayyih	'whose [daughter] is that girl?'
and also:		
	aynū ḥaggiš ar-rajjāl	'where is your f.s. man?'

A *ḥagg* + noun phrase can also be used to express other relationships such as amount (cf. *Syntax* pp. 220-224):

	zalaṭ ḥagg mīyat alf	'money amounting to 100,000'
and origin:		
	kalām min ḥagg ṣan^c^ā	'speech of San^c^ā' [i.e. San^c^ānī]'

The full set of *ḥagg* + pronoun suffixes is:

	singular	plural
1.	*ḥagg-ī*	*ḥagg-anā*
2. m.	*ḥagg-ak*	*ḥagg-akum*
2. f.	*ḥagg-iš*	*ḥagg-akin*
3. m.	*ḥagg-ih*	*ḥagg-ahum*
3. f.	*ḥagg-ahā*	*ḥagg-ahin*

6. *Negation of pronouns*

In Lesson 4 we saw that independent pronouns can be pre-negated by the single morpheme *miš*, to give the equivalent of 'not me', 'not you', etc. Independent pronouns differ from other nouns, however, in that they can also be negated by

[3] Note also that *al-bayt ḥaggahā* implies that 'she' actually possesses the house, whereas *baytahā* does not necessarily imply possession - she may simply rent the house.

the discontinuous morpheme *mā* - *-š* or by *mā* to produce, for example, the equivalent of 'I not', 'you not', etc. The full set of negated independent pronouns is:

	singular	plural
1.	*m-anī-š*	*m-iḥna-š*
2. m.	*m-anta-š*	*m-antū-š*
2. f.	*m-antī-š*	*m-antan-š*
3. m.	*mā-hū-š*	*mā-hum-š*
3. f.	*mā-hī-š*	*mā-hin-š*

Note that *-ayn* of *antayn* 'you f.pl.' is reduced to *-an* before the negative suffix *-š* (cf. Lesson 9), and that 'I not' is realised as *m-anī-š* rather than as **m-anā-š*.

7. *Adverbs: 'here' and 'there'*

The two main adverbs of place or locative adverbs are *hānā* 'here', and *hānāk* 'there'. 'Here' can also be expressed by the word *hinīyih*, and 'there' by the word *hinayka*. 'Here' can also be expressed by the prepositional phrase ***min*** *hānā* or ***min*** *hinīyih* as in the second dialogue in this lesson.

8. *Modal adjectives: 'possible', 'necessary', 'ought'*

Certain adjectives commonly function as modal elements in Arabic. These include *mumkin* 'possible', *lāzim* 'necessary', *mafrūḍ* 'supposed; ought', and *ḍurūrī* 'necessary; essential' (cf. *Syntax* pp. 167-169). When followed by an imperfect verb these elements give the sense of 'may', 'should', 'have to' or 'must':

mumkin	+ *asāfir*	+ *baᶜd usbūᶜayn*	*mumkin asāfir baᶜd usbūᶜayn*
'possible'	'I-travel'	'after two-weeks'	'I may travel in two weeks'

lāzim	+ *asāfir*	+ *baᶜd usbūᶜayn*	*lāzim asāfir baᶜd usbūᶜayn*
'necessary'	'I-travel'	'after two-weeks'	'I must travel in two weeks'

The modal adjective *mafrūḍ* may take the definite article, as in:

al-mafrūḍ	+ *asāfir*	+ *baᶜd usbūᶜayn*	*al-mafrūḍ asāfir baᶜd usbūᶜayn*
'ought'	'I-travel'	'after two-weeks'	'I ought to travel in two weeks'

Sentences which begin with a modal adjective are negated by *miš* or *maš* before the modal adjective:

miš + mumkin asāfir ba^cd usbū^cayn [neg] 'I may travel after two weeks'	*miš mumkin asāfir ba^cd usbū^cayn* 'I cannot travel after two weeks'
miš + lāzim asāfir ba^cd usbū^cayn [neg] 'I must travel after two weeks'	*miš lāzim asāfir ba^cd usbū^cayn* 'I need not travel after two weeks'

Similarly, these sentences are put into the past by adding *kān* before the adjective:

kān	+ *lāzim*	+ *asāfir*	*kān lāzim asāfir*
[past]	'necessary'	'I travel'	'I had to travel'
kān	+ *mumkin*	+ *yijī*	*kān mumkin yijī*
[past]	'possible'	'he comes'	'he could/was able to come'

When these sentences are negated in the past, it is the verb *kān* which is negated:

mā kānš lāzim asāfir	'I did not have to travel'
mā kānš mumkin yijī	'he was not able to come'

9. *Nouns of place*

In English there is nothing about the word 'restaurant' to tell us that it is a place in which food is eaten, nor indeed is there anything about the word 'food' to relate it to the verb 'eat'. In Arabic, however, nouns are very closely related to their corresponding verbs such that it is possible to guess the meaning of a certain noun if the related verb is known.

As we have seen earlier (Lesson 4), in Arabic words consist of a *root* of consonants and a *pattern*. Thus the verb *širib* 'to drink' consists of the consonants *š-r-b* in the pattern **KiTiB**, and the noun *zawāj* 'wedding m.' consists of the consonants *z-w-j* in the pattern **KaTāB**. In addition, certain patterns are associated with certain types of words. There are three common patterns for the noun of place (cf. Thematic Vocabulary, Lesson 3): ma**KTaB** *(*ma**KTiB***)*, ma**KTaB**ih, and mi**KTāB**ih. Nouns of place of the pattern ma**KTaB** and ma**KTiB** are masculine:

verb	gloss	noun of place	gloss
ṣana^c	to make	*maṣna^c*	factory
katab	to write	*maktab*	office
jilis	to sit	*majlis*	council

Nouns of place of the pattern ma**KT**a**B**ih and mi**KT**ā**B**ih are feminine:

verb	gloss	noun of place	gloss
daras	to learn	*madrasih*	school
katab	to write	*maktabih*	library
^{c}ilim	to know	*mi^{c}lāmih*	traditional school
ġassal	to wash	*miġsālih*	laundry
xabaz	to bake bread	*mixbāzih*	bakery

Nouns of these three patterns all take the broken plural pattern ma**K**ā**T**i**B**[4] (cf. Lesson 4):

singular	plural	gloss
maktab	*makātib*	office
majlis	*majālis*	council
maṭ^{c}am	*maṭā^{c}um*	restaurant
madrasih	*madāris*	school
maktabih	*makātib*	library
mi^{c}lāmih	*ma^{c}ālim*	traditional school
miġsālih	*maġāsil*	laundrette
mixbāzih	*maxābiz*	bakery

A fourth pattern, **K**a**TT**ā**B**ih[5] is also, but less commonly, used as a noun of place. Nouns of this pattern are feminine and take the sound feminine plural ending *-āt*:

verb	gloss	noun of place	gloss
ṣarraf	to change money	*ṣarrāfuh*	money changers
ġassal	to wash	*ġassālih*	laundrette

[4] **maKāTuB** when the second or third consonant in the root is emphatic.

[5] **KaTTāBuh** when one of the consonants in the root is emphatic.

10. *Transitive verbs: double objects*

In English some verbs take two objects, for example the verb 'give' in sentences such as 'I gave her a present' where the first object is 'her' and the second object is 'a present'. Certain verbs in Arabic also take two objects; as in English, when a verb takes two objects, the first object usually refers to a person while the second object refers to something inanimate (cf. *Syntax* pp. 141-143). Examples include:

labbasnā l-bint fustān	'we dressed the girl in a dress'
laggimīhā zibādī	'feed f.s. her yoghurt'
ᶜazzimī l-marih akl injlīzī	'invite f.s. the woman for English food'

11. *Objects: 'one of...', 'some of...'*

Objects are often introduced by *min* in Ṣanᶜānī Arabic, particularly when the object is a demonstrative pronoun or a *ḥagg* phrase (cf. 5. above), as in:

atḥākā min ḥagg al-yaman	'I speak Yemeni [lit: of that which belongs to Yemen]'
hin yiᶜmalayn min hāḏā	'they f. do that [lit: of that]'

When a definite plural count noun follows *min* (rather than a pronoun or a *ḥagg* phrase), the meaning changes from VERB X to VERB one of X. Compare:

	labbasnāhā gargūš	'we dressed her in a bonnet'
with		
	labbasnāhā min al-garāgiš	'we dressed her in one of the bonnets'

When a definite non-count noun follows *min*, the meaning changes from VERB X to VERB some [of the] X. Compare:

	laggimīhā zibādī	'feed f.s. her yoghurt'
with		
	laggimīhā min az-zibādī	'feed f.s. her some [of the] yoghurt'

Thematic Vocabulary

Travel

^{c}alā ḥisāb(ak)	at (your m.s.) own expense
bāṣ pl. *-āt*	bus m.
bījū pl. *-āt*	Peugot taxi f.
bi-nafar	by person [i.e. in a shared taxi]
dabbāb pl. *-āt*	small bus m.
dawrih pl. *-āt*	trip f.
masāfih pl. *-āt*	distance f.
maṭār pl. *-āt*	airport m.
mūṭūr pl. *-āt*	motorbike m.
rijl pl. *arjul*	peddle [of bicycle] m.
safar	travel; journey m.
safīnih pl. *safāyin*	ship f.
sawwāḥ pl. *-īn*	tourist m.
saykal pl. *-āt*	bicycle m.
sayyārih pl. *-āt*	car f.
taḏkirih pl. *taḏākir*	ticket f.
ṯaman	price; fare m.
ṭayyāruh pl. *-āt*	plane f.

Exercises

1. *Gap filling*

Provide the correct pronouns in the following topical sentences:

Example: *al-bint kam l___fī l-bilād (šahr) ———> al-bint kam lahā fī l-bilād*

i. *ar-rajjāl kam l___ min maratih? (ṯamān)*

ii. *al-ustāḏ kam l___fī briṭāniyā? (šahrayn)*

iii. *aṭ-ṭullāb kam l___ hānā? (yawmayn)*

iv. *ibniš kam l___ hānāk? (ṯalāṯ asābī^{c})*

v. *al-makālif kam l___fī ṣan^{c}ā? (sanatayn)*

2. Answer the above questions in full using the information provided in brackets.

Example: *al-bint kam l___ fī l-bilād (šahr)* —–> *gad lahā šahr fī l-bilād.*

3. *Sentence completion*

Complete the following sentences.

Example: *kull aṭ-ṭullāb?* ———> *aywih, aṭ-ṭullāb kulluhum*

i. *kull al-banāt? aywih,* ______________________

ii. *kull al-bayt? aywih,* ______________________

iii. *kull al-gāt? aywih,* ______________________

iv. *kull al-ḥarāwī? aywih,* ______________________

v. *kull al-muġanniyīn? aywih,* ______________________

vi. *kull as-saltih? aywih,* ______________________

vii. *nafs al-gā*^{c}*? aywih,* ______________________

viii. *nafs as-sūg? aywih,* ______________________

ix. *nafs al-gariyih? aywih,* ______________________

4. *Relative clauses*

Link the following pairs of clauses using *allaḏī* or *allī* and adding a referential pronoun in the relative clause where necessary. In the example, the relative pronoun and the referential pronoun are highlighted in **bold**:

Example: *absarti l-gāt? / ištarayt al-gāt ams.*—–> *absarti l-gāt* ***allaḏī*** *štarayt***ih** *ams?*

i. *gad absart al-bint / al-bint gad sāfarat al-yawm.*___________

____

ii. *ištarayt az-zinnih / az-zinnih fī s-sūg.*________________

iii. *sāfartu l-bilād / al-bilād garīb min hānā.*________________

iv. *ašti tḥākā ma*^{c} *al-ustāḏ / al-ustāḏ yištaġil fī jāmi*^{c}*at ṣan*^{c}*ā.* ___

____

v. *ar-rajjāl hānā / asāfir ma^c ar-rajjāl lā bārīz (Paris).* ________

____

5. *Possession*

Change the following annexion phrases into phrases involving *ḥagg*.

Example: *zinnatī* ——> *az-zinnih ḥaggī*

i. *kitāb al-wald.* ________________________________

ii. *jambiyatak.* ________________________________

iii. *^{c}allāgiyat al-marih.* ____________________________

iv. *bint marat aš-šayx.* ____________________________

v. *bilād an-nās.* ________________________________

vi. *bintiš.* ____________________________________

vii. *rajjāliš.* __________________________________

6. *Negation*

Negate the following sentences.

Example: *anā dārī* ——> *m-anīš dārī*

i. *az-zalaṭ fī l-ġurfih.* ____________________________

ii. *al-bayt kabīr gawī.* ____________________________

iii. *hū min al-kuwayt.* _____________________________

iv. *zawj al-marih ma^{c}āhā.* ________________________

v. *ašti štarī gāt min bāb al-yaman.* __________________

vi. *ma^{c}ak sayyārih.* _______________________________

vii. *al-gāt ḥālī gawī.* _____________________________

viii. *mumkin ajī ba^{c}d yawm.* ________________________

7. *Word order*

Reorder the following sets of words to produce meaningful sentences in Ṣanᶜānī Arabic:

i. *gawī, gad, kaṯīr, hū, al-yawm.*

ii. *niddī, lāzim, lahā, al-xāṭam, nafs.*

iii. *yištī, kān, gāt, yištarī, ams.*

iv. *sayyārih, maᶜānā, kān, kabīrih.*

v. *al-bilād, mumkin, nisāfir, šahr, baᶜd.*

vi. *min, al-yaman, ništī, ḥagg, nitḥākā.*

vii. *alaggim, min, al-bint, ar-ruzz.*

viii. *az-zinnih, ḥālī, ḥagg, gawī, bintiš.*

8. *Translation*

Translate the following groups of sentences into Ṣanᶜānī Arabic:

A. Use *nafs*

i. Do you m.pl. want Jamāl Street itself?

ii. Does he want the same man?

iii. Does she want the actual market-place?

B. Use *lāzim*

i. They m. have to leave the children in Britain.

ii. He has to chew *gāt* everyday.

iii. She has to prepare lunch.

C. Use *kān* + a modal adjective

i. She was supposed to come today.

ii. He could have come yesterday.

iii. She had to prepare lunch.

D. Use *kam* + *lā* + pronoun

i. How long has your f.s. daughter been in Yemen?

ii. How long have you m.s. been in France?

iii. How long have your m.pl. children been in Yemen?

E. Use two objects

i. Feed m.s. her potatoes.

ii. I dressed her in a nice dress.

iii. She gave the bride a wedding present.

LESSON 11

Kayf asīr al-jāmi^{c} al-kabīr?

Dialogue 1 *kayf asīr al-jāmi^{c} al-kabīr?*

sawwāḥ: salām ^{c}alaykum yā ^{c}izzī.

ṣubī: ^{c}alaykum as-salām.

sawwāḥ: law samaḥt, gul lī kayf asīr al-jāmi^{c} al-kabīr fī l-madīni l-gadīmih. mišū ba^{c}īd min hānā, mā?

ṣubī: illā, gadū ba^{c}īd šwayyih, gadū bayn bāb al-yaman wa-sūg al-bagar, w-iḥna d̲alḥīn fī bāb ṣabāḥ.

sawwāḥ: w-aynī sūg al-bagar? axṭī min hānā ṭawālī?

ṣubī: māšī, lā tuxṭīš min hānā, lā xuṭīt hākad̲ā ṭawālī tūṣal mīdān at-taḥrīr. aḥsan šī tirkab taks min hānā lā bāb al-yaman, wa-tudxul al-bāb wa-tsīr min al-bāb ṣalā sūg al-bagar wa-tliff yamnih gabl sūg al-bagar wa-l-jāmi^{c} hākad̲ā ^{c}alā yasratak.

sawwāḥ: wa-kam adfa^{c} sawwāg at-taks?

ṣubī: ^{c}alā-mā tištī, xamsīn girš, sittīn, sā^{c}-mā tirkab kull yawm. aw min mīdān at-taḥrīr tirkab dabbāb, tirkab bi-nafar, wa-tiddī mā bi-lā ^{c}ašarih gurūš.

sawwāḥ: ḥayyāk allāh.

ṣubī: allāh yiḥayyīk, ma^{c}a s-salāmih.

sawwāḥ: fī 'aman allāh.

Dialogue 2 *^{c}ādāt al-^{c}īd*

^{c}ādāt al-yaman tijāh al-^{c}īd, tijāh al-^{c}īd bi-t̲amān aw ^{c}ašar iyyām yinaffiḏ̣ū, yixarrijū kull šī wa-ynaḏ̣ḏ̣ufu l-bayt, yika^{cc}ikū ka^{c}k al-^{c}īd, wa-yištaraw ja^{c}ālat al-^{c}īd, wa-ja^{c}ālat al-^{c}īd mikawwanih min az-zabīb wa-l-lawz wa-š-šiklīt wa-l-fustug wa-d-dixišš wa-^{c}aṣīr. wa-l-^{c}iyyāl yitġassilū tijāh al-^{c}īd bi-yawm yitḥammamū yitmaššaṭū ša^{c}ruhum, wa-l-banāt yitnaggašayn nagš wa-yitḥannayn. wa-yawm

al-^{c}īd al-ab maṯalan yizūr binti l-mitzawwijih, wa-ba^{c}d al-ġadā' al-bint al-mitzawwijih tuzūr abūhā w-ummahā wa-jaddahā wa-jaddathā, wa-yiddaw zalaṭ yigassimūh la-l-makālif yi^{c}aswibū ^{c}asb, wa-l-jihhāl yākulu l-ja^{c}āli llaḏi nsawwīhā fī ṣuḥūn. al-jahhāl ti^{c}jibhum al-ja^{c}ālih gawī. w-iḏā mā kaffāš yawm al-^{c}īd, iḏa l-usrih mā gad kammalatš yawm ṯānī yukūn mā zāl ^{c}īd ^{c}indanā yawm ṯānī yawm ṯāliṯ ṯalāṯ iyyām al-^{c}īd, wa-ygassimū wa-ysīrū wa-yjaw.

Vocabulary

^{c}ādih pl. *-āt*	custom f.	*aḥsan šī*	the best thing m.
a^{c}jab - yi^{c}jib	to please (s.o.)	*^{c}alā*	on; against
^{c}alā-mā	as adjt.	*^{c}asb*	money given as present m.
^{c}aṣīr	juice m.	*^{c}aswab - yi^{c}aswib*	to give *^{c}asb*
ayy	any	*(^{c}asb)*	as a present
bāb pl. *abwāb*	gate; door m.	*bagar*	cattle coll. m.
ba^{c}īd	far	*bayn*	between; in
dafa^{c} - yidfa^{c}	to pay (s.o., s.th.)	*daxal - yudxul*	to enter; go into
dixišš	roast chick peas m	*fustug*	pestachios m.
gabl	before	*gadīm*	old
gassam - yigassim	to divide out (s.th.)	*girš* pl. *gurūš*	Riyal m.
hākaḏā	like this	*ḥattā*	until; up to
^{c}īd pl. *a^{c}yād*	festival; holiday m.	*iḏā*	if
illā	but yes!	*ja^{c}ālih*	sweets coll. f.
jadd pl. *ajdād*	mat. grandfather m.	*jaddih* pl. *-āt*	mat. grandmother f.
jāmi^{c} pl. *jawāmi^{c}*	mosque m.	*ka^{cc}ak - yika^{cc}ik*	to make cake
kaffā - yikaffī	to be enough	*ka^{c}k*	[type of] cake m.
kammal - yikammil	to finish; complete	*laff - yiliff*	to turn
law	if	*law samaḥt*	please [lit: if you allow]
mā	isn't it?	*madīnih* pl. *mudun*	town; city f.
mā zāl	it is still	*mīdān at-taḥrīr*	Liberation Squ. m.
mukawwan / mikawwan	made up of	*naḏḏaf - yinaḏḏuf*	to clean (s.th.)
nafar pl. *anfār*	person m.	*naffaḏ - yinaffiḏ*	to dust
nagš	cosmetic painting m.	*rikib - yirkab*	to ride (s.th.)
ṣaḥn pl. *ṣuḥūn*	plate m.	*ṣalā*	towards; to
samaḥ - yismaḥ	to allow (s.o., s.th.)	*ša^{c}r*	hair m.
šiklīt	chocolate m.	*ṣubī* pl. *ṣubyān*	boy, youth m.

taks pl. *-iyāt*	taxi m.	*t̲amān* pl. *t̲awāmin*	week m.
ṭawālī	straight on	*tġassal - yitġassil*	to wash o.s.
tḥammam - yitḥammam	to bathe	*tḥannā - yitḥannā*	to henna o.s.
tijāh	before	*tmaššaṭ - yitmaššaṭ*	to comb o.s.
tnaggaš - yitnaggaš	to tatoo o.s.	*usrih* pl. *usar*	family f.
xarraj - yixarrij	to take (s.th.) out	*xuṭī - yuxṭā*	to walk
yamnih	right	*yasrih*	left
yawm t̲ānī	the next day	*zalaṭ*	money m.

Grammar

1. *Pronunciation: t and ṭ*

The letters *t* and *ṭ* are pronounced as *t* and *ṭ* (i.e. as voiceless sounds) before or after another consonant and when doubled (see Introduction), as in:

sawwāg ***at-taks***	'the taxi driver'
wa-tsīr *min al-bāb*	'and you m.s. go from the gate'

At the beginning of a sentence and between vowels, however, the letters *t* and *ṭ* are pronounced as *d* and *ḍ*:

	ᶜalā-mā ***dištī***	'as you m.s. like'
cp.	*ᶜalā-mā* ***tštī***	'as you m.s. like'
	hū ***ḍālub*** *šāṭur*	'he is a clever student'
cp.	***aṭ-ṭālub*** *šāṭur*	'the student m. is clever'

2. *Vocative*

yā ᶜizzī is one of many terms used to attract the attention of someone whose name is unknown. *ᶜizzī* is said to be the nickname of the Prophet Muhammad. Other neutral terms include:

yā wald	'boy!'
yā zaᶜkamih	'girl!'
yā bint	'girl!'

A common jocular phrase to attract someone's attention is:

yā ra^{c}wī 'farmer!'

where *ra^{c}wī* means literally peasant or farmer. Other (slightly) derogatory terms include *yā gabīlī* 'tribesman!'. Downright rude terms include *yā ḥimār* 'donkey!'

3. *Elative: 'more...', '...er'*

The elative gives the sense of *more* of that described by the adjective. It is formed from an adjective on the pattern **aKTaB**, as in:

adjective	elative	gloss
jamīl	*ajmal*	'more beautiful'
bixayr	*abxar*	'better'
gadīm	*agdam*	'older'
zġīr	*azġar*	'younger; smaller'

Where the adjective has a final weak letter (i.e. *w* or *y*), the pattern of the elative is **aKTā**, as in:

adjective	elative	gloss
bāgī	*abgā*	'more constant'
ġālī	*aġlā*	'more expensive'

Where the adjective has two identical consonants, the pattern of the elative is **aKaTB**, as in:

adjective	elative	gloss
xafīf	*axaff*	'lighter'
jadīd	*ajadd*	'newer'

Some elatives, such as *aškal* 'better', do not have an adjective from which they are derived.

4. *Superlative: 'the most...'*

The superlative gives the sense of something being *most* that described by the adjective. To form the superlative, the elative either takes the definite article *al-*:

al-ajmal 'the most beautiful'
al-aškal 'the best'

or it is the first term (the annexed term) in an annexion phrase (cf. Lesson 8). In this case, the second term (the annex) is either *singular indefinite*:

aškal šī 'the best thing'
akbar bint 'the oldest girl'

or *plural definite*, as in:

abxar aṭ-ṭuyūr 'the best of the birds'
azġar al-ᶜiyyāl 'the youngest of the boys'

5. *'But yes!'*

Unlike French and German, English has no specific word with which to answer a negative question negatively: we would say, 'But yes!', or simply, 'Yes!' in response to a question such as, 'He isn't coming, is he?'. In Ṣanᶜānī Arabic, the equivalent to French 'si' or German 'doch' is *illā*:

w-aynū ṣāluḥ, mā gad jāš? 'where is Salih, hasn't he come?'
illā, gad jā 'yes! He has come'

6. *Tag questions*

A common tag question in Ṣanᶜānī is made by simply adding the negative particle *mā* to the end of a sentence. Unlike English where 'is it?' is used after negative sentences and 'isn't it?' after positive sentences, the same term, *mā,* is used whether the preceding sentence is negative - as in *mā gad jāš* 'he hasn't come', or positive *gad jā* 'he has come':

mā gad jāš, mā 'he hasn't come, has he?'
gad jā, mā 'he has come, hasn't he?'

7. *Negative command*

The negative command is formed by adding *lā* (or, less commonly, *mā*) before the imperfect verb and optionally suffixing *-š*:

lā	+ *timšī*	+ *(š)*	*lā timšīš*
[neg]	'you m.s. walk'	[neg]	'don't walk!'
lā	+ *tirkabī*	+ *(š)*	*lā tirkabīš*
[neg]	'you f.s. ride'	[neg]	'don't ride!'
lā	+ *tisīrū*	+ *(š)*	*lā tisīrūš*
[neg]	'you m.pl. go'	[neg]	'don't go!'
lā	+ *tudxulayn*	+ *(š)*	*lā tudxulanš*[1]
[neg]	'you f.pl. go in'	[neg]	'don't go in!'

8. *Negation with mā*

Negation involving *mā… -š* or *lā… -š* may alternatively involve simply *mā* or *lā*:

m-anā dārī	'I don't know'
ᶜalā sibb mā yuxruj	'so that it m. does not come out'
lā tudxul	'don't come in!'

Certain common expressions may only take the *mā* form (without *-š*), as in:

m-anī ᶜilm	'I don't know'
mā darānī	'I don't know'

9. *Adverbs: 'a day before …'*

'A day, week, month, etc. before or after X' is generally expressed in Ṣanᶜānī Arabic by saying 'after/before X by a day/week':

tijāh al-ᶜīd	+ *bi-ṯamān*[2]	*tijāh al-ᶜīd bi-ṯamān*
'before the-festival'	'by-a-week'	'a week before the festival'

[1] cf. Lesson 7 for contraction of *-ayn* to *-an* before suffix.

[2] The word *ṯamān* 'week' is related to the number *ṯamāniyih* 'eight', and is also used in the sense of eight [days].

ba^{c}d al-ġadā'	+ *bi-sā^{c}ah*	*ba^{c}d al-ġadā' bi-sā^{c}ah*
'after lunch'	'by-an-hour'	'an hour after lunch'

10. *Verbs: 'to like'*

There are two common ways of expressing the sense of liking something: either by using the verb *yi^{c}jib* 'to please' + object pronoun where the subject of *yi^{c}jib* is the 'liked' object, or, less commonly, by using the verb *ḥabb - yiḥibb* 'to like, love'. Compare the two ways of expressing 'I like Yemen a lot':

al-yaman ti^{c}jibnī gawī
'Yemen' 'pleases-me' 'very [much]'

[bayn-]aḥibb al-yaman gawī
'I-like' 'Yemen' 'very [much]'

In the first example, Yemen is the subject of the verb, and in the second example Yemen is the object of the verb.

11. *Initial weak verbs: waja^c, wuṣul, yibis*

Initial weak verbs are verbs like *waja^c* 'to hurt', *wuṣul* 'to arrive' and *yibis* 'to become dry' which begin with an initial *w* or *y*. These verbs behave like sound verbs in the perfect aspect (cf. Lesson 6), but behave like weak verbs in the imperfect. Here the vowel of the imperfect prefix and the first consonant of the verbal stem combine to form a long vowel - *ū* in the case of initial-*w* verbs and *ī* in the case of initial-*y* verbs. Here is the full paradigm of the common verb *wuṣul - yūṣal* 'to arrive' in the imperfect aspect:

	singular	plural
1.	*awṣal*[3]	*nūṣal*
2. m.	*tūṣal*	*tūṣalū*
2. f.	*tūṣalī*	*tūṣalayn*
3. m.	*yūṣal*	*yūṣalū*
3. f.	*tūṣal*	*yūṣalayn*

The active participle of *wuṣul* is *wāṣul* 'arriving; one who arrives'. Here is the full paradigm of *yibis - yības* 'to become dry' in the imperfect aspect:

[3] The first singular form is the one exception to this rule. This form treats the initial weak verbs as sound verbs - that is to say, the first consonant remains as a consonant.

	singular	plural
1.	*ābas*	*nības*
2. m.	*tības*	*tībasū*
2. f.	*tībasī*	*tībasayn*
3. m.	*yības*	*yībasū*
3. f.	*tības*	*yībasayn*

The active participle of *yibis* is *yābis* 'dry; drying'.

12. *Verbal nouns*

Arabic does not have the concept of an infinitive verb. It does, however, have verbal nouns which are often used in the same context as an inflected verb and may be translated into English as an infinitive (cf. Lesson 5). Verbal nouns have a variety of patterns, depending on the particular verb. The following table gives examples of some of the common verbal noun patterns (for more patterns cf. *Syntax* p. 436); the verb from which the verbal noun is derived is given in the third masculine singular form in the perfect aspect:

pattern	verb	gloss	verbal noun	gloss
KaTB	*akal*	'he ate'	*akl*	'eating'
	nisī	'he forgot'	*nasy*	'forgetfulness'
KiTB	*libis*	'he wore'	*libs*	'wearing; clothes'
KaTaB	*bakā*	'he cried'	*bakā*	'crying'
	xirim	'he longed for'	*xaram*	'longing'
KaTBih	*hirib*	'he fled'	*harbih*	'fleeing; flight'
KuTūB	*xaraj*	'he went out'	*xurūj*	'going out; exit'
	daxal	'he entered'	*duxūl*	'entering; entrance'
	wuṣul	'he arrived'	*wuṣūl*	'arrival'
KaTūB	*gaṣṣ*	'he cut'	*gaṣūṣ*	'cutting'
KiTāBih	*daras*	'he learnt'	*dirāsih*	'learning; study'
	girī	'he learnt'	*girāyih*	'learning; study'
KaTīBih	*dawā*	'he talked'	*dawīyih*	'talk'
KiTBān	*nisī*	'he forgot'	*nisyān*	'forgetfulness'
ma**KTaB**	*ṭuluᶜ*	'he went up'	*maṭlaᶜ*	'ascension'
ma**KTaBih**	*ᶜirif*	'he knew'	*maᶜrafih*	'knowledge'

13. *Cognate objects*

One common use of the verbal noun in Arabic is as a *cognate* object. Arabic makes great use of cognate objects. To the English speaker these cognate objects often appear to be unnecessary, since they do not materially affect the meaning:

*gad akalat **akl** kaṯīr*	'she has eaten a lot'
*gad ġaddāh **ġadā** ḥālī*	'he gave him a nice lunch'
*gad naggašatnī **nagš** ḥālī*	'she has tatooed me nicely'

In a similar way, cognate *participles* are used as adverbs to verbs of movement:

*gad daxalū **dāxil***	'they m. went inside'
*gad xarajū **xārij***	'they m. went out'
*gad nazalū **nāzil***	'they m. went downstairs'
*gad ṭuluᶜū **ṭāluᶜ***	'they m. went up'
*gad daxxalūhā **dāxil***	'they m. took her inside'
*gad xarrajūhā **xārij***	'they m. took her outside'
*gad nazzalūhā **nāzil***	'they m. took her downstairs'

14. *Conditional clauses*

Conditional clauses either describe real and fulfillable conditions, or unreal and unfulfillable conditions. Real conditions are described in sentences such as:

If he goes outside, he will catch cold.

where the possibility of him catching cold is still real; unreal conditions, on the other hand, are described in sentences such as:

If he had gone outside last week, he would have caught cold.

where the possibility of catching a cold is no longer real. The conditional particle in English is 'if'. In Ṣanᶜānī Arabic there are several terms for 'if': *lā*, *iḏā* and *in* are used where the condition is fulfillable, while *law* and *lā* are used where the condition is not fulfillable. The first set of particles, *lā*, *i̱dā* and *in,* are often followed by a verb in the perfect, or by a prepositional or nominal clause optionally introduced by *kān*. Thus, real conditional clauses can be constructed by putting *lā*, *i̱dā* or *in* at the beginning of an appropriate declarative sentence; if the declarative sentence is verbal the verb can be either in the imperfect or the perfect in the conditional clause; if the declarative sentence is nominal the verb *kān* can be (optionally) added:

declarative sentence	conditional clause
al-wazīr min hānāk	*i̱dā (kān) al-wazīr min hānāk, (yisabbirū nā'ib min hānā)*
'the minister is from there'	'if the minister is from there, (they make a deputy from here)'
yiddaw liš šī	*lā ddaw liš šī, lāzim tiraddīhā bi-nafs an-naw*^{c}
'they give you something'	'if they m. give you f.s. something, (you have to give her the same type of thing back)'
wāḥid yixazzin	*i̱dā wāḥid yixazzin, (gadū ḥālī)*
'someone chews'	'if someone chews (*gāt*), (it is nice)'
bih mawt	*lā (kān) bih mawt, (lāzim tisīrayn)*
'there is death'	'if there is a funeral, (you f.pl. have to go)'

The same principle applies for unreal conditional clauses using *law* or *lā*; however, the verb of the main clause (bracketed in the examples of real conditional clauses above) is often preceded by uninflected *kān* when *law* is followed by the verb in the perfect or by *kān*:

law kān bi-l-yaman, kān bi-l^{c}*ab bi-l-ġubār*	'if he was in Yemen, he would play in the dust'
lā 'absartih, kān gult lih	'if I had seen him, I would have told him'

In unreal conditional clauses the verb of the main clause is usually in the perfect:

law šī[4] *šams, kānat ams*	'if there were sun, it would be yesterday'

[4] *šī* is often used after conditional particles where *bih* would be used in non-conditional sentences.

law šī mišš, mā xarajnā 'if there had been any brains, I wouldn't have gone out'

Thematic Vocabulary

Buildings and places

bayt pl. *biyūt*	house m.
dār pl. *dūr*	house f.
fundug pl. *fanādig*	hotel m.
gahwih pl. *gahāwih*	coffee shop m.
gaṣr pl. *guṣūr*	palace m.
ḥānūt pl. *ḥawānīt*	shop m.
jāmi^{c} pl. *jawāmi*^{c}	mosque m.
jāmi^{c}*ah* pl. *-āt*	university f.
lūkandih pl. *-āt*	small, cheap hotel; rest-house f.
madīnih pl. *mudun*	town; city f.
madrasih pl. *madāris*	school f.
maḥaṭṭuh pl. *-āt*	station f.
maktab pl. *makātib*	office m.
maktabih pl. *makātib*	library; bookshop f.
mal^{c}*ab* pl. *malā*^{c}*ib*	playground m.
markaz pl. *marākiz*	centre m.
masjid pl. *masājid*	mosque m.
maṭ^{c}*am* pl. *maṭā*^{c}*um*	restaurant m.
mīdān pl. *mayādīn*	square m.
mi^{c}*lāmih* pl. *ma*^{c}*ālim*	traditional school f.
nūbih pl. *nuwab*	round, defensive tower f.
raṣduh pl. *-āt*	main, asphalted road f.
šāri^{c} pl. *šawāri*^{c}	street m.
sifārih pl. *-āt*	embassy f.
timṯāl pl. *tamāṯīl*	statue m.
wizārih pl. *-āt*	ministry f.
zugāg pl. *azgāg*	alley; lane m.
zugzugī pl. *zagāzig*	alley; lane m.

Exercises

1. *Greetings*

Give an appropriate reply to the following greetings:

i. *salām ᶜalaykum!* ________________

ii. *tiṣbaḥī ᶜala l-xayr!* ________________

iii. *kaṯṯar allāh xayrukum!* ________________

iv. *akramak allāh!* ________________

v. *al-ḥamdu li-llāh ᶜala s-salāmih!* ________________

2. *Gap filling*

Complete the following sentences, correctly inflecting the verb given in brackets.

Example: *aštī* __________ *taks (yirkab)* —> *aštī* ***arkab*** *taks*

i. *as-sawwāg mumkin* __________ *la l-bāb (yisīr).*

ii. *ummī lāzim* __________ *baṭāṭ al-yawm (yištarī).*

iii. *tištī* __________ *mšakkal, yā ᶜabd al-wahhāb? (yišrab)*

iv. *lāzim* __________ *yā Sarah (yizūrnā).*

v. *yištaw* __________ *ᶜasb (yiᶜaswib).*

vi. *iḥna lāzim* __________ *tijāh al-ᶜīd bi-yawm (yitġassil).*

3. *Negative commands!*

Negate the following imperatives using *lā*, then *lā ... š*.

Example: *irkab taks min hānā!* —> *lā tirkab(š) taks min hānā!*

i. *sīrī yamnih hākaḏā!* ________________

ii. *udxulū min bāb al-yaman!* ________________

iii. *uḏwayn ḏalḥīn yā banāt!*________________

iv. *xallīhum ᶜind abūhum!* ________________________________

v. *jī yawm al-xamīs!* ________________________________

4. *Question and answer*

Provide full sentence answers to the following questions, using the information given in brackets:

Example: *kam lak min bilādak?* (one month) —> *gad lī šahr min bilādī*

i. *marat aḥmad gad maᶜāhā ᶜiyyāl?* (no) ____________________

ii. *zamīlatiš gad maᶜāhā ᶜiyyāl?* (yes, a boy and a girl) ________

____

iii. *ayyaḥīn tisāfirū maṣr?* (on Thursday) ____________________

iv. *lilmā tixazzinayn gāt xayrāt?* (you like *gāt*) ______________

____

v. *al-ᶜaṣīr miš ḥālī?* (yes, it is very nice) ____________________

5. *Find the plural*

Find the meaning and the plural form of the following nouns:

i. *bāb* ii. *ᶜīd* iii. *maklaf* iv. *ṣbuᶜ* v. *marrih* vi. *bilād* vii. *ḥarīw* viii. *jāhil* ix. *yad* x. *širšaf* xi. *ustāḏ* xii. *gamīṣ* xiii. *šāriᶜ* xiv. *ṯamān*

6. *Present > past*

Put the following sentences into the past using the appropriate form of *kān*.

Example: *bih ġubār kaṯīr fī l-madīnih* —> *kān bih ġubār kaṯīr fī l-madīnih*

i. *ibnī maᶜ abūh.* ________________________________

ii. *gad maᶜānā ṯintayn banāt.* ________________________________

iii. *al-gāt ġālī marrih hāḏi s-sanih.* ____________________

iv. *antī mitzawwijih, mā?* ____________________

v. *aš-šarṭ ṯalāṯīn alf bass fī 'ibb.* ____________________

vi. *ar-rijāl bi-tḥākaw xayrāt.* ____________________

7. *Declarative > conditional*

Make the following declarative sentences into conditional clauses using either *lā* or *iḏā*, then add add the main clause supplied in brackets.

Example: *ma^c^ānā zalaṭ xayrāt (ništari šyā ḥālī) ——> lā šī ma^c^ānā zalaṭ xayrāt, ništari šyā ḥālī*

i. *as-safīr min ^c^adan (yisabbirū nā'ib* [= deputy] *min hānā)* ___

____

ii. *gad bih ^c^iris al-yawm (nisīr al-ḥaflih)* ____________________

iii. *nisawwī ḥaflih la l-bint (^c^a-yjaw nās kaṯīr)* ____________________

____

iv. *arja^c^ al-bilād ba^c^d yawmayn (atfarraṭ ġudwuh)* ____________________

____

8. *Translation*

Translate the following groups of sentences into Ṣan^c^ānī Arabic:

A. Use *^c^ād* + pronoun

i. Are you f.s. married or still single, Khadija?

ii. Is he married or still single?

iii. Is she married or still single?

B. Use *gabl / ba^c^d … bi-…*

i. We clean the whole house a week before the festival.

ii. They m. travel to Aden a week after the festival.

iii. You f.s. must go two days after Ramadan [= *ramaḍān*].

C. Directions

i. Turn m.pl. left before the mosque.

ii. Turn f.s. right after Liberation Square.

iii. Turn m.s. left, then walk straight on until you reach the gate.

D. Ordinal numbers

i. You m.s. must buy the first book.

ii. You f.s. must buy the second book.

iii. They m. must buy the third book.

LESSON 12

Al-ittiṣāl bi-t-tilifūn

Dialogue 1

Ann: *ṣbaḥtū, mumkin akallim xadījih?*

Salwa: *man ištīhā?*

Ann: *Ann.*

Salwa: *dagīgih wāḥidih.*

Dialogue 2

Louise: *salām ^{c}alaykum.*

Najla: *^{c}alaykum as-salām. man ma^{c}ī?*

Louise: *hāḏā Louise, aštī ḥākī ṣabrī.*

Najla: *ṣabrī mā bih ḥaddū, yā Louise, gad xaraj.*

Louise: *ayyaḥīn yuḏwī luh?*

Najla: *anā m-anī ^{c}ilm, yimkin ba^{c}d sā^{c}ah.*

Louise: *nāhī, gulī lih yitṣal bī ^{c}ind-mā yuḏwī?*

Najla: *ṭayyub, ša-ddī lih xabar.*

Dialogue 3

John: *msaytū.*

Muhammad: *massākum allāh bi-l-xayr.*

John: *aštī xābir mḥammad.*

Muhammad: *ma^{c}ākum mḥammad. man ma^{c}ī?*

John: *hāḏā John min London.*

Muhammad: *aywih, John! kayf ad-dunyā, yā 'axī?*

John: *ad-dunyā sābir w-allāh.*

Muhammad: *w-ayn ant? gad ant fī l-yaman awlā gadak titṣal min brīṭānīyā?*

John: *anā fī ṣan^{c}ā ḏalḥīn, jālis fī fundug dār al-ḥamd.*

Muhammad: *ant mā zid tištaġil ^{c}ind axūk fī London?*

John: *illā! gad jīt hānā ziyārih rasmīyih.*

Muhammad: *kam lak hānā ḏalḥīn?*

John: *mā b-lā sā^{c}atayn, ^{c}ādanī jīt min al-maṭār.*

Muhammad: *al-ḥamdu li-llāh ^{c}ala s-salāmih!*

John: *āmīn!*

Muhammad: *gasmak jīt lāzim tizūrnā fī l-bayt.*

John: *ṭab^{c}an bi-kull surūr! nafsī zūrkum. mumkin ajī ġudwuh?*

Muhammad: *anā miš fāḍī ġudwuh. bayn-asāfir Paris al-usbū^{c} al-gādim, wa-ġudwu ṣ-ṣubḥ ḍarūrī sīr al-jawāzāt ajaddid ḥaggi l-jawāz, wa-ba^{c}d aḍ-ḍuhr gad ma^{c}ī maw^{c}id fī l-wizārih ^{c}ind nā'ib al-wazīr. anā 'āsif gawī w-allāh.*

John: *^{c}ādī, allāh yi^{c}īnak.*

Muhammad: *allāh karīm. gul lī, šī ma^{c}ak mišwār yawm al-jum^{c}ah?*

John: *yawm al-jum^{c}ah hāḏā mā biš ma^{c}ī šī min as-sā^{c}ah wāḥidi ḍ-ḍuhr.*

Muhammad: *ṭayyub, jī lā ^{c}indanā yawm al-jum^{c}a s-sā^{c}ah wāḥidih wa-nuṣṣ law-mā ttimm aš-šuġl, nitġaddā sawā wa-ba^{c}da nsīr nixazzin fī bayt Tim.*

John: *nāhī, 'absirak yawm al-jum^{c}ah, in šā' allāh. tiṣbaḥ ^{c}ala l-xayr, yā mḥammad.*

Muhammad: *w-ant min ahl al-xayr, yā John.*

Vocabulary

^{c}ādī	that's okay; normal	*^{c}afwan*	sorry; excuse me
dagīgih pl. *dagāyig*	minute f.	*dār al-ḥamd*	[name of hotel f.]
ḍarūrī	essential	*ḍuhr*	noon m.
dunyā	world f.	*fāḍī*	free
fundug pl. *fanādig*	hotel m.	*gādim*	previous
gasmak	since you m.s.	*ḥākā - yiḥākī*	to talk (to s.o.)
^{c}ilm	knowledge m.	*^{c}ind-mā*	when adjt.
itṣal - yitṣal	to telephone; call	*jaddad - yijaddid*	to renew (s.th.)
jālis	staying	*jawāz* pl. *-āt*	passport m.
al-jawāzāt	[term for ministry of the interior f.]	*kallam - yikallim*	to talk (to s.o.)

maṭār pl. *-āt*	airport m.	*maw*^{c}*id* pl. *mawā*^{c}*id*	appointment m.
mišwār pl. *mašāwir*	errand; s.th. to do m.	*nafsī*	I really want to
nā'ib pl. *nuwwāb*	deputy m.	*rasmī*	official
ṣābir	good	*sawā*	together
štaġal - yištaġil	to work	*šuġl*	work m.
surūr	delight m.	*tamm - yitimm*	to finish (s.th.)
tġaddā - yitġaddā	to have lunch	*xabar*	information m.
(yiddī lih xabar)	he (will) let him know	*xābar - yixābir*	to talk (to s.o.)
xaraj - yuxruj	to go out	*yimkin*	perhaps
zid	again; more	*ziyārih* pl. *-āt*	visit f.

Grammar

1. *Greetings*

A common greeting between people who know each other fairly well is *kayf ad-dunyā*, literally 'how is the world?' The reply is *ad-dunyā ṣābir*, literally 'the world is good'.

When someone says they have been working hard, or that they have a lot of work to do it is usual to use a phrase like *allāh yi*^{c}*īnak* 'may God help you m.s.' or *allāh yi*^{c}*īniš* 'may God help you f.s.'. The usual reply is *allāh karīm* 'God is generous' or *āmīn*, a word which is related to our Amen.

The phrase *al-ḥamdu li-llāh* ^{c}*ala s-salāmih* 'thanks be to God for safety' is said to someone who has just had a safe journey. The usual reply to this is *āmīn*.

In the late afternoon or evening the first speaker will often finish a conversation with the phrase *tiṣbaḥ* ^{c}*ala l-xayr* lit. 'wake up m.s. in goodness'. The reply is *w-ant min ahl al-xayr* 'and you m.s. are from the people of goodness'. These phrases are equivalent to our expression 'good night'. The verb *tiṣbaḥ* inflects for gender and number, and similarly the pronoun is *antī* for a woman, and *antū* and *antayn* for plural.

2. *Adverbs: 'hopefully'*

The phrase *in šā' allāh* (also pronounced as *in šallāh*) is very common in all dialects of Arabic. Literally it means 'if God wills', but in context it is closer to our phrase 'hopefully'. However, *in šā' allāh* is used far more frequently in Arabic than 'hopefully' is in English.

3. *'I would really like to', 'I wish'*

One common way of expressing a sense of wish or desire is the word *nafs* + pronoun followed by the imperfect verb. The imperfect verb inflects for the person indicated by the suffix on *nafs*:

nafsi bsiriš	'I really want to see you f.s.'
nafsak tizūr al-yaman	'do you m.s. wish to visit Yemen?'

4. *'Since', 'because', 'on account of the fact that...'*

The term *gasm* followed by a pronoun suffix means 'since/because/on account of the fact that...' It is often followed by the perfect verb, as in:

gasmak jīt (lāzim tizūrnā)	'since you have come you must visit us'

It can also be followed by an adverb or a prepositional phrase, as in:

gasmak hānā (lāzim tizūrnā)	'since you are here you must visit us'

and

gasmak fi l-yaman (lāzim tizūrnā)	'since you are inYemen you must visit us'

5. *Adverbs: 'only'*

There are several ways of expressing 'only' in Ṣanᶜānī Arabic. Two common expressions are *bass* and *mā bi-lā* (often pronounced *mā b-lā).*

Bass follows the limited term, as in:

šahr bass	'only a month'
ištarayt wāḥid bass	'I only bought one'

Mā bi-lā precedes the limited term, as in:

mā bi-lā šahr	'only a month'
mā bi-lā wāḥid	'only one'
mā bi-lā sīr anā wa-hī	'I am just going with her'

6. *Word order: ḥagg*

A phrase involving *ḥagg* [for possession] usually comes after the possessed noun, as in: *al-bayt ḥaggī* 'the house belonging to me; my house', but it can also come before the possessed noun, in particular when *ḥagg* takes a pronoun suffix (*Syntax* p. 224), and as in the example in this lesson:

ḥaggi l-jawāz 'my passport'

When the *ḥagg* phrase precedes the possessed noun the idea of possession is often (though not necessarily) emphasised (*Syntax* p. 223). In some cases the speaker may be biding time because they cannot remember the name of the possessed thing, in a similar way to 'where's your ..., your ...', and 'where's my ..., oh, what's it called?!' in English.

aynū ḥaggiš ar-rajjāl 'where is he, your husband?'

7. *Adverbs: 'again', 'more' and 'no longer'*

'Again', 'more' and 'no longer' can be expressed very neatly in Ṣanᶜānī Arabic by the particle *zid* before a verb in the perfect or the imperfect depending on whether the speaker is referring to an event in the past or in the present/future. *zid* does not change for person, number or gender:

zid nixābirhā 'let's talk to her again'

zid absartahā 'I saw her again'

In order to express the sense of 'no longer' or 'not again' the negative particle *mā* precedes *zid*:

mā zid nixābirhā 'we will not talk to her again'

mā zid absartahā 'I no longer saw her'

The negative particle *-š* is also commonly suffixed to *zid*, as in:

mā zidš agūl 'I no longer say'

8. *'He's not here...'*

A very common phrase used to express 'so-and-so is not here' is *mā bih ḥadd* 'there is no one' followed by the appropriate independent pronoun:

mā bih ḥaddū	'he is not here'
mā bih ḥaddī	'she is not here'
mā bih ḥaddum	'they m. are not here'
mā bih ḥadd ant	'you m.s. are not here'

Often the phrase *mā bih ḥadd* is preceded by a noun, or by the name of the person who is not here, as in:

ṣabrī mā bih ḥaddū	'Sabri is not here'
jamīlih mā bih ḥaddī	'Jamila is not here'

In this case the pronoun can be left off *ḥadd*:

ṣabrī mā bih ḥadd	'Sabri is not here'
jamīlih mā bih ḥadd	'Jamila is not here'

When an independent pronoun precedes the phrase *mā bih ḥadd*, a pronoun does not also follow *ḥadd*:

anā mā bih ḥadd	'I'm not there'
hum mā bih ḥadd	'they m. are not here'

The phrase *mā bih ḥadd* does not usually have a past form. When you say in Arabic, for example, 'you came and I wasn't there':

antū jītū w-anā mā bih ḥadd	'you m.pl. came and I wasn't there'

the phrase *w-anā mā bih ḥadd* is felt to have applied at the time indicated in the main verb *jītū*, i.e. in the past. Similarly, in a sentence which refers to the future, such as 'I shall come and you won't be there':

anā ᶜad-jī w-ant mā bih ḥadd	'I shall come and you m.s. won't be there'

the phrase *w-anā mā bih ḥadd* is felt to apply at the time indicated in the main verb *ᶜad-jī*, and therefore to apply at some future time.[1]

9. *Verbs: 'to finish doing ...'*

Two different verbs are used to express 'to finish'. These verbs are *kammal - yikammil* and *tamm - yitimm*. In order to say 'to finish doing s.th.' *kammal* or *tamm* is followed by a verb in the imperfect, or by a (usually verbal, cf. Lesson 11) noun, as in:

	tammaynā nitġaddā	'we finished having lunch'
or		
	tammaynā l-ġadā	'we finished lunch'
	tammaynā nudrus	'we finished studying'
or		
	tammaynā d-dirāsih	'we finished study'
	kammalnā ništaġil	'we finished working'
or		
	kammalnā š-šuġl	'we finished work'

10. *Imperfect: 'he should call me'*

There is no one word to translate English 'should' or 'would' (cf. Lesson 5). In general, the imperfect aspect can express the sense of 'should' or 'would', as in *yitṣal* in the following two examples:

gulī lih yitṣal bī	'tell f.s. him he should call me'
gālū yitṣal bī	'they said he would call me'

And as in *yijī* and *yištarī* in the following examples:

gulī lih yijī	'tell f.s. him he should come'
gulī lih yištarī lī baxūr	'tell f.s. him he should buy me incense'

'Would' can also be expressed by the imperfect with the future prefix:

[1] This is due to Arabic *tense subordination*. For details on tense subordination in Ṣanᶜānī Arabic see *Syntax* pp. 85-91.

gālū ^{c}a-yjī	'they said he would come'
gāl ^{c}a-yštarī lī baxūr	'he said he would buy me incense'

11. *Telling the time*

The time is expressed by the word *as-sā^{c}ah* 'the hour' followed by the appropriate number (cf. *Syntax* p. 323, Lesson 8):

as-sā^{c}ah + *wāḥidih* 'the-hour' 'one'	*as-sā^{c}ah wāḥidih* 'one o' clock' or 'the time is one'
as-sā^{c}ah + *ṯintayn* 'the-hour' 'two'	*as-sā^{c}ah ṯintayn* 'two o' clock' or 'the time is two'

In the times from three o' clock to ten o' clock, the number does not take the ending *-ih* because it comes after a feminine noun (cf. Lesson 15):

as-sā^{c}ah + *ṯalāṯ* 'the-hour' 'three'	*as-sā^{c}ah ṯalāṯ* 'three o' clock' or 'the time is three'
as-sā^{c}ah + *arba^{c}* 'the-hour' 'four'	*as-sā^{c}ah arba^{c}* 'four o' clock' or 'the time is four'
as-sā^{c}ah + *xams* 'the-hour' 'five'	*as-sā^{c}ah xams* 'five o' clock' or 'the time is five'

With eleven o' clock and twelve o' clock the number takes its independent form (i.e. without final *-ar*, cf. Lesson 15):

as-sā^{c}ah ḥid^{c}āš	'eleven o' clock' or 'the time is eleven'
as-sā^{c}ah iṯn^{c}āš	'twelve o' clock' or 'the time is twelve'

To say 'so much past' the hour you give the hour, for example, *as-sā^{c}ah ṯalāṯ* then *wa-* followed by the fraction of the hour. The fractions have the pattern **KuTB** and, with the exception of 'half' *nuṣṣ* and, perhaps, 'sixth' *suds*, take the same consonants as the corresponding whole number:

whole number	fraction
ṯalāṯ	*ṯulṯ*
arba^{c}	*rub*^{c}
xams	*xums*
sitt	*suds*
sab^{c}	*sub*^{c}
ṯamān	*ṯumn*

A time like 4.20 is expressed as *as-sā*^{c}*ah arba*^{c} *wa-ṯulṯ* 'literally: the hour is four and a third'. 4.30 is expressed as *as-sā*^{c}*ah arba*^{c} *wa-nuṣṣ* 'literally: the hour is four and a half'. A time like 4.10 will be expressed as *as-sā*^{c}*ah arba*^{c} *wa-*^{c}*ašar* 'literally: the hour is four and ten (minutes)'. 4.25 is expressed as *as-sā*^{c}*ah arba*^{c} *wa-nuṣṣ illā xams* 'literally: the hour is four and a half except for five (minutes).' After the half hour mark the time is usually expressed as being the coming hour except for a fraction or so many minutes: thus, 4.40 is expressed as *as-sā*^{c}*ah xams illā ṯulṯ* 'literally: the hour is five except for a third'. 4.45 is expressed as *as-sā*^{c}*ah xams illā rub*^{c} 'literally: the hour is five except for a quarter'. 4.50 is expressed as *as-sā*^{c}*ah xams illā* ^{c}*ašar* 'literally: the hour is five except for ten (minutes)'. The exception to this occurs immediately after the half hour mark where 4.35 is expressed as *as-sā*^{c}*ah arba*^{c} *wa-nuṣṣ wa-xams* 'literally: the hour is four and a half and five'.

12. *Yemeni time*

When people are referring to the time, they may add the word *yamanī,* as in *as-sā*^{c}*ah ṯalāṯ yamanī* to mean three o' clock *Yemeni* time. Yemeni time differs from international (or English) time in that Yemeni one o' clock is equivalent to English seven o' clock, Yemeni two o' clock to English eight o' clock, Yemeni three o' clock to English nine o' clock, and so on. When arranging social appointments, it may be useful to ask *as-sā*^{c}*ah ṯalāṯ yamanī wallā 'injlīzī* 'three o' clock Yemeni time or English time?' or you may find that you are either six hours late or six hours early!

13. *Verb forms*

Unlike English, the Arabic verb system is remarkably regular. There is one basic verb type which in the perfect aspect has the pattern CVCVC (where C = consonant and V = vowel). A verb which has this particular pattern is said to be a *form I* verb. Form I verbs which we have encountered so far include:

perfect	imperfect[2]	gloss
katab	*yuktub*	'to write'
jamac	*yijmac*	'to collect'
cirif	*yicraf*	'to know'
širib	*yišrab*	'to drink'
xisir	*yixsir*	'to spend; lose'
kubur	*yikbar*	'to become big; to become older'
zuġur	*yizġar*	'to be small; to be young'

Hollow verbs, such as *gāl* 'to say' and *sār* 'to go', doubled verbs, such as *jass* 'to sit' *tamm* 'to finish' and *dagg* 'to knock', and third weak verbs, such as *dirī* 'to know' and *nisī* 'to forget' are also considered to be form I verbs.

14. *Derived verb forms II - IV*

By lengthening consonants or vowels, or by adding consonants to the beginning of the verb or within the verb, a number of verb forms can be *derived* from the basic form I. In contrast to form I verbs, derived verbs always have the vowels *a-a* in the perfect aspect.

14.1. Form II

Form II is derived by doubling the second consonant: it has the pattern CaCCaC in the perfect and yiCaCCVC[3] in the imperfect. Form II verbs include:

perfect	imperfect	gloss
ġassal	*yiġassil*	'to wash (s.o./s.th.)'
labbas	*yilabbis*	'to dress (s.o.)'
naggaš	*yinaggiš*	'to tatoo (s.o.) with antimony'
sammā	*yisammī*	'to call (s.o.; s.th.)'
sannab	*yisannib*	'to stand'
sawwā	*yisawwī*	'to do (s.th.)'
xazzan	*yixazzin*	'to chew'

[2] The imperfect vowels of form I verbs are not wholly predictable and should be learnt at the same time as the perfect verb is learnt.

[3] V is most commonly *i* in the imperfect, as in the examples given here. This final imperfect vowel is *a* in a few form II verbs, and may be *u* where the verb has an emphatic consonant - *ṭ*, *ṣ* or *ḍ*, e.g. *yiṭawwul* 'to lengthen; to be long'.

14.1.1. Verbal noun of form II verbs

The verbal noun of form II verbs is formed on one of the patterns below. Different verbs take different patterns, and some verbs (such as *xazzan - yixazzin* 'to chew') may take more than one verbal noun pattern.

pattern	verbal noun	verb	gloss
KaTTāB	*xazzān*	*xazzan*	chewing (*gāt*)
	ġassāl	*ġassal*	washing
	bayyāḏ̣	*bayyaḏ̣*	whitening; whiting
KuTTāB	*nuffāḏ̣*	*naffaḏ̣*	dusting
KiTTāB	*firrās*	*farras*	closure
taKTīB	*tadxīn*	*daxxan*	smoking
	taxzīn	*xazzan*	chewing (*gāt*)
taKTūB	*taṣlūḥ*	*ṣallaḥ*	fixing
tuKTāB	*tuṣlāḥ*	*ṣallaḥ*	fixing

14.2. Form III

Form III verbs are derived by lengthening the first vowel: form III has the pattern CāCaC in the perfect and yiCāCVC[4] in the imperfect. Form III verbs include:

perfect	imperfect	gloss
ḥākā	*yiḥākī*	'to talk to'
rāᶜā	*yirāᶜī*	'to wait [for]'
sāfar	*yisāfir*	'to travel'
xābar	*yixābir*	'to talk to'
wāfag	*yiwāfag*	'to agree'
jāwab	*yijāwab*	'to answer'

14.2.1. Verbal noun of form III verbs

The verbal noun of form III verbs is formed on one of the patterns below. As for form II verbal nouns, different verbs take different patterns, and certain verbs may take more than one verbal noun pattern:

[4] As for form II, the final imperfect vowel of form III verbs is most commonly *i*, but is *a* in a few verbs, as in *yiwāfag*.

pattern	verbal noun	verb	gloss
KaTāB	*jawāb*	*jāwab*	reply; answer
	ᶜagāb	*ᶜāgab*	punishment
KiTāBih	*ḥikāyih*	*ḥākā*	tale; recount
maKāTaBih/	*maᶜāgabih*	*ᶜāgab*	punishment
muKāTaBih[5]	*muṣādamuh*	*ṣādam*	collision

14.3. Form IV

Form IV verbs take an initial vowel and no vowel between the first and second consonants: form IV has the pattern aCCVC in the perfect and yiCCVC in the imperfect. This verb form is not very common in Ṣanᶜānī Arabic:

perfect	imperfect	gloss
abṣar	*yibṣir*	'to see'
abrad	*yibrid*	'to cool'
aḥlak	*yiḥlak*	'to die'
aᶜjab	*yiᶜjib*	'to please'
aṭlag	*yuṭlug*	'to set free'
axlaṣ	*yixliṣ*	'to take off'

14.3.1. Verbal noun of form IV verbs

The verbal noun of form IV verbs has one basic pattern, iKTāB:

pattern	verbal noun	verb	gloss
iKTāB	*ixlāṣ*	*axlaṣ*	taking off; removal
	iṭlāg	*aṭlag*	setting free

15. *Active participles of verb forms II - IV*

Active participles (cf. Lesson 13 for passive participles) from certain verbs are often used in place of the corresponding verb in Ṣanᶜānī Arabic. In contrast to active and passive participles from the basic form I verb (cf. Lesson 7), participles from derived verbs take the same pattern as the corresponding imperfect verb. The only difference between say *yisannib* 'he stands' and *misannib* 'standing' is that

[5] muCāCaCuh where one of the root consonants is an emphatic.

the active participle takes initial *m*. Common active participles from derived verbs include:

active particle	gloss
misannib	'standing'
mixaddir	'being in a doped state'
mixazzin	'chewing'
misāfir	'travelling'
muwāfag	'agreeing; agreed'
mirā^{c}*ī*	'waiting'
mu^{c}*jib*	'pleasing'
mumkin	'possible'

The *i* of *mi-* (*u* of *mu-*) is often not pronounced in rapid speech (see below). Active participles of derived verbs take the endings *-ih* for feminine singular, *-īn* for masculine plural and *-āt* for feminine plural, as in:

hū msannib	'he is standing'
*hī msannib***ih**	'she is standing'
*hum misannib***īn**	'they m. are standing'
*hin misannib***āt**	'they f. are standing'

Quadriliteral verbs (cf. Lesson 7) such as *gambar* 'to sit' take the same imperfect pattern - yiCaCCVC - and the same active participle pattern - m(i)CaCCVC - as form II verbs, as in:

ana mgambar	'I am sitting'
ana mgawzab	'I am squatting'

Thematic Vocabulary

Communications

al-barīd	the post m.
al-ittiṣālāt	communications f.
ḍarf pl. *ḍurūf*	envelope m.
duwalī	international
faks pl. *-āt*	fax m.
maḥallī	local
maktab al-barīd	post-office m.
maktūb pl. *makātīb*	letter m.

ragm pl. *argām [at-tilifūn]*	[telephone] number m.
rāsal - yirāsil	to correspond (with s.o.)
risālih pl. *rasā'il / rasāyil*	letter f.
ṣawwar - yiṣawwur	to [photo]copy
ṣundūg pl. *ṣanādīg [al-barīd]*	post box [as in post-box number] m.
*ṭābu*ᶜ pl. *ṭawābu*ᶜ	stamp m.
tilifūn pl. *-āt*	telephone m.
xuṭṭ / xaṭṭ pl. *xuṭūṭ*	[telephone] line m.

Exercises

1. *Possessive pronouns*

Complete the table below by suffixing the correct possessive pronoun to the prepositions and nouns. The top left-hand corner is completed by way of example:

	fi	*gafā*	*ma*ᶜ	ᶜ*alā*	*umm*
anā	*fīnī*				
iḥna					
antī					
antayn					
hū					
hin					

2. *Tell the time!*

Read the following times out loud in Ṣanᶜānī Arabic:

i. 9.00. ii. 1.00. iii. 4.00. iv. 5.00. v. 7.00. vi. 2.30. vii. 8.45. viii. 9.55.

3. *Sentence formation*

Put the following single words into meaningful sentences. Where verbs are involved inflect as appropriate:

Example: *naggaš* ——> *ummī gad naggašatnī nagš ḥālī*

i. *xābar* ______________________________

ii. *zid* ______________________________

iii. *gasmak* ______________________________

iv. *nafsī* ______________________________

v. *mumkin* ______________________________

vi. *ḍarūrī* ______________________________

4. *Verb inflection*

Complete the table below by inflecting the verbs appropriately. The top left-hand corner is completed by way of example:

	absar	*sammā*	*dagg*	*gāl*	*xābar*
anā	*absart*				
iḥna					
antī					
antū					
hī					
hin					

5. *Possession*

Change the following phrases into noun + *ḥagg* phrases.

Examples: *bint man al-bint tayyih* ——> *ḥagg man al-bint tayyih*
kitābak ——> *al-kitāb ḥaggak*

i. *sirwāliš* ____________________

ii. *ġadākum* ____________________

iii. *bilādih* ____________________

iv. *ibn man al-wald ḏayyā?* ____________________

v. *kitāb al-bint* ____________________

6. *Relative clauses*

Link the following pairs of sentences by using the relative pronoun *allaḏī*, etc. Add a referential pronoun in the relative clause where necessary. In the example the relative pronoun and the referential pronoun are highlighted in **bold**.

Example: *ayn as-sirwāl / ištarayt as-sirwāl ams* ———> *ayn as-sirwāl* ***allī*** *štarayt**ih** ams*

i. *ayn al-bint / jibtī l-bint ma*^{c}*iš ams* ____________________

ii. *ayn al-kitāb / katabtī l-kitāb* ____________________

iii. *ayn al-bayt / muḥammad sākin fī l-bayt* ____________________

____

iv. *ayn az-zalaṭ / ṭaraḥt az-zalaṭ hinīyih* ____________________

v. *ayn al-marih / jītī ma*^{c} *al-marih ams* ____________________

7. *Word order*

Put the following groups of words into the correct order to produce meaningful sentences:

i. *yawm, šā-jī, ar-rabū*^{c}*, 'in, allāh, liš, šā'*

ii. *ᶜalā, allāh, al-ḥamd, li-, l-ᶜāfiyih*

iii. *t̲alāt̲, rubᶜ, as-sāᶜah, d̲alḥīn, wa-*

iv. *lāzim, yijaw, kān, xams, wa-, as-sāᶜah, nuṣṣ*

v. *illā, gad, abī, xarajū, as-sāᶜah, xams*

vi. *al-wald, maᶜ, ayn, allad̲ī, -ih, gad, abī, xarajū, as-sāᶜah, sitt*

8. *Translation*

Translate the following groups of sentences into Ṣanᶜānī Arabic:

A. Time

i. I must go to the ministry at eight o' clock.

ii. They m. must go the the ministry at nine o' clock.

iii. You m.pl. must go to the ministry at eleven o' clock.

B. Use *zid*

i. I saw her again at seven o' clock.

ii. My husband will not go to Yemen again.

iii. He no longer visits us.

C. Days of the week

i. You m.pl. see your children on Wednesday.

ii. I will see you m.s. on Tuesday.

iii. They m. will see her on Sunday.

D. Use the imperfect

i. Tell m.s. him he should visit me.

ii. Tell her she should speak to me.

iii. They f. said he would come today.

LESSON 13

al-ġadā fi l-yaman

Dialogue 1 *as-saltih*

Amira: *ṭawwal ᶜumriš yā najlā, rawwaynī kayf tisawway al-ġadā fi l-yaman.*

Najla: *min ᶜaynī, al-ġadā ḥagg al-yaman gadū mkawwan min as-saltih.*

Amira: *ahamm šī as-saltih, mā?*

Najla: *aḥna fī bilādnā lāzim nisawwī saltih.*

Amira: *mā tḥuṭṭī baynahā?*

Najla: *baynahā kull šī, baynahā marag wa-makarūnih wa-ruzz wa-šwayyat širkih awlā dijāj, lā šī dijāj, wa-nsawwī fawghā ḥilbih maxḏūbuh.*

Amira: *kayf tuxḏubi l-ḥilbih?*

Najla: *abuzz šwayyat ḥilbih maṭḥūnuh ka-ḏayyāhā, aḏarrīhā fī ṭāsu zġīrih w-askub fawgahā galīl mā, wa-baᶜd kaḏā 'axallīhā ḥawālī ṯulṯ sāᶜah nuṣṣ sāᶜah, wa-baᶜdā skub bāgi l-mā' minnahā wa-xḏub al-ḥilbi l-mablūlih bi-l-yad ka-ḏayyā law-mā ykūn lawnahā ḥālī wa-gad istawat sawā.*

Amira: *anā ma stirš axḏub al-ḥilbih sawā.*

Najla: *antī w-allahī miš ālifīh. law kuntī 'ālifīh tigdarī.*

Dialogue 2 *az-zaḥāwug*

Amira: *kayf tiᶜmalī zaḥāwug yā najlā?*

Najla: *zaḥāwug aṭ-ṭamāṭis?*

Amira: *aywih, gawā gulī lī mā baynih.*

Najla: *awwal šī tḥuṭṭi ṭ-ṭamāṭis fi l-mazḥagih. gad absarti l-mazḥagih?*

Amira: *aywih, al-mazḥagih ḥajar ka-ḏayyā mā?*

Najla: *nāhī, hāḏā ḥajar kabīrih wa-ḥajar zġīrih. tuḥuṭṭī fi l-mazhagi ṭ-ṭamāṭis wa-l-bahārāt wa-ṯ-ṯawmih wa-l-kammūn wa-tizḥagīh law-mā ykūn sā'il. bih nās bi-yākulūh min al-ḥajar ᶜala l-kidam. al-kidam allaḏī yibīᶜūhā fi l-gāᶜ. anā law anā *ḥāmil kunt ākul kull az-zaḥāwug fī l-mazḥagih. w-anā ḥāmil kān yi^{c}jibnī l-ākul zaḥāwug wa-kidam wa-bisbās kaṯīr. ḏalḥīn ma gdarš ākulih.*

Amira: *wa-n-nās ^{c}āduhum bi-staxdamu l-mazḥagih?*

Najla: *mā bi-staxdamūš al-mazhagi l-ḥajar xayrāt sā^{c} al-xallāṭ. ḏalḥīn yuḥuṭṭu l-bahārāt wa-ṭ-ṭamāṭis wa-l-kull dāxil al-xallāṭ wa-yuxluṭūh hākaḏā wa-bass.*

Dialogue 3 *al-malūj*

Amira: *antū fī l-yaman gad ma^{c}ākum xubz wa-malūj mā?*

Najla: *aywih, wa-l-malūj yixtalif ^{c}an al-xubz ḥattā fī l-iṣlāḥ. al-malūj nisawwī bi-l-yad, amma l-xubz dagg dagg dagg bi-hāḏīk al-maxbazih, lākin bi-nisbih la-l-malūj yitmaddid ^{c}arḏ at-tannūr bi-l-yad. maṯalan nibuzz guṭ^{c}at ^{c}ajīnih wa-nsabbirhā wa-nxallīha mdawwirih, ba^{c}da njirr šwayyat ḥilbih mablūlih sa^{c}am mišī maxḏūbuh wa-nimsaḥhā ba^{c}dā nif^{c}alhā fī t-tannūr ^{c}asibb wāḥid yigdar yimaddidhā ka-ḏayyāhā.*

Amira: *antī m^{c}iš tannūr ġāz?*

Najla: *aywih, m^{c}ī tannūr ġāz jadīd afḏal min al-gadīm ashal wa-l-kull, lākin zārat nās yifaḏḏulu t-tannūr al-ḥaṭab, at-tannūr al-gadīm ya^{c}nī.*

Dialogue 4 *aṭ-ṭabīx*

Najla: *aṭ-ṭabīx yitġassil al-baṣal wa-yitgaṭṭa^{c} hākaḏā zġīr zġīr, wa-nḥammi l-baṣal fawg an-nār, lāzim nixalli l-baṣal aḥmar šwayyih. ba^{c}dā nuskub fawgih min aṣ-ṣalṣuh hāḏī llī tijī fī ^{c}ilbih ma^{c} galīl mā' ^{c}alā sibb tūga^{c} sā'ilih fa-ṣ-ṣalṣuh tukūn gawiyih, wa-nsawwī ḥawā'ij wa-milḥ dāxil aṣ-ṣalṣuh wa-ṭab^{c}an al-bāmiyih, aṭ-ṭabīx lāzim al-bāmiyih.*

Amira: *wa-ṯ-ṯawmih, antū gad ma^{c}ākum ṯawmih min gabl aṯ-ṯawrih awlā min ba^{c}dahā?*

Najla: *aṯ-ṯawmih hāḏī mawjūdih min zamān, lāzimhā. y-allāh, ṣāluḥ yidagdag ^{c}ala l-bāb lāzim aftaḥ lih.*

Vocabulary[1]

afḍal	preferable	*ahamm*	more important
aḥmar	red	^{c}*ajīnih*	dough f.
ālif	experienced	*ammā / mā*	as for
^{c}*arḍ*	breadth m.	*ashal*	easier
bāgī	remaining m.	*bahārāt*	spices
bazz - yibuzz	to take (s.th.)	*dagdag - yidagdag*	to knock
ḏarrā - yiḏarrī	to sprinkle (s.th.)	*dāxil*	in; inside
faḍḍal - yifaḍḍul	to prefer (s.th.)	*fataḥ - yiftaḥ*	to open (s.th.)
fawg	on; on top of	*fi*^{c}*il - yif*^{c}*al*	to do; make (s.th.)
galīl	little m.	*gawī*	strong; thick
ġāz	gas m.	*gidir - yigdir*	to be able; can
guṭ^{c}*ah* pl. *guṭa*^{c}	piece f.	*ḥajar* pl. *ḥijār*	stone; mortar f.
ḥammā - yiḥammī	to heat (s.th.)	*ḥaṭab*	wood m.
ḥaṭṭ - yiḥuṭṭ	to put (s.th.)	*ḥattā*	even
ḥawā'ij	spices	^{c}*ilbih* pl. ^{c}*ilab*	tin; box f.
iṣlāḥ	making (e.g. bread)	*jadīd* pl. *judud*	new
kaḏā	like that	*ka-ḏayyā(hā)*	like that
kammūn	cumin m.	*lākin*	but
lawn pl. *alwān*	colour m.	*mā'*	water m.
mablūl	wet	*maddad - yimaddid*	to spread (s.th.)
maṭḥūn	ground adj.	*mawjūd*	present; available
maxbazih pl. *maxābiz*	padded bread applicator f.	*maxḍūb*	beaten
mazḥagih pl. *mazāḥig*	stone on which tomatoes are ground		
midawwir	rounded	*misiḥ - yimsaḥ*	to wipe (s.th.)
nār pl. *nīrān*	fire f.	*rawwā - yirawwī*	to show (s.o., s.th.)
sabbar - yisabbir	to prepare (s.th.)	*sā'il*	liquid adj.
sakab - yuskub	to pour (s.th.)	*ṣalṣuh*	sauce f.
satar - yistir	to be able; can	*sawā*	properly
stawā - yistawī	to be ready	*staxdam - yistaxdim*	to use (s.th.)
tannūr pl. *tanāwīr*	traditional oven f.	*ṭāsuh* pl. *ṭīsān*	bowl f.
ṯawm	garlic coll. m.	*ṯawmih*	piece of garlic f.
ṯawrih pl. *-āt*	revolution f.	*tgaṭṭa*^{c} *- yitgaṭṭa*^{c}	to be cut up
tmaddad -yitmaddid	to be spread	*wuga*^{c} *- yūga*^{c}	to become; turn out
xalaṭ - yuxluṭ	to mix (s.th.)	*xallāṭ* pl. *-āt*	electric mixer m.
xtalaf - yixtalif (^{c}*an)*	to differ (from s.th.)	*zaḥag - yizḥag*	to crush (s.th.)

[1] Revise the thematic vocabulary in Lesson 6.

zamān	time m.	*zārat* + noun	some ...

Grammar

1. *Greetings*

The phrase *ṭawwal ᶜumriš* to a woman, (less commonly *ṭawwal ᶜumrak* to a man) literally means 'may [God] make your life long'. It is used to ask someone for help and can be idiomatically translated as 'please'. The usual response is *min ᶜaynī* (literally: 'from my eye') which translates idiomatically as 'of course!' or 'with pleasure!' Another way of expressing the sense of 'please' is *gawā*, a word which is used most often by children.

2. *Colours*

The basic colour adjectives are formed on the same pattern as the elative (cf. Lesson 11) - namely aKTaB, as in:

abyaḏ	'white'
aḥmar	'red'
aṣfar	'yellow'
aswad	'black'
axḏar[2]	'green'

The feminine colour adjective is formed on the pattern KaTBā:

sawdā	'black f.'
ḥamrā	'red f.'
ṣafrā	'yellow f.'
xaḏrā	'green f.'

In order to say 'to become white, etc.' or 'to make white, etc.', a form II verb is used:

bayyaḏ	'to become/make white'
ḥammar	'to become/make red'
ṣaffar	'to become/make yellow'
sawwad	'to become/make black'
xaḏḏar	'to become/make green; to wet'

[2] *axḏar* is also used in the sense of 'wet' as in: *as-sirwāl axḏar* 'the trousers are wet'.

Non-primary colour adjectives are derived from other nouns by adding the relational ending *-ī* (cf. Lesson 4), as in:

noun	colour	gloss
zayt	*zayt-ī*	oil-coloured, possibly petrol
kuḥl	*kuḥl-ī*	antimony [dark or navy blue]
burtagāl	*burtagāl-ī*	orange
raṣṣāṣ	*raṣṣāṣ-ī*	lead-coloured [i.e. grey]

Feminine non-primary colour adjectives are produced by adding the feminine ending *-ih*. However, as with many adjectives which end in *-ī* the feminine ending *-ih* is often not pronounced (cf. Lesson 7).

3. *The comparative: '...-er than'*

In order to say that something is 'more X than' something else the elative is followed by *min* + noun, as in:

al-jadīd afḏal min al-gadīm	'the new is better than the old'
al-xamīrih abgā min al-marih	'yeast is more constant than women'
al-gāt aġlā min al-akl	'*gāt* is more expensive than food'

In order to say 'redder' or 'yellower' than X you simply put *min* + noun after the colour adjective because the colour already has the same pattern as the elative, aKTaB:

*as-sijāyir aṣfar min al-madā*ᶜ*ah*	'cigarettes are yellower than the waterpipe'
bintī abyaḏ minniš	'my daughter is whiter than you'

4. *Emphasis of final words*

Words meaning 'like that' and, less commonly, demonstratives and locatives, can be emphasised at the end of an utterance by adding the sound *-hā*:

ka-ḏayyāhā	'like that!'

hākaḏāhā	'like that!'
hāḏāhā	'that!'
hānāhā	'here!'

Similarly, the feminine singular imperative may take the ending *-yih* to express emphasis - particularly, but not exclusively, when an imperative is repeated:

ibsirī bsirī bsirīyih	'look, look, look f.s.!'
šūfī šūfī šūfīyih	'look, look, look f.s.!'

5. *Reflexive and passive verb forms*

There are two common passive and reflexive verb forms. One involves prefixing *(i)t-* to the corresponding transitive or causative verb. When the corresponding transitive or causative verb is *form II* the passive or reflexive verb form is *form V*:

t	+ *ġaṭṭā*	*tġaṭṭā*
[pass]	'he covered'	'it m. was covered'
t	+ *gaṭṭa*^{c}	*tgaṭṭa*^{c}
[pass]	'he cut'	'it m. was cut up'
t	+ *maddad*	*tmaddad*
[pass]	'he spread out'	'it m. was spread out'
t	+ *ġassal*	*tġassal*
[pass]	'he washed'	'it was washed; he washed himself'
t	+ *zawwaj*	*tzawwaj*
[refl]	'he married'	'he got married; he was married'
t	+ *ġaddā*	*tġaddā*
[refl]	'he gave s.o. lunch'	'he had lunch'

When the corresponding transitive or causative verb is *form III*, as in the examples below, the reflexive verb form is *form VI*:

t	+ *ḥākā*	*tḥākā*
[refl]	'he talked [to s.o.]'	'he talked'

t	+ *xābar*	*txābar*
[refl]	'he talked [to s.o.]'	'he talked'

t	+ *jābar*	*tjābar*
[refl]	'he talked [to s.o.]'	'he talked'

The second passive verb form involves insertion of *-t-* immediately after the first consonant. This verb pattern is known as *form VIII*:

transitive	passive
sawwā 'he did'	*stawā* 'it was done/ready'
ḥabas 'he imprisoned'	*ḥtabas* 'he was imprisoned'
sakab 'he poured'	*stkab / stakab* 'it m. was spilled'

Note that some non-reflexive, non-passive verbs also take this verb form, as in:

štaġal	'he worked'

Where the first letter of the basic form I verb is *w* or *y* this letter disappears in the derived form and the *t* may be pronounced as a geminate *tt*:

form I	form VIII
wuṣul 'he arrived'	*ittaṣal / tṣal* 'he contacted'

Finally, the passive can be formed by changing the vowels of the basic (active) form I verb from *a-a* or *i-i* to *u-i* or *i-i* in the perfect, and from *i-a, i-i,* or *u-u* to *u-a* in the imperfect, as in:

active	passive
sarag 'he stole'	*surig* 'it m. was stolen'

zara^c 'he cultivated'	*ziri*^{c} 'it m. was cultivated'
^{c}*irif* 'he knew'	^{c}*urif* 'it m. was known'
sgā 'he irrigated'	*sugī* 'it m. was irrigated'
yi^c*raf* 'he knew'	*yu*^{c}*raf* 'it m. was known'
yuḍrub 'he hit'	*yuḍrab* 'he was hit'

6. *Imperfect of form V, VI and VIII verbs*

The imperfect of form V, VI and VIII verbs is formed simply by adding the appropriate imperfect prefix (and suffix) to the perfect verb:

yi	+ *tġaddā*	*yitġaddā*
[imp]	'he had lunch'	'he has lunch'
yi	+ *tḥākā*	*yitḥākā*
[imp]	'he talked'	'he talks'
yi	+ *tjābar*	*yitjābar*
[imp]	'he talked'	'he talks'
yi	+ *ḥtabas*	*yiḥtabas*
[imp]	'he was imprisoned'	'he is imprisoned'

In some form V verbs, the final vowel of the imperfect verb may be *i* rather than *a*, as in:

yitmaddid	'it m. is spread out'
yitġassil	'it m. was washed'
yitzawwij	'he was married'

7. *The passive participle: '...-ed'*

The passive participle is often used as an adjective in Ṣan^{c}ānī Arabic. As with the active participle (cf. Lesson 7, Lesson 12), the pattern of the passive participle depends on the verb form from which it is derived.

7.1. Form I

The passive participle of the basic verb has the pattern maKTūB when the verb has three 'sound' letters, or has a weak letter at the beginning of the verb:

verb	passive participle	gloss
xaḏ̣ab	*maxḏ̣ūb*	'beaten'
ball	*mablūl*	'wet'
hamm	*mahmūm*	'troubled'
wajad	*mawjūd*	'found; present'

The passive participle of verbs which end in a weak letter - i.e. *y* or *w* - is formed on the pattern maKTī:

verb	passive participle	gloss
ġalā	*maġlī*	'boiled'
banā	*mabnī*	'built'

The passive participle of hollow verbs is formed on the pattern maKāB:

verb	passive participle	gloss
gāl	*magāl*	'said; saying'
kān	*makān*	'place'

7.2. Participles of derived verbs

The passive and active participle of derived verbs are (almost) identical (cf. Lesson 12). The only *possible* difference is that the last vowel of the passive participle is more likely to be *a*, while the last vowel of the active participle is more likely to be *i*. Usually, however, it is only the context which tells the listener whether a particular participle is active or passive. Two passive participles of form II verbs are found in the dialogues in this lesson, namely:

m(i)dawwir	'rounded'
m(i)kawwan	'made up of; consists of'

Passive participles of form III verbs are rare. The passive participle of form IV verbs is also rare. One example of a form IV passive participle is:

mu^{c}*jab*	'pleased'

The passive participle of form V, VI and VIII verbs is identical to the corresponding imperfect verb except for the fact that the first letter is *m-* in the participle (cf. Lesson 12):

imperfect	participle
yitmaddid 'it m. is spread out'	*mitmaddid* 'spread out'
yitzawwij 'he gets married'	*mitzawwij* 'married'
yitsāmaḥ 'he is tolerant'	*mitsāmaḥ* 'tolerant; accommodating'
yiḥtabis 'he is imprisoned'	*miḥtabis* 'imprisoned'

Note that many nouns have participle shapes: a drink of mixed fruit juices is called *mišakkal*; a letter is called *maktūb* from *katab* 'to write'; a mat on which to wash the dead is called *muġtsal*; a thin pastry pocket of eggs, onion and tomatoes is *muṭabbag*; thin, flaky flat bread is *mlawwaḥ*.

8. *Modal verbs: 'to be able to do…'*

There are two common verbs for 'to be able to do …' in San^{c}ānī Arabic: *satar/yistir* and *gidir/yigdir*. Like *yištī* 'he wants' these verbs usually take a following imperfect verb, as in:

tigdirī tuxḏubī	'you f.s. can beat fenugreek'
tistir tuxbuz	'she can bake bread'

These two modal verbs are most commonly used in the negative: in order to say 'cannot' the modal verb is negated, as in:

ma stirš axbuz	'I cannot bake bread'
mā nigdirš nuktub sawā	'we cannot write properly'
mā tigdirīš tuxḏubī	'you f.s. cannot beat fenugreek'

The negative suffix *-š* is optional and may be left off:

mā tigdirī tuxḏubī	'you f.s. cannot beat fenugreek'

9. *Adjunctions involving -mā*

Adjunctions involving *-mā* are very common in Ṣan^{c}ānī Arabic. The most common adjunctions of time are *law-mā* 'when; until', *lammā* 'when; until', *ḥīn-mā* 'when', *^{c}ind-mā* 'when', *ḥāl-mā* 'when', *ba^{c}d-mā* 'after', and *gabl-mā* or *tijāh-mā* 'before'. *law-mā* generally means 'when' when it introduces an initial clause, and 'until' when it introduces a final clause:

law-mā tkūn jāhiz, nisāfir	'when you m.s. are ready, we will go'
nuxḏubhā bi-l-yad, law-mā gadi stawat sawā	'we beat it by hand until it is properly done'

In general, adjunctions ending in *-mā* are followed by a verb, as in:

wa-txallay šwayyih law-mā yintahī	'leave f.s. it a little until it is finished'
bi-yirja^{c}ū min al-migbār ba^{c}d-mā yigbirūh	'they return from the burial after burying him'
ḥāl-mā yisīr yiḥijj	'when he goes on the pilgrimage'

law-mā can also be followed by *gad* + pronoun (as in *law-mā gadi stawat sawā* 'until it is properly done', cf. also *Syntax* p. 341). When no verb is available, for example in clauses such as *ant jāhiz* 'you m.s. are ready' and *hī ^{c}āṭušuh* 'she is thirsty', the imperfect of the verb *kān* is used:

law-mā tkūn jāhiz	'when you m.s. are ready'
law-mā tkūn ^{c}āṭušuh	'when she is thirsty'

If the verb has an explicit subject, the subject follows the verb:

law-ma tṣaffi l-mari d-dijājih 'when the woman cleans the chicken'

Other common adjunctions involving *-mā* include *^{c}alā-mā* 'as', *sā^{c}-mā* 'as; like', and *ka-mā* 'as; like':

^{c}alā-mā tišti 'as you m.s. like'

sā^{c}-mā tirkab kull yawm 'as you m.s. ride everyday'

ka-mā is usually followed by a verb in the perfect aspect:

ka-mā štaytī 'as you f.s. like'

ka-mā gult liš 'as I told you f.s.'

The adjunctions *sā^{c}-mā* and *^{c}alā-mā* differ from other adjunctions in that they often takes a following independent pronoun rather than a complete clause:

hī tišrab sā^{c}-manā 'she smokes like me [i.e. like I do]'

hū yitḥākā sā^{c}-maḥnā 'he speaks like us'

ana tḥākā sā^{c}-mā hum 'I speak like them m.'

tibsirhum ^{c}alā-mā hum 'you see them as they [really] are'

10. *Annexion: 'some'*

'Some' is most commonly expressed by the word *zārat* as the first term in an annexion phrase. The annex is either *indefinite plural*, as in:

zārat nās 'some people'

or *indefinite singular*, as in:

zārat ḥīn
'some' 'time'
zārat ḥīn
'sometimes'

zārat marih
'some' 'woman'
zārat marih
'some women'

zārat *wāḥid* 'some' 'one'	*zārat wāḥid* 'some people; the odd one'

The annex can also be a *pronoun* (and therefore *definite*) to give the sense of 'some of ...', as in:

zārat *hum* 'some' 'them m.'	*zārathum* 'some of them'

When the annex is otherwise definite, the word *ba^{c}ḏ* is used in place of *zārat*:

ba^{c}ḏ *an-nās* 'some' 'the-people'	*ba^{c}ḏ an-nās* 'some [of the] people'
ba^{c}ḏ *al-gur'ān* 'some' 'the-Qur'an'	*ba^{c}ḏ al-gur'ān* 'some of the Qur'an'

11. *More on ḥagg*

ḥagg is not simply used for possession. *ḥagg* + noun can also be used in place of a relational (*nisbih*) adjective (cf. Lesson 4), and is sometimes preceded by *min* 'of':

mā biš laban (min) ḥagg al-bagar = ...laban bagarī
'there is no cow's yoghurt'

wa-ragṣat al-bara^c ḥagg ar-rijāl = ragṣat al-bara^c ar-rijālī
'the men's *bara^c* dance'

kalām ḥagg al-yaman = kalām yamanī
'Yemeni speech'

Where the relational adjective could occur on its own, so the *ḥagg* phrase can occur on its own, and not following a noun:

lākin ḥagg al-yaman yukūn lih šamm aḥsan = lākin al-yamanī...
'but the Yemeni has a better smell'

12. *Adverbs: 'properly'*

The word *sawā* has two distinct adverbial meanings: in an earlier lesson it has been listed with the meaning 'together', as in *nitġaddā sawā* 'we will have lunch together' and *nixazzin sawā* 'we will chew together'. It is also used in the sense of 'properly':

lāzim tuxḏubī l-ḥilbih sawā	'you f.s. must beat the fenugreek properly'

This is particularly the case with imperatives:

uktub sawā	'write m.s. properly!'
igrā sawā	'learn/read m.s. properly!'

Thematic Vocabulary

Kitchen equipment

birmih pl. *biram*	clay cooking pot f.
ḏabbat ġāz	gas cannister f.
ḏaġġāṭ pl. *-āt*	pressure cooker m.
furn pl. *afrān*	modern oven with stove; baker's oven m.
ġāz	gas m.
gumgumī pl. *gamāgim*	tin can m.
kitlī pl. *katālī*	tea-kettle m.
madagg pl. *-āt*	pestle m.
madallih pl. *-āt*	large water jar f.
magaṣṣ pl. *-āt*	scissors m.
maglā pl. *magālī*	stone cooking pot m.
mal^{c}agih pl. *malā^{c}ig*	spoon f.
mal^{c}agih ^{c}ūdī	wooden spoon f.
maxbazih pl. *maxābiz*	padded bread applicator used to make *xubz* as opposed to *malūj* f.
mazḥagih pl. *mazāḥig*	stone for crushing herbs, vegetables or salt f.
suxār	black on side of cooking pot m.
tannūr pl. *tanāwīr*	traditional round oven f.
tannūr ḥaṭab	traditional round wood-burning oven f.
tannūr ġāz	modern round gas oven [same shape as above] f.
ṭāsuh pl. *ṭīsān*	tin or iron container or plate f.

Exercises

1. *Greetings*

Give an appropriate reply to the following greetings:

i. *mā liš šī?* ______________________________

ii. *tiṣbaḥū ^{c}ala l-xayr!* ______________________________

iii. *msaytū!* ______________________________

iv. *kayf ḥālak?* ______________________________

v. *allāh yi^{c}īnak!* ______________________________

vi. *ṭawwal ^{c}umriš!* ______________________________

vii. *al-ḥamdu li-llāh ^{c}ala s-salāmih!* ______________________________

2. *Substitution*

Replace the relational adjective in the following sentences by a phrase involving *ḥagg*.

Example: *bayn-aḏakkir* [= remember] *ar-ragṣ hāḏa n-nisā'ī* ——> *bayn-aḏakkir ar-ragṣ hāḏa* ***ḥagg an-nisā***

i. *as-salti ṣ-ṣan^{c}ānī ykūn lahā šamm aḥsan.* ______________________________

____

ii. *bass al-bākistānī mā ḥibbahā.* ______________________________

iii. *al-bagarī ḥālī gawī.* ______________________________

iv. *gadak širibt al-gahwi l-yamanī.* ______________________________

v. *al-yamanī 'aškal min al-faransī.* ______________________________

3. *Superlative*

Replace the definite noun phrase by a superlative phrase.

Example: *at-tannūr al-gadīmih* ——> *agdam tannūr*

i. *al-bint aṭ-ṭawīluh.* ____________________

ii. *al-wald az-zaġīr.* ____________________

iii. *al-bint al-ḥāliyih.* ____________________

iv. *al-waragi l-xafīfih.* ____________________

v. *al-akl al-ġālī.* ____________________

4. *Tell the time!*

Read the following times out loud in Ṣanᶜānī Arabic:

i. 4.30 ii. 5.40 iii. 7.50 iv. 6.15 v. 10.20 vi. 11.05 vii. 8.45 viii. 9.30

5. *Declarative sentence > conditional clause*

Change the following declarative sentences into conditional clauses, then add the main clause given in brackets:

Example: *bih mā'(nišrabih)* ——> *lā šī mā, nišrabih*

i. *tugūlī 'ahamm šī saltih (asawwīhā liš).* ____________________

ii. *tuxḏubī l-ḥilbih sawā (tiṭlaᶜ ḥālī).* ____________________

iii. *axallīhā nuṣṣ sāᶜah ṯulṯ sāᶜah (yikūn aškal).* ____________________

____

iv. *tištī baṣal wa-ṯawm (ša-ddī liš).* ____________________

6. *Negation*

Negate the following sentences:

Example: *ša-xbuz xubz al-yawm.* ———> *mā ša-xbuzš xubz al-yawm.*

i. *antī širibtī gahwih min ḥagg al-yaman.* ____________________

ii. *at-tannūr al-ġāz aḥsan min at-tannūr al-ḥaṭab.* __________

____

iii. *kān al-mafrūḍ nisabbir al-ġadā.* ________________________

iv. *bih nās yi^c^jibhum aš-šay al-aswad.* ______________________

v. *lāzim nisīr fī-sā^c^.* ______________________________________

7. *Word order*

Put the groups of words below into the correct order to produce meaningful sentences:

i. *^c^umriš, yā, ṭawwal, bintī, kayf, rawwaynī, saltih*

ii. *yitġassal, al-baṣal, wa-, lāzim, yitgaṭṭa^c^*

iii. *al-jay, absiriš, mā, al-usbū^c^, ša-stirš*

iv. *al-akl, min, fī, aġlā, hānā, faransā*

v. *^c^a-yjī, gālū, ams, lī, ġudwuh, gad*

LESSON 14

Ad-dirāsih fi l-yaman

Dialogue 1 *liš al-guwih!*

Amira: *ḥayyā liš al-ḥayāh!*

Louise: *liš ḥayāt ad-dunyā!*

Amira: *wayniš? anā mrā^{c}ī liš min aṣ-ṣubḥ w-antī mā tjay illā wa-gadu s-sā^{c}ah ṯalāṯ. ummi tṣalū bī gālū jay ṣtabaḥī, bass gult luhum māšī Louise ^{c}a-tjī.*

Louise: *anā 'āsifih w-allāhi, tṣalū bī fi l-bayt gālū lāzim asīr al-ma^{c}had akallim al-mudīr, fa-xuṭīt min baytī la-l-ma^{c}had wa-d-dunyā šams. w-allāhi gadanā ti^{c}ibt gawī!*

Amira: *liš al-guwih!*

Louise: *mā ma^{c}nā liš al-guwih?*

Amira: *liš al-guwih ma^{c}nathā lā bi-ti^{c}malī šī wa-bi-tištaġilī ^{c}amal kaṯīr y-allāh allāh yiddī liš al-guwih ^{c}ala l-^{c}amal allī bi-tsawway, w-anti tgūlī lī liš al-^{c}āfiyih. sa^{c}am antī liš al-guwih w-anā gad lī l-^{c}āfiyih!*

Dialogue 2 *al-mi^{c}lāmih wa-l-jāmi^{c}*

Salwa: *mḥammad gad t^{c}allam fi l-mi^{c}lāmih wa-hū zġīr sā^{c} hāḏā!*

Sarah: *māhī l-mi^{c}lāmih hāḏa?*

Salwa: *ma-ntīš dārī māhī l-mi^{c}lāmih, yā Sarah?*

Sarah: *māšī, gawā gulī lī māhī.*

Salwa: *al-mi^{c}lāmih sā^{c}-mā tgūlī madrasih fīhā sabbūrih yuktub al-mu^{c}allim ^{c}alayhā, lākin allaḏī kānū min awwal yudrusū fi l-mi^{c}lāmih kānū yiddaw mugābil.*

Sarah: *wa-l-mugābil mā hū?*

Salwa: *al-mugābil sā^{c}-mā tgūlī zalaṭ, bass miš kaṯīr - mablaġ ramzī 'aṣlan. kān bih min riyālayn, min riyāl, xamsih bi-l-kaṯīr. wa-yawm al-xamīs yiddaw la-š-*

šaybih hāḏa l-mu^{c}allim ka^{c}k awlā šī.

Sarah: *^{c}ād bih ma^{c}ālim fī l-yaman?*

Salwa: *rubbamā fī r-rīf, lākin miš hānā fī ṣan^{c}ā. ma^{c}ānā madāris ^{c}ādī ḏalḥīn sā^c-mantū.*

Sarah: *wa-ma^{c}ākum tadrīs fī l-jāmi^c mā?*

Salwa: *aywih.*

Sarah: *at-tadrīs fī l-jāmi^c miš bi-dūn mugābil?*

Salwa: *illā, at-tadrīs fī l-jāmi^c bi-dūn mugābil. ya^{c}nī bi-ṭla^c wāḥid min aš-šuyūx yigarrī ṯalāṯih, arba^{c}ah jahhāl aw ḥattā l-kubār yigarrīhum.*

Sarah: *yigarrīhum al-gur'ān?*

Salwa: *aywih, yigarrīhum tilāwat al-gur'ān aw aḥādīṯ awlā figh aw ayy naw^c. at-tilāwih ma^{c}nathā girāyih ayy at-tajwīd. wa-l-mu^{c}allim fī l-mi^{c}lāmih ismih saydanā. allaḏī bi-drus fī l-jāmi^c mā yidfa^{c}š wa-lā šī.*

Dialogue 3 *al-jāmi^{c}ah*

Sarah: *wa-d-dirāsih fī l-jāmi^{c}ah, iḏā 'adrus anā fī l-jāmi^{c}ah hānā kam adfa^c fī sanih?*

Salwa: *mā b-lā mablaġ rasmī ramzī min miyatayn girš. ḏaḥḥīn anā law aštī drus fī briṭāniyā fī jāmi^{c}at Durham kam adfa^c fī sanih?*

Sarah: *ad-dirāsih fī briṭāniyā ġālī, gad tidfa^{c}ī arba^{c}ah wallā xams alf istirlīnī.*

Salwa: *kam yiṭla^c riyāl?*

Sarah: *gad yiṭla^c ḥawālī miyatayn alf.*

Salwa: *mā šā' allāh, at-tadrīs fī briṭāniyā ġālī marrih! gaṣdī jay antī hānā tudrusī!*

Sarah: *yā rayt w-anā hānā ṭawālī nudrus sawā!*

Vocabulary[1]

ᶜamal	work m.	*bi-dūn*	without
daras - yudrus	to learn; study	*dirāsih*	learning f.
figh	jurisprudence m.	*garrā - yigarrī*	to teach (s.o., to read)
gaṣdī	I mean	*gawā*	please
girāyih	reading; learning f.	*al-gur'ān*	the Qur'an m.
guwih	strength f.	*ḥadīṯ* pl. *aḥādīṯ*	Prophetic tradition m.
ḥayāh pl. *-āt*	life f.	*istirlīnī*	Sterling
kabīr pl. *kubār*	grown-up; adult m.	*mablaġ* pl. *mabāliġ*	amount m.
maᶜhad pl. *maᶜāhid*	institute m.	*maᶜnā* pl. *maᶜānī*	meaning m.
muᶜallim pl. *-īn*	teacher m.	*mudīr* pl. *mudarā*	manager m.
mugābil	fee; money paid to teacher/school m.	*murāᶜī (lā)*	waiting (for s.o.)
ramzī	token adj.	*rīf* pl. *aryāf*	countryside m.
rubbamā	maybe	*sabbūrih*	blackboard f.
šams	sun m.	*šaybih* pl. *šayabāt*	old man m.
saydanā	[teacher in *miᶜlāmih*]	*šayx* pl. *šuyūx*	learned man m.
tadrīs	teaching m.	*tajwīd*	Qur'an reading m.
tᶜallam - yitᶜallam	to learn	*ṭawālī*	all the time
tiᶜib - yitᶜab	to become tired	*tilāwih*	recitation f.
ṭuluᶜ - yiṭlaᶜ	to get up; start doing s.th.; work out at		

Grammar

1. *Greetings*

The greeting *ḥayyā liš al-ḥayāh* 'may you have life' with the reply *liš ḥayāt ad-dunyā* 'may you have the life of the world' is used between women who know each other well.

The phrase *liš (lak* m.*) al-guwih* 'may you have strength' is used to someone who has a lot of work to do, particularly if they are tired. The reply is *liš (lak* m.*) al-ᶜāfiyih* 'may you have health'.

[1] Also revise thematic vocabulary in Lesson 11.

2. *The relative pronoun: 's/he who'*

The relative pronoun *alladī,* etc. is often used without a preceding noun to mean 's/he who', 'the one who', 'that which', or 'those who' (cf. *Syntax* p. 416-417). If a verb follows it may take masculine singular agreement, even if the actual referant is feminine or plural. For example:

alladī bi-drus fi l-jāmi^c	'those who study in the mosque'
alladī ma yxazzin gāt yākul lubbān	'those who do not chew *gāt* eat gum'
alladī zawjahā māt mā tuxrujš min al-bayt ṭūlat al-larba^cīn yawm	'she whose husband dies does not leave the house for the whole forty days'
allī ^camalhā min al-bidāyih kān yfakkir ašyā ḥālī gawī	'those who worked on it from the beginning were thinking of lovely things'

When the actual referant is plural, however, the verb may agree for plurality:

lākin alladī kānū min awwal yudrusū fī l-mi^clāmih kānū yiddaw mugābil	'but those who studied in the *mi^clāmih* in the olden days used to pay a fee'

3. *Indefinite relative clauses*

In Lesson 10 we saw that two statements referring to a common *definite* entity could be linked by the relative pronoun *alladī*, etc. Two statements which refer to a common *indefinite* entity can also be linked, but they are linked without the relative pronoun: unlike English *who, which*, etc., where the relative pronoun is optional irrespective of whether the relativised noun is definite or indefinite, *alladī* is only used after a definite noun.[2] In other ways, however, indefinite relative clauses are identical to definite relative clauses: where the common indefinite noun is the subject of a sentence in the second statement, the second mention of the noun is simply omitted:

absart rajjāl / hānāk rajjāl	'I saw a man' 'there is a man'

becomes

[2] The analysis in *Syntax* does not consider *alladī*, etc. to be a relative pronoun, but describes it as the *clausal definite article* (*Syntax* p. 230).

	absart rajjāl hānāk	'I saw a man [who was] there'
	sākin fī bayt / bayt ba^{c}īd min hānā	'[I] live in a house' 'a house far from here'
becomes		
	sākin fī bayt ba^{c}īd min hānā	'[I] live in a house [which is] far from here'
	kān bih marih / marih sabbarat al-ġadā	'there was a woman' 'a woman made lunch'
becomes		
	kān bih marih sabbarat al-ġadā	'there was a woman who made lunch'

Where the noun in the second statement is not the subject, it is replaced by a referential pronoun in the relative clause: the referential pronoun is an object pronoun where the noun would be the object of a verb:

	sākin fī bayt / ištarayt bayt ams	'[I] live in a house' 'I bought a house yesterday'
becomes		
	*sākin fī bayt ištarayt**ih** ams*	'[I] live in a house [which] I bought yesterday'
	hāḏī 'ajmal bint / absart bint	'this is the prettiest girl' 'I saw a girl'
becomes		
	*hāḏī 'ajmal bint absarta**hā***	'this is the prettiest girl I have seen'

and by a possessive pronoun where the noun would be the 'object' of a preposition or the annex in an annexion phrase:

	al-mi^{c}lāmih madrasih / fī l-madrasih sabbūrih	'the *mi^{c}lāmih* is a school' 'in the school is a blackboard'
becomes		
	*al-mi^{c}lāmih madrasih fī**hā** sabbūrih*	'the *mi^{c}lāmih* is a school which has [lit: in which is] a blackboard'
	hāḏā sabbūrih / yuktub al-mu^{c}allim ^{c}alā sabbūrih	'this is a blackboard' 'the teacher writes on a blackboard'
becomes		
	hāḏā sabbūrih yuktub	'this is a blackboard which the

al-mu^callim ^calayhā	teacher writes on [it]'

4. *The comparative: 'more X'*

In Lesson 13 we saw that the comparative is formed by the elative aKTaB + *min*. Another common way of conveying the sense of comparison is by the *uninflected* adjective followed by the elative *akṯar* or *azyad* 'more' + *min*. This is similar to the English construction 'more X' as in 'more studious', 'more industrious', 'more boastful'. For example:

al-bint mariḍ azyad min ar-rajjāl	'the girl is ill more than the man [i.e. sicker than the man]'
at-tadrīs fī briṭāniyā ġālī 'azyad min hānā	'schooling in Britain is expensive more than here [i.e. more expensive than here]'

Alternatively, a noun such as *ḥamā* 'heat' in the following example can be followed by *akṯar* or *azyad*:

ḥudaydih ḥamā 'akṯar min ti^cizz	'Hudayda is hot more than Taizz [i.e. hotter than Taizz'
briṭāniyā bard azyad min al-yaman	'Britain is cold more than Yemen [i.e. colder than Yemen]'

5. *'I mean ...'*

To say 'someone means' something, the word *gaṣd* 'intention' takes the appropriate pronoun suffix and the word is followed by a verb in the imperfect aspect (cf. *Syntax* p. 168):

gaṣdī yisāfir al-yaman	'I mean he should travel to Yemen'
gaṣdak mā tištīš tisāfir	'do you m.s. mean you don't want to travel?'

6. *'I wish!'*

yā rayt (+ *wa-* + sentence) expresses the sense of 'I wish!' where the wished-for event or activity cannot be fulfilled. The sentence following *wa-* is in the present tense - either by being verbless (as in the first example below), or by having a verb in the imperfect:

yā rayt w-antī hānā fī lundun!	'I wish you f.s. were here in London!'
yā rayt w-ant tisāfir ma^{c}ānā!	'I wish you m.s. were travelling with us!'
yā rayt w-anā fī l-bayt jālisih!	'I wish I f. was staying at home!'

7. *'Since yesterday', 'for two days'*

In order to say that you have been doing, and you are continuing to do, something for a certain length of time, English uses the near past 'has been doing' followed by 'for' if you express the length of time, or 'since' if you are mentioning the point at which you started doing something, as in:

I have been dancing **for ten years.**

or

I have been dancing **since I was five.**

In Arabic (as in most European languages) the present tense is used if the action is still being done. This is expressed either by the imperfect prefixed by *bayn-* or *bi-*, or by the active participle. In order to say 'since' - i.e. the time when you started doing something -, the preposition *min* is used, as in:

anā mrā^{c}ī liš min aṣ-ṣubḥ	'I have been waiting for you since the morning'
bayn-axazzin min aṣ-ṣubḥ	'I have been chewing since the morning'

In order to express 'for' - i.e. the length of time you have been doing something - the phrase *gad l-* + pronoun is most commonly used followed by the length of time:

ana mxazzin gad lī šahr	'I have been chewing for a month'
gadū ^{c}ārifih gad lih sanih	'he has known him for a year'

As we have seen earlier (Lesson 10), verbless sentences are generally used to express 'being' in this type of sentence:

gadū fī l-yaman min al-ᶜīd	'He has been in Yemen since the festival'
gad lī šahr min zawjī	'I have been away from my husband for a month'
gad lak kam fī l-yaman	'How long have you been in Yemen'

8. *Masculine plural for respect*

In Lesson 1 we saw that the masculine plural is used when the referent is singular male or female in fixed greetings, such as *as-salām ᶜalay**kum*** 'peace be upon you', and as a sign of respect. The use of the masculine plural for parents in particular (and also for relations of the same generation as parents) is not restricted to greetings, but is used whenever the parent is mentioned or addressed.[3] Consider the following examples:

abī gad sāfarū tiᶜizz	'my father travelled to Taizz'
ummī yuxbuzū xubz	'my mother is baking bread'
y-abī jaw zūrūnā	'father! Come and visit us!'
y-ummī jaw iṣṭabaḥū ᶜindanā	'mother! Come and have breakfast with us!'

People of an older generation will also often refer to themselves as 'we' and use the masculine plural in verbs and adjectives:

ddaw lanā naks	'give m.pl. me the waterpipe'
gadiḥna b-xayrīn	'I am well'

[3] Compare this usage to French 'tu' and German 'du' where the *familiar* pronoun is used to address parents.

9. *Verb form X*

The derived verb form X takes initial *ista-* in the perfect, *yista-* in the imperfect. It often carries the sense of finding something to be, eg. strange, as in:

adjective	verb
ġarīb 'strange'	*istaġrab - yistaġrib* 'to find s.th. strange'

With some verbs it has the sense of seeking something implied in the basic (form I) verb, as in:

form I	form X
fihim 'he understood'	*istafham* 'he sought information / understanding'

It may also imply making something do what is implied in the basic form I verb:

form I	form X
^{c}amal 'he worked'	*ista^{c}mal* 'he used'

10. *Adverbs: 'perhaps'*

The sense of 'perhaps' is commonly expressed by *gad* followed by an imperfect verb, as in the dialogue in Lesson 13:

gad yiṭla^{c} miyatayn alf	'it may come to 200,000'

Another way of expressing 'perhaps' is by the adverb *rubbamā* at the beginning of the sentence, as in:

rubbamā ysāfir al-yawm	'perhaps he will travel today'

A third way of expressing 'perhaps' is by the verb *yimkin* (Lesson 12 vocabulary, cp. *mumkin* Lesson 10) at the beginning of the sentence, as in:

yimkin yisāfir al-yawm 'perhaps he will travel today'

The sense of 'may have ...-ed' is generally expressed by *gad* + *yukūn* + perfect verb, as in:

zawjiš gad yukūn itṣal biš 'your husband may have phoned you f.s.'

11. *Generic nouns*

In English, a noun can have one of *three* types of definition: when reference is made to a *specific* specimen of a class, the noun may take either the indefinite article or the definite article:

A tiger is sleeping in the cage.

or

The tiger is sleeping in the cage.

When reference is *generic* and is being made to the *class* as opposed to a specific *specimen* of the class, either zero article may be used with the noun in the plural:

Tigers are dangerous animals.

or the definite or indefinite article may be used with the noun in the *singular*:

The tiger is a dangerous animal.

A tiger is a dangerous animal.

When generic reference is made to an abstract noun in English, as in 'music', 'education', 'trade', etc., zero article is used with the noun in the singular:

Music is very calming.

Trade is always slow.

Education is better than idleness.

In Arabic, by contrast, there are only *two* types of definition: either a noun is indefinite and therefore has no article:

jirr lak gāt 'get yourself some *gāt*!'

or a noun is definite and has the definite article:

al-gāt ḥālī gawi l-yawm	'the *gāt* is very nice today'

When the speaker wants to make generic reference to the class, rather than specific reference to a specimen of the class, the noun is felt to be *definite*, and takes the definite article. Examples include the nouns in the following sentences (also see examples in Lesson 13, 3.):

as-safar mut^{c}ib	'Travel is tiring'
iḏā l-kalām fuḍḍuh fa-s-sukūt ḏahab	'If speech is silver, then silence is gold'
al-girāyih aškal min al-xazzān	'Learning is better than chewing'
al-bayt al-yamanī ḥālī	'Yemeni houses are nice'

12. *'Not except ...', 'only...'*

The sense of 'not except ...' or 'not ... but' is expressed by the negative particle *mā* (optionally with the negative suffix *-š*) and the restrictive particle *illā*. The restrictive particle *illā* restricts the scope of the verb, noun or prepositional phrase (cf. *Syntax* pp. 264-265). The example in the dialogue in this lesson is:

w-antī mā tjay illā wa-gadu s-sā^{c}ah ṯalāṯ	'you f.s. don't come except [i.e. until] it is three o' clock!'

Other examples include:

ma štīš illā hāḏā	'I don't want anything but this m.'
mā širibtš illā bunn	'I drank nothing but coffee'

13. *Emphatic negation: 'not at all !'*

Emphatic negation is expressed by the emphatic particle *wa-* plus *lā* (cf. *Syntax* p. 264). *wa-lā* can then negate either a verb or a noun. Two very common expressions include:

wa-lā yihimmak	'don't let it worry you m.s.!'

wa-lā wāḥid	'none at all! / not a one!'

Where the object of a verb is negated using *wa-lā*, the verb is negated by *mā* and optionally by the negative suffix *-š*:

antī mā tibsirī(š) wa-lā šī	'you f.s. can't see a thing!'
*mā yidfa*ᶜ*š wa-lā šī*	'he doesn't pay a thing'

The noun in an existential sentence can be negated using *wa-lā*. In this case *bih* is negated using *mā* and ... *š*:

mā biš wa-lā girš	'there is not a single *riyāl*!'

wa-lā can also be used as an emphatic tag to a negative sentence. In this case it translates as 'at all!' The main sentence stress tends to fall on the final word *-lā*. Compare:

	ma štīš hāḏā	'I don't want that!'
with		
	ma štīš hāḏā wa-lā	'I don't want that at all!'

Also compare:

	ma bsartš ḥadd	'I didn't see anyone'
with		
	ma bsartš ḥadd wa-lā	'I didn't see anyone at all!'
and		
	ma yḥibbš al-yaman	'he doesn't like Yemen'
with		
	ma yḥibbš al-yaman wa-lā	'he doesn't like Yemen at all!'

Exercises

1. *Verb inflection*

Inflect the bracketed verb(s) in each of the following examples.

Example: *abī* ______ᶜ*indanā (jā' yitġaddā)* ——> *abī* ***jaw yitġaddaw*** ᶜ*indanā*

i. *ummī gad* __________ *dijāj fi s-sūg (ištarā).*

ii. *uxtī fāyizih* ___________ *zinnih sawdā (yilbas).*

iii. *ibn axī* ___________ *fī s-sa*ᶜ*ūdī (bi-štaġil).*

iv. *xabīratī gad* ___________ *nifās (māt* = died*).*

2. *Gap filling*

Fill in the gaps by putting the adjective in brackets into its corresponding comparative:

Example: *hāḏi z-zinnih* _______ *min tayyih (raxīṣ)* ——> *hāḏi z-zinnih arxaṣ min tayyih.*

i. *al-maraysī* _______ *min aṭ-ṭaḥīn (ġālī).*

ii. *hāḏa l-bayt* _______ *min ḏayyā (aswad).*

iii. *al-bank* _______ *min al-jawāzāt (garīb).*

iv. *aṭ-ṭamāṭīs* _______ *min al-baṣal (aḥmar).*

v. *xālatī jīhān* _______ *min uxtahā salwā (zġīr).*

vi. *al-wizārih* _______ *min maktab al-barīd (ba*ᶜ*īd).*

3. *Substitution*

Replace the following statements by wishes.

Example: *aḥnā fī l-yaman.* ——> *yā rayt w-aḥnā fī l-yaman!*

i. *ummī gad sāfaru l-bilād.* ______________________________

ii. *abī gad ištaraw sayyārih jadīdih.*__________________________

iii. *al-wald mā gad jāš yizūr uxtih.*___________________________

iv. *sūg al-gāt mišū ba*ᶜ*īd min hānā.*__________________________

v. *antī sākinih hānā fī l-yaman.*____________________________

4. *Gender change*

Change the gender in the following examples from masculine to feminine. Where necessary replace masculine nouns by feminine nouns.

Example: *gad sāfarū safar ṭawīl* ——> *gad sāfarayn safar ṭawīl.*

i. *ᶜiyyāl salwā jaw yiṣṭabaḥū ᶜindanā 'ams.* ________________

ii. *ibnak bi-lᶜab* [= plays] *fī t-turāb.* ________________

iii. *gad absart ar-rijāl yiṣīḥū* [= shout] *fī š-šāriᶜ?* ________________

____

iv. *yawm al-jumᶜah yiṣallaw fī l-jāmiᶜ.* ________________

v. *ibnī bi-ydrus fī l-jāmiᶜah.* ________________

5. *Form X verbs*

Construct form X verbs from the following basic verbs and adjectives. Guess their meanings:

Example: *ġarīb* ———> *istaġrab* 'to consider strange; to be surprised'

i. *ᶜasir* [= difficult] ________________

ii. *sahl* ________________

iii. *raxīṣ* [= cheap] ________________

iv. *ġālī* ________________

v. *ḥālī* ________________

vi. *fagīr* [= poor] ________________

vii. *bārid* ________________

6. *Relative clauses*

Link the following pairs of sentences to produce a main clause and relative clause:

Example: *kān bih marih / marih kannasat baytahā* ——> *kān bih marih kannasat baytahā*

i. *absart rajjāl / rajjāl yisāfir min al-yaman.* ________________

ii. *hāḏā nafs al-bint / jibtī l-bint min awwal.* ________________

iii. *hāḏī 'ajmal malābis / šallaytū malābis.* ________________

iv. *antī sabbartī 'aškal ġadā / akalt ġadā fi l-yaman.* __________

____

v. *kān bih rajjāl / rajjāl ištarā lih gāt.* ________________

7. *Verb inflection*

Complete the table below by inflecting the verbs in the imperfect. The top left-hand corner has been completed by way of example:

	yistaġrib	*yitġassal*	*yuṭbux*	*yibuzz*
ummī	*yistaġribū*			
abī				
axwatī				
bintī				
aš-šaybih				
al-banāt				

8. *Translation*

Translate the following groups of sentences into Ṣanᶜānī Arabic:

A. Use *wa-lā*

i. I haven't got a single *riyāl*!

ii. He doesn't like Yemen at all!

iii. I can't see a thing!

B. Use *gad* + *yikūn*, *yimkin*, or *rubbamā*

i. There are perhaps traditional schools in the town.

ii. Perhaps my father will come today.

iii. Maybe my sister is at home.

C. Use *min*

i. He has been waiting for me since yesterday.

ii. I have been in Yemen since the festival.

iii. She has been in Yemen since last month.

D. Use a relative clause

i. This is the most expensive *gāt* I have seen.

ii. Did you see the man I bought the dress from yesterday?

iii. I gave the same present that you f.s. gave.

LESSON 15

Al-bayt al-yamanī

Dialogue 1 *al-makān al-yamanī*

Tim: *ḥayy allāh man jā'!*

Salih: *allāh yiḥayyīk!*

Tim: *al-makān fī l-bayt al-yamanī, gul lī mā šaklih yā ṣāluḥ?*

Salih: *al-makān ḥagganā s^{c}am?*

Tim: *aywih, al-makān ḥaggukum.*

Salih: *hāḏa l-makān ḥagganā makān ya^{c}nī kabīr, mišū zuġayrī, fa-hū ṭūluh ^{c}arḏuh ṯalāṯih mitr fī xamsih hākaḏā, ṯalāṯih mitr fī xamsi mtār. fī l-makān ḥagganā 'arba^c ṭīgān, ṯintayn ṭīgān bi-ṭullayn ^{c}ala š-šāri^c wa-ṯintayn ṭīgān bi-ṭullayn ^{c}ala l-ḥawī. ṭab^{c}an hāḏa l-makān bi-nilja' lih li-l-xazzān. ma^{c}ī fī l-makān hāḏā tiliviziyūn abū šanab wa-fīdiyū w-msajjilih, wa-hū mafrūš bi-mafāriš wa-firiš ya^{c}nī ^{c}alā šakl aṭ-ṭābu^c al-yamanī ma^c al-wasāyid, wa-fīh al-madāki', ya^{c}ni llī bi-nxazzin ^{c}alayhin bi-ntkī' ^{c}alayhin. wa-ma^{c}ī madā^{c}ah fī l-wasaṭ ṭab^{c}an. wa-l-madā^{c}ah hāḏā kull wāḥid yi^{c}rafhā fī l-yaman. hāḏi l-madā^{c}ah bi-šakl gaṣabuh hākaḏā ṭawīluh wa-min nāzil ^{c}alā šakl kurih, ^{c}alā šakl al-jawzih jawz al-hind hāḏā wa-bi-tkūn markūzih ^{c}alā jallās. al-jallās ^{c}a-ykūn ṣaḥn mdawwar aw yikūn bi-šakl allī hū mawjūd ma^{c}ī fī l-madā^{c}ah, bi-š-šakl aṯ-ṯulāṯī hākāḏā. al-madā^{c}ah maṣnū^{c}ah min al-xšab. wa-fī l-madā^{c}ah ṭab^{c}an hāḏā ^{c}alā-mā gult anā gabl šwayyih innahū bi-šakl al-jawzih, jawz al-hind. jawz al-hind hāḏā a^{c}tagid innū bi-yiḥfarūhā min dāxil bi-yiḥfarūhā yixallawhā zayy al-kurih, bi-hāḏa š-šakl, bass mistadīrih lā mistaṭīluh, wa-min šān tiḥwī hāḏa l-kurih hāḏā 'aw nsammīh iḥna l-jawzih. al-jawzih hāḏā tiḥwī al-mā'. al-mā' allī yikūn fīhā, al-mā' ḥagg al-madā^{c}ah hāḏā. ṭab^{c}an al-mā ḥna nbaddil kull yawm, kull yawm abaddil al-mā' li'annī bayn-ašrab yawmīyih. bayn-abaddil al-mā' ḍarūrī al-mā' tabdīlih fī l-madā^{c}ah lannū law mā baddilš fīhā l-mā' ṭab^{c}an ^{c}a-tības, ya^{c}nī ^{c}a-tības bass bi-sur^{c}ah u-mā ^{c}a-tkunš kwayyisih, fa-tabdīlih ḍarūrī. ṭab^{c}an fa-min ^{c}ind hāḏa l-*

jawzih mamdūdih zayy al-gaṣabuh ^{c}alā fawg bass min al-xšab maxzūgih fī l-wasaṭ. wa-fī rāshā bi-yirtkiz al-būrī, iḥna nsammīh al-būrī hāḏā ḥagg an-nār. ṭab^{c}an al-būrī maṣnū^{c} min at-trāb. hāḏa l-būrī zayy-mā tigūl innahū šī bi-ntruḥ fīh at-titin. wa-ba^{c}dā t-titin hāḏā ṭab^{c}an at-titin bi-nbillih wa-nxallīh axḍar šwayyih, ma nxallīš yābis wa-lā nxallīh axḍar gawī. fa-bī-kūn titin mablūl bi-l-mā' wa-niṭraḥ fawgih an-nār niġaṭṭīh kullih bi-n-nār min šān yiṭla^{c} naks kwayyis ṭab^{c}an. wa-ba^{c}dayn fīh gaṣabuh, al-gaṣabuh mamdūdih ya^{c}nī ṭab^{c}an al-gaṣabuh mumkin tijirr gaṣabuh mitr mitrayn ṯalāṯih arba^{c}ah ya^{c}nī ma^{c}ī ṯalāṯ amtār xams amtār hāḏa l-gaṣabu bi-tkūn gadī l-gaṣabu l-kwayyisih. xams amtār kwayyisih. wa-l-gaṣabuh bi-tudxul fī xuzgī wasṭ al-jawzih. al-jawzih hāḏā mġallafih bi-n-naḥḥās. fīhā xuzgī min an-naḥḥās bi-tṭraḥ fīh al-mišrab ḥagg al-gaṣabuh.

Tim: *kam as-sā^{c}ah yā ṣāluḥ?*

Salih: *gadu s-sā^{c}ah wāḥidih wa-nuṣṣ.*

Tim: *w-allāh! ġudwuh ma^{c}ī mtihān lāzim aḍwī 'adrus.*

Salih: *masra^{c}! jiss ^{c}indanā, nijirr lanā gāt, nitġaddā wa-nxazzin sawā. ant kawdak bi-tudrus!*

Tim: *ma gdirš w-allāh! šā-jī lak al-xamīs lā mā biš ma^{c}ak mišwār.*

Salih: *nāhī, jī l-xamīs!*

Dialogue 2 *hāḏawlā ṯalāṯih matākī'*

Abd al-Salam: *hāḏawlā' ibsirī, hāḏawlā ṯalāṯih matākī'. wāḥid iṯnayn ṯalāṯih arba^{c}ah, hāḏawlā l-matākī l-larba^{c}ah min al-xirag, tamām. wa-ḏayyik al-matkā' wāḥid iṯnayn ṯalāṯih, hāḏawlā s-sfinj, tamām. wa-m^{c}iš hānā ^{c}ašar wasāyid wāḥidih ṯintayn ṯalāṯ arba^{c} xams sitt sab^{c} ṯamān tis^{c} ^{c}aš, ^{c}ašar wasāyid. hāḏawlā hin min al-xirag. wa-m^{c}ānā bsirī hāḏa l-jambīyih ḥālī wāḥidih jambīyih, wa-lā ^{c}a-tšūfī l-^{c}ugūd hinḏālahin wāḥid iṯnayn ṯalāṯih arba^{c}ah, arba^{c}ah ^{c}ugūd, wa-xamz ṭīgān. hāḏawlā xams ṭīgān, lākin Iain hū ḏā ma^{c}ih iṯnayn giṭārāt, giṭār iṯnayn.*

Janet: *wa-ṣ-ṣafīf. kam m^{c}ākum ṣufwaf ?*

Abd al-Salam: *m^{c}ānā ṣufwaf fī l-bayt hāḏā, wāḥid iṯnayn ṯalāṯih arba^{c}ah xamsih sittih, sittih ṣufwaf. hāḏawlā ṣ-ṣufwaf illī yuṭruḥū fīhin al-ašyā' wa-hāḏawlāk, wa-ṯalāṯih arba^{c}ah ṣufwaf ḥagg aṭ-ṭīgān. sittih ṣufwaf waḥdahin wa-ṯalāṯih w-arba^{c}ah ṣufwaf ḥagg aṭ-ṭīgān. sittih ṣufwaf waḥdahin wa-ṯalāṯih arba^{c}ah ṣufwaf ḥagg aṭ-ṭīgān ma^{c} al-^{c}ugūd, tamām. wa-ṭ-ṭīgān hāḏawlā wa-l-baradāt ma^{c}ānā ṯalāṯ baradāt, wa-mdā^{c}ah, wāḥidih, wa-būrī, wa-ṯintayn msajjilāt.*

Janet: *wa-kam ma^{c}ākum šabābīk?*

Abd al-Salam: *šabābīk ma^{c}ānā wāḥid iṯnayn ṯalāṯih šabābīk, u-d-darājīn kull ṭarḥah bih sab^{c} darājīn, sab^{c} sab^{c}. al-labwāb fī l-bayt, fī kull ṭarḥah arba^{c}ah abwāb, abwāb ḥagg al-lamkinih. wāḥid bāb ḥadīd, wa-ṯintayn šijar xārij aš-šāri^{c}. ibsirī b-bustān ḥagganā hānā kān malān šijar. ma^{c}ānā ṯalāṯ abwār, al-labwār hāḏawlā ḥagg al-mā', kānayn aṯ-ṯalāṯi l-labwār hāḏawlā bi-saggayn al-bustān bi-kullih. wa-m^{c}ānā fī kull bīr barik, kull bīr ma^{c}āhā wāḥidih barik. wa-hāḏa l-bīr illī hnīyih ma^{c}āhā ṯalāṯih aḥwāḍ zuġār, wa-barik wāḥidih. gadī al-kabīrih. al-laḥwāḍ az-zuġār hāḏawlā bi-yuxruj minnahin al-mā'. mā' bi-yinzil wa-yjī lā wasṭ al-barik allī bi-ṭla^{c} minnahā šaḏarawān. gad absarti š-šaḏarawān min ḥagg al-mafraj? hāḏā bi-nzil minnahin, wa-ṯ-ṯānīyih gadī hinīyihā. mā m^{c}āhā illā barik wāḥidih, bi-yuxruj minnahā l-mā' wa-ysaggi l-bustān. wa-ṯ-ṯāliṯih hāḏīk mā ma^{c}āhā llā barik wāḥidih. wa-hāḏā fī l-ḥārah ḥagganā bih ma^{c}ānā yimkin sab^{c}ah biyūt. hāḏā s-sab^{c}a l-biyūt kullahin ḥagg usratī. kull al-usrih ya^{c}nī axwat abī wa-xawāt abī wa-hāḏā, kull wāḥid ma^{c}ih bayt.*

Vocabulary

abū šanab	satellite m.
axḏar	wet
ball - yibill	to wet (s.th.)
barik pl. *birkān*	pool; pond f.
bi-sur^{c}ah	quickly
bustān pl. *basātīn*	garden m.
fidiyū pl. *-āt*	video m.
gaṣabuh pl. *gaṣīb*	pipe f.
ḥadīd	iron m.
ḥārah pl. *-āt*	area f.
^{c}agd pl. *^{c}ugūd*	arched window m.
baddal - yibaddil	to change (s.th.)
bardih pl. *baradāt*	curtain f.
bīr pl. *abwār*	well f.
būrī pl. *-āt*	waterpipe top m.
darajih pl. *darājīn*	stair f.
firiš	furnishings m.
giṭār pl. *-āt*	guitar m.
ḥafar - yiḥfar	to dig a hole; bore
ḥawā - yiḥwī	to contain (s.th.)

ḥawḍ pl. *aḥwāḍ*	trough m.	*ḥawī* pl. *ḥwāyā*	yard m.
^{c}*irif - yi*^{c}*raf*	to know (s.th.)	*jallās* pl. *jalālīs*	waterpipe stand m.
jarr - yijirr	to take (s.th.)	*jawz al-hind*	coconut m.
jawzih	coconut f.	*kawdak*	you're always!
kurih	ball f.	*kwayyis*	good
li'ann / lann	because	*liji' - yilja' (lā)*	to resort (to s.th.)
madā^{c}*ah* pl. *madāyi*^{c}	waterpipe f.	*mafāriš*	furnishings
mafrūš	furnished	*makān* pl. *amkinih*	main sitting room m.
malān	full	*mamdūd*	stretched
markūz	supported	*maṣnū*^{c}	made
masra^{c}	early; soon	*matkā* pl. *matākī*	cushion support; arm rest m.
maxzūg	having a hole	*mġallaf*	covered; wrapped
min šān	so that	*mišrab* pl. *mašārib*	mouthpiece m.
mistadīr	round	*mistaṭīl*	long
mitr pl. *amtār*	metre m.	*msajjilih* pl. *-āt*	tape recorder f.
mtiḥān pl. *-āt*	exam m.	*naks*	smoke m.
nāzil	below; downstairs	*rtkaz - yirtkaz*	to be set up; on top
šaḏarawān pl. *-āt*	fountain m.	*ṣafīf* pl. *ṣufwaf*	shelf m.
saggā - yisaggī	to water; irrigate (s.th)	*šajarih* pl. *šijar*	tree f.
šakl pl. *aškāl*	shape; form m.	*sfinj*	foam m.
šubbāk pl. *šabābīk*	latticed cooler m.	*tabdīl*	replacement m.
ṭābu^{c}	habit; custom m.	*tadxīn*	smoking m.
^{c}*tagad - yi*^{c}*tagid*	to believe (s.th.)	*ṭall - yuṭull (*^{c}*alā)*	to look down (on s.th.)
tamām	okay?	*ṭaraḥ - yiṭraḥ/yiṭruḥ*	to put (s.th.)
ṭarḥah pl. *ṭaraḥāt*	floor; level f.	*tiliviziyūn* pl. *-āt*	television m.
titin	tobacco m.	*tkā' - yitkī (*^{c}*alā)*	to sit, lean (on s.th.)
ṭūl	length m.	*ṯulāṯī*	triangular
waḥdahin	on their f. own	*wasaṭ / wasṭ*	middle m.
wusādih pl. *wasāyid*	mattress f.	*xārij*	outside
xazzān	chewing m.	*xirag*	rags f.
xašab / xšab	wood m.	*xuzgī* pl. *xizgān*	hole m.
yābis	dry	*yibis - yības*	to become dry
zayy	like prep.	*zayy-mā*	as; like adjt.
zuġayrī	small		

Grammar

1. *Greetings*

The greeting *ḥayy allāh man jā'!* 'may God keep he who comes alive' with the return greeting *allāh yiḥayyīk!* 'may God keep you m.s. alive' is used between men who generally know each other fairly well.

2. *Filler words: 'I mean…'*

Adjectives usually immediately follow the noun they modify, as in *al-kabīr* in:

al-makān al-kabīr	'the big room'

However, two types of filler word can interrupt a noun-adjective sequence. These are the manner demonstratives *hākaḏā* or *ka-ḏayyā* 'like that', and the filler words *yā sa^{c}am, sa^{c}am* and *ya^{c}nī* 'i.e.', 'I mean' or 'that is to say'. Both types of filler word are exemplified in the first dialogue in this lesson (cf. also *Syntax* p. 217):

makān ya^{c}nī kabīr	'a big room'
gaṣabuh hākaḏā ṭawīluh	'a long pipe'

Another type of filler word, which acts like a tag, is the word *tamām* 'okay?' used typically at the end of a sentence in order to involve the listener more:

arba^{c}ah ṣufwaf tamām	'four shelves, okay?'

3. *'Without'*

'Without' is usually expressed by the phrase *bi-ġayr,* less commonly by *bi-dūn*:

al-bint bi-ġayr umm sā^c al-gamīṣ bi-ġayr kum	'a girl without a mother is like a dress without sleeves'
mā biš bayt bi-ġayr tiliviziyūn	'there is no house without a television'

4. *Word order: prepositional phrase plus noun*

After a phrase involving *ma^c* in the sense of 'to have', the locative adverb *hānā* or *hinīyih* ‘here’ usually precedes the noun:

m^{c}iš hānā ^{c}ašar wasāyid	‘you f.s. have here ten back cushions’

Similarly, a prepositional phrase also precedes the noun, as in:

ma^{c}ī fi l-makān hāḏā tiliviziyūn	‘in this room I have a television’
wa-m^{c}ānā fi kull bīr barik	‘in every well we have a pool’

This is particularly the case when the prepositional object is a possessive pronoun:

al-bayt ma^{c}ānā fīhā msajjilih	‘the house, we have a tape recorder in it’

Similarly, when a transitive verb requires a preposition, the prepositional phrase precedes the object when the object is an explicit noun, (cf. *Syntax* pp. 149-150):

niddī lak mushil	‘we will give you a purgative’
lā ddit lā bint axrāṣ	‘if she gives a girl earrings’

5. *Numbers and number-noun agreement*

In Lesson 6 we considered the cardinal numbers from 3 - 10. Here we look at the count form of the numbers and the use of numbers with weights, time and measures. There are two forms of the numbers 3 - 10: a *masculine* form (which is identical to the count form given in Lesson 6); and a *feminine* form. These two forms are given in the table below:

No.	masculine	feminine
3	*ṯalāṯih*	*ṯalāṯ*
4	*arba^{c}ah*	*arba^{c}*
5	*xamsih*	*xams*
6	*sittih*	*sitt*
7	*sab^{c}ah*	*sab^{c}*
8	*ṯamāniyih*	*ṯamān*
9	*tis^{c}ah*	*tis^{c}*
10	*^{c}ašarih*	*^{c}ašar*

In order to say 'three [to ten] X', the number is followed by an indefinite *plural* noun. Additionally, the number takes the masculine form when the *singular* of the following noun is masculine, as in:

ṯalāṯih šabābīk 'three latticed coolers'
where the singular *šubbāk* is masculine.

sittih ṣufwaf 'six shelves'
where the singular *ṣafīf* is masculine.

When the singular of the following noun is feminine, however, the number takes a shortened form (without the final *-ih* ending), as in:

ṯalāṯ abwār 'three wells'
where the singular *bīr* is feminine.

sab^c darājīn 'seven steps'
where the singular *darajih* is feminine.

In order to say '*the* three [upto ten] X', either the definite number is followed by a definite plural noun, as in:

aṯ-ṯalāṯ al-labwār 'the three wells'

as-sab^ca l-biyūt 'the seven houses'

Or, more emphatically, the definite number follows the definite noun, as in:

al-labwār aṯ-ṯalāṯ 'the three wells'

al-biyūt as-sab^cah 'the seven houses'

6. *'A sink with taps'*

To translate English 'with' in the sense of 'X with taps', 'X with forty pages' where the noun following 'with' is an integral part of X, the word *abū* [= father in other contexts] is used with a following *singular* noun (cf. *Syntax* pp. 219-220). In the phrase *tiliviziyūn abū šanab* 'satellite television', in the first dialogue in this lesson, *abū šanab* is not a translation of the word 'satellite', but rather a description of a satellite and means literally 'with antennae'. Examples include:

maġsal abū ḥanafī 'sink with taps'

bazz abū xaṭṭ	'material with stripes'
gamīṣ abū ragabih	'dress with a collar [lit: neck]'

Abū is often used before a number to express the number of, for example, pages in the case of a book, or milligrams in the case of tablets:

daftar abū miyih	'exercise book with 100 [pages]'
ḥubūb abū miyatayn	'tablets of 200 [milligrams]'

7. *Arithmetic*

For addition, the conjunction *wa-* 'and' and the verb *yisāwī* 'makes; equals' are used:

xamsih wa-wāḥid yisāwī sittih	'five and one equals six'

For subtraction, *nāgiṣ* 'minus' and the verb *yisāwī* 'makes; equals' are used:

sittih nāgiṣ wāḥid yisāwī xamsih	'six minus one equals five'

For multiplication, the preposition *fī* 'in' and the verb *yisāwī* are used:

ṯalāṯih fī ṯalāṯih yisāwī tisᶜah 'three times three equals nine'

For division the preposition *ᶜalā* 'on' and the verb *yisāwī* are used:

sittih ᶜalā ṯalāṯih yisāwī ṯnayn 'six divided by three equals two'

8. *'It'*

The dummy subject 'it' is usually expressed by *hū* in Ṣanᶜānī Arabic (cf. *Syntax* p. 413), as in:

*mā gad jāš illā wa-gad**ū** s-sāᶜah sitt*	'he didn't come until it was six o' clock'
itṣalū bī law-mā gadū maġrib	'they m. called me when it was sunset'

gadū laylat ad-duxūl	'it is the consummation night'

When time is involved, 'it' can be expressed by *hī* (*ibid*):

gadī s-sā^{c}ah xams	'it is five o' clock'

9. *Adverbs: 'always!'*

A common plaintive way of expressing the fact that you, or someone else is always doing something involves the word *kawd* + pronoun followed by the imperfect verb with the habitual prefix *bi-*, as in:

ant kawdak bi-tudrus	'you m.s. are always studying!'
anā wa-zawjī kawdanā bi-ntigāla^c	'my husband and I are always arguing!'
anā kawdī bayn-aṣabbin	'I am always washing!'

10. *Agreement with inanimate plurals*

When a noun is an inanimate plural, the agreeing verb, adjective or pronoun is feminine plural when the noun referents are considered to be separate, individual instances (cf. Lesson 3; Lesson 4; *Syntax* p. 104), as in:

wa-fīh madāki', ya^{c}nī llī bi-nxazzin ^{c}alayhin bi-ntkī' ^{c}alayhin	'and there are supports, I mean those we chew on, we lean on'
sittih ṣufwaf waḥdahin	'six shelves on their own'
kānayn at-ṯalāṯ al-labwār bī-saggayn …	'the three wells used to water…'

When the noun referents are considered to be a collectivity or the noun is generic, however, the verb, adjective or pronoun is feminine *singular (ibid)*, as in:

as-sayyārāt tuṣtum yawmī	'cars crash daily'
al-ayyām galīlih	'the days are few/there are few days'

ba^cd ayyām kaṯīrih	'after many days'

11. *Reflexive verbs*

In Yemeni Arabic, a number of verbs take the preposition *lā* plus a pronoun suffix which is co-referential with the subject of the verb (cf. *Syntax* p. 202-203). These verbs have a similar function to the type of reflexive verbs found in colloquial English, such as: 'get yourself back by midnight', 'wash yourself!', and 'I'll buy myself a new coat'; and in French, such as: 'je me lave', 'je m'appele…', 'je m'en vais', etc. Reflexivity is found in a number of verbs of motion, such as:

ša-ḍwī lī l-bayt	'I will go home'
sār lih	'he went'

Reflexivity is also found in other transitive and intransitive verbs. The example in the first dialogue in this lesson is:

nijirr lanā gāt	'we'll get ourselves *gāt*'

Other typical examples include:

niwaggif lanā taks	'we'll hail ourselves a taxi'
aštarī lī baxūr	'I will buy myself some incense'
titġaddā lahā	'she has lunch'

As in English, when a verb can be either reflexive or non-reflexive, the reflexive imperative tends to have more force than its non-reflexive counterpart (cf. *Syntax* p. 203). Compare the following two pairs:

	imšaw lakum	'be gone with you m.pl.!'
versus		
	imšaw	'go away m.pl.!'
	jirr lak gāt	'get yourself some *gāt*!'
versus		
	jirr gāt	'get some *gāt*!'

12. *Presentational particles: 'here it is!'*

Sanᶜānī Arabic has a number of *presentational* particles. These particles translate English phrases such as 'here it is!', 'here they are!', and 'there they are!'. Sanᶜānī Arabic has two sets of presentational particles: a near set which roughly corresponds to phrases such as 'here it is!'; and a far set which roughly corresponds to phrases such as 'there it is!' (see Lesson 16). The main presentational particle is *ḏā*. This is often preceded by the pronoun *hū* or *hī*:

hū ḏā	'here he is!'
hī ḏā	'here she is!'

hū ḏā is also be used in the sense 'there you are!' or 'here you are!':

Iain hū ḏā maᶜih iṯnayn giṭārāt	'Iain, there you are, he has two guitars!'

Where the subject is plural, *ḏā* usually takes following *lā* + pronoun:

al-banāt hin ḏālāhin	'the girls, there they are!'
al-ᶜiyyāl hum ḏālāhum	'the boys, there they are!'

For further examples and further discussion of presentational particles cf. *Syntax* pp. 422-423.

Thematic Vocabulary

The house

ᶜagd pl. *ᶜugūd*	upper arched window, now with coloured glass m.
badrūm pl. *-āt*	cellar m.
dawr pl. *adwār*	floor [e.g. first floor] m.
daymih pl. *diyam*	traditional kitchen f.
dihlīz pl. *dahālīz*	hall; place m.
dīwān pl. *dawāwīn*	sitting room [often best room] m.
dūlāb pl. *dawālīb*	drawer m.
gamarīyih / gamarī pl. *-āt*	top round window in alabaster f.
gindīl pl. *ganādīl*	lightbulb m.
ġurfih pl.*ġuraf*	room f.
ḥammām pl. *-āt*	modern-style bathroom m.

ḥanafī pl. *-āt* — tap f.
ḥāwī pl. *ḥwāyā* — yard m.
ḥijrih pl. *ḥijar* — hall f.
jūb^{w}*ā* pl. *ajbīyih* — roof f.
kaššāf pl. *-āt* — torch m.
mafraj pl. *mafārij* — room with a view in which *gāt* chews are held m.
maġsal pl. *maġāsil* — modern-style sink m.
makān pl. *amkinih* — sitting room m.
masḥalih pl. *masāḥil* — verticle draining surface f.
maṭbax pl. *maṭābux* — modern-style kitchen m.
mistaraḥ pl. *-āt* — traditional bathroom m.
muṭhār pl. *-āt* — traditional bathroom m.
ṣafīf pl. *ṣufwaf* — shelf m.
šāgūs pl. *šawāgīs* — small rectangular or square window which opens fully for ventilation. Sometimes in the middle of a *gamarīyih* m.
sāḥil pl. *sawāḥil* — traditional sink; washing floor m.
šubbāk pl. *šabābīk* — latticed cooler which juts out on outer wall of house and is used to keep food cool. Can be made of wood or mud m.
ṭāguh pl. *ṭīgān* — large window which opens f.
ṭarḥah pl. *ṭaraḥāt* — floor [e.g. first floor] f.
ṭayramānuh pl. *-āt* — small room at top of house; watch-out room f.

Exercises

1. *Greetings*

Give an appropriate reply to the following greetings:

i. *ḥayy allāh man jā'!* ____________________
ii. *ḥayyāš allāh!* ____________________
iii. *akramak allāh!* ____________________
iv. *msaytū!* ____________________
v. *allāh yi*^{c}*īnak!* ____________________

2. *Arithmetic*

Work out the following sums orally in Ṣanᶜānī Arabic:

i. 2 + 3 ____________________

ii. 4 - 3 ____________________

iii. 5 x 2 ____________________

iv. 6 ÷ 6 ____________________

v. 12 ÷ 6 ____________________

3. *Tell the time!*

Read the following times out loud in Ṣanᶜānī Arabic:

i. 10.30 ii. 9.15 iii. 6.45 iv. 5.40 v. 4.20 vi. 5.55 vii. 11.00 viii. 12.00

4. *Sentence formation*

Use the following words and phrases in complete sentences:

Example: *yā rayt wa-* ————> *yā rayt w-antī hānā fī tiᶜizz!*

i. *yā rayt wa-* ____________________

ii. *gaṣdī* ____________________

iii. *kawdak* ____________________

iv. *yištī* ____________________

v. *istaġrab* ____________________

vi. *mā bi-lā* ____________________

vii. *bi-ġayr* ____________________

5. *Verb inflection*

Complete the table below by correctly inflecting the verbs. The top left-hand corner has been completed by way of example:

	yixallī	*yuṭull*	*yuxṭā*	*yištī*
ant	*tixallī*			
anā				
antī				
hum				
hin				

6. *Negation*

Negate the following sentences:

Example: *gāl innū ^{c}a-yjī* ———> *mā gālš innū ^{c}a-yjī*

i. *lāzim asīr al-jāmi^{c}ah.* ____________

ii. *at-tadrīs fī l-jāmi^{c} bi-dūn mugābil.* ____________

iii. *ġudwuh gad ma^{c}ī mtihān.* ____________

iv. *zid tištī gahwih?* ____________

v. *ma^{c}ānā madāris ^{c}ādī.* ____________

vi. *^{c}ād agul lak jī!* ____________

7. *'Only ...'*

Say 'only' in the following sentences using *mā ... illā.*

Example: *šā-jī lak al-xamīs.* ——> *mā šā-jī lakš illa l-xamīs.*

i. *addī lhum šwayyat gāt.* ____________

ii. *ti^{c}malī baynahā samn.* ____________

iii. *ništī gahwih.* ____________

iv. *ištarā jarīdat aṯ-ṯawrih.* ______________________________

v. *uxtī fāyizih tištī txazzin.* ______________________________

8. *Numbers*

Look around your room and say how many of the following (between one and ten) you have in Ṣanᶜānī Arabic:

Example: books ———> *gad maᶜī xamsih kutub fī l-ġurfih*

i. doors

ii. tables

iii. windows

iv. pens

v. shelves

vi. scissors

9. *Translation*

Translate the following groups of sentences into Ṣanᶜānī Arabic:

A. Use *kawd* + pronoun

i. My daughter is always cooking!

ii. Your husband is always travelling!

iii. You m.s. are always reading!

B. Use *yā rayt wa-*

i. I wish my daughter were here in Ṣanᶜā'!

ii. I wish you f.s. lived in Yemen!

iii. I wish my son were well!

C. Use *hū* or *hī*

i. It is ten to three.

ii. It is early.

iii. It is sunset.

D. Use a reflexive verb

i. We must get ourselves home!

ii. Be gone with you m.s.!

iii. He bought himself *gāt*.

E. Use *abū*

i. I want an exercise book with 40 pages.

ii. I want 50 mg tablets.

iii. I want a dress with stripes.

F. Use *min*

i. I want some rice.

ii. I want some bread.

iii. I want one of the exercise books.

LESSON 16

Al^{c}āb ṣan^{c}ānī

Dialogue 1 *ḥabs wa-l-lamān*

Ibrahim: *al-li^{c}bih ḥabs wa-l-lamān hī 'ismahā ḥabs wa-l-lamān awlā lāḥigih. law-mā yjaw al-^{c}iyyāl yigūlū ḥayyā nil^{c}ab lāḥigih wallā ḥabs wa-l-lamān. hāḏīk nafs al-li^{c}bih. yif^{c}alū hānā xuṭṭ min ^{c}ind an-nās hāḏawlāk lā hinīyih ^{c}alā 'asās innū xamsih anfār wa-xamsih xuṣūm, fa-yiddaw al-li^{c}bih bi-filis dāyir ^{c}asibb man yidayyir yil^{c}ab fī l-amān. yif^{c}alū hānā xuṭṭ ismih amān, wa-nafs al-xuṭṭ hāḏā 'ismih ḥabs. wa-ba^{c}dā yil^{c}abū bi-filis dāyir wa-jā ^{c}ind ḏayya l-farīg ad-dāyir aw al-filis ḥasab aṭ-ṭalab. maṯalan anā jī 'anā wa-farīg w-antī wa-farīg. agūl mā tištay fils wallā dāyir, gūlī.*

Janet: *fils.*

Ibrahim: *iḏā jā fils ^{c}indiš tudxulī l-amān. iḥnā nibda' nilaḥḥigiš iḥnā ba^{c}dā yudxul al-xamsih hāḏā fī l-amān wa-l-xamsih hāḏā yijlisū xārij al-amān, wa-ba^{c}dā yibda'ū yuxrujū ^{c}alā wāḥid wāḥid min al-amān wa-hāḏawlā yibda'ū yilaḥḥigūhum aw yitxaṣṣaṣ bi-l-wāḥid yilaḥḥigih. yuxruj wāḥid min al-amān, wa-wāḥid min allī xārij yilaḥḥigih law-mā yimsakih. wa-'in ma ystarš yimsakih yirja^c al-amān, al-muhimm hū yuhrub wa-hum yilaḥḥigūh w-iḏā šibiḥūh yišillūh al-ḥabs. wa-xalāṣ yijlis hānāk law-mā yijaw aṣḥābuh yingiḏūh. fa-yuxrujū ^{c}adad xayrāt maṯalan ṯalāṯih arba^{c}ah ^{c}alā sibb yif^{c}alū lahum šalīyih wa-wāḥid yisīr kaḏā wāḥid yisīr kaḏā wāḥid yisīr kaḏā wa-yisīrū ṣalayh sa^{c}am ṣalā ḏayyā fī l-ḥabs wa-yjarribū yilḏa^{c}ū yadih wa-hū yimudd lā ^{c}indahum bi-šarṭ innū ma yxrujš min al-ḥabs, min al-xuṭṭ sa^{c}am. wa-law-mā misikūh hū yuhrub li-l-amān. 'in yistar yisīr al-amān gadū ḏakka, wa-'in hū ma ystirš šibiḥūh wa-rijji^{c}ū l-ḥabs marrih ṯānī, wa-nafs al-afrād allaḏī xarajū ma^{c}ih in yistarū riji^{c}ū ma yistarūš iḥtabasū. al-muhimm al-xamsih allī kānū fī l-amān law-mā gadum fī l-ḥabs al-farīg aṯ-ṯānī yudxul al-amān, wa-hāḏāk yijī yuxruj yibda' yilaḥḥigih min jadīd wa-hākaḏā xalāṣ.*

Dialogue 2 ***yā masā, jīt amassī ^{c}indukum!***

Abd al-Salam: *wa-fī ramaḏān al-^{c}ašī šā-kallimak ^{c}an al-jahhāl hāḏawlā, yuxrujū yimassaw hāḏā ṭabī^{c}ah kull yawm fī ramaḏān ba^{c}d al-lakl. yijtama^{c}u l-laṭfāl, wa-yiruḥū yimassaw yiduggū ^{c}ala l-bayt wa-yimassaw ^{c}alayh wa-^{c}ind-mā yimassaw nurjum lahum filūs girš giršayn ṯalāṯih wa-hāḏā, hāḏī kānat minn awwal bi-kaṯīr, ḏaḥḥīn gad bida'at mā ^{c}ad fīš. wa-l-masā hāḏā law-mā yijtama^{c}ū jihhāl xamsih arba^{c}ah kam-mā kān yiruḥū yiduggu l-bayt wa-ygūlū lā ṣāḥub al-bayt: yiruḥū l-jahhāl fī l-bayt hāḏawlā fī sinn ibnak yiṣayyuḥū, yijībū anāšīd, wa-ygūlū:*

yā masā jīt amassī ^{c}indukum

wāḥid yiṣayyuḥ hākaḏā w-allī gafāh aṯ-ṯalāṯih aw al-arba^{c}ah yiṣīḥū:

limi' limi'

wa-hū yigūl:

yā masā as^{c}ad allāh hal-masā limi' limi'
yā masā irjimū min ^{c}indukum limi' limi'

yiṣayyuḥū bi-hāḏa ṭ-ṭarīguh yijībū anāšīd. ṣāḥub al-bayt hū yisma^{c}hum, ṭab^{c}an yirtāḥ bi-l-laṭfāl az-zġār hāḏā yijīb lahum flūs, hāḏī ṭabī^{c}ah ^{c}ādī ya^{c}nī mā biš fīhā ^{c}ayb aw ayy ḥājih inn ant tugūl l-awlādak ^{c}ayb lā truḥš wallā šī. al-jīrān yixallawhum zayy-mā tgūl farḥat al-awlād bi-hāḏāk al-wagt min al-maġrib, wa-^{c}ād fīh al-anāšīd tigūl iḏā mā ḥadd jāwab min al-bayt min al-bayt mā ḥadd yijāwab wa-hum ^{c}ārifīn innū fīh nās fī l-bayt yigūlū:

ḥarrik w-inḏug māšī xirīnā bāb al-bayt

yiṣayyuḥū hākaḏā yifajji^{c}ū 'iḏā mā tiḥarrik wa-tirjum lahum min al-filūs ḥarrik w-inḏug ^{c}irift inḏug ya^{c}nī irmī māšī xirīnā bāb al-bayt, ya^{c}nī 'iḏā mā rijimt lā n-nās šī wlā ayya ḥājih iḥna bi-n^{c}ammil lak xarā bāb al-bayt ^{c}ārif mā ma^{c}nā xarā.

James: *aywih.*

Abd al-Salam: *al-bawl iḏā mā rijimta lnāš wa-lā riyāl wa-lā jibt lanā ayy ḥājih iḥna bi-nbul lak fī l-bāb. hāḏā hū l-ma^{c}nā ḥaggahā w-a^{c}tagid inn al-masā hāḏā, yā masā hāḏā ^{c}indana ḥna nsammīh nirūḥ nimassī. 'a^{c}tagid innū mitwājid fī duwal ^{c}arabīyih kaṯīr a^{c}tagid fī maṣr u-fī duwal ^{c}arabīyih kaṯīr wa-hāḏā. u-miš*

^{c}ārif min ayn jā' innamā 'aḏakkirih wa-^{c}ādaḥna zuġār. hāḏā hū ḥagg al-masā' wa-hāḏā ramaḏ̣ān.

Vocabulary

^{c}adad pl. *a^{c}dād*	number m.	*amān*	safety; den m.
^{c}ammal - yi^{c}ammil (lā)	to do (s.th., to s.o.)	*as^{c}ad*	to make (s.o.) happy; to bless
asās pl. *usus*	basis m.	*^{c}ašī / ^{c}ašīyih*	evening f.
^{c}ayb	shame m.	*bāl - yibūl*	to urinate
bawl	urine m.	*dagg - yidugg / yidigg*	to knock, hit (s.th.)
ḏakka	there he is!	*ḏakkar - yiḏakkir*	to remember (s.th.)
dawlih pl. *duwal*	state; country f.	*dayyar - yidayyir*	to have a turn
fajja^{c} - yifajji^{c}	to frighten; surprise (s.o.)		
fard pl. *afrād*	person m.	*farḥah* pl. *faraḥāt*	joy; pleasure f.
farīg pl. *furūg*	team m.	*fīh*	there is
fil(i)s dāyir	heads or tails	*fī sinn …*	(at) the age of …
gafā	behind	*gurnih* pl. *guran*	corner f.
ḥabs	prison m.	*ḥasab / ḥasb*	according to
ḥayyā	come on!	*hirib - yuhrub*	to flee; escape
ḥtabas - yiḥtabis	to be imprisoned	*innamā*	however adjt.
jalas - yijlis	to sit; stay	*jār* pl. *jīrān*	neighbour m.
jarrab - yijarrib	to try (s.th.)	*jāwab - yijāwab*	to answer (s.o.)
jtama^{c} - yijtama^{c}	to get together; meet	*kam-mā*	as many as; however much adjt.
laḏa^{c} - yilḏa^{c}	to strike (s.th.) lightly	*laḥḥag - yilaḥḥig*	to chase (s.o.)
lāḥigih	catch f.	*li^{c}bih* pl. *al^{c}āb*	game f.
li^{c}ib - yil^{c}ab	to play (s.th.)	*limi'*	why
madd - yimudd	to stretch out	*maġrib*	sunset m.
masā	evening m.	*māšī*	otherwise; or else
massā - yimassī	to play *yā masā*	*min jadīd*	again [lit: from new]
misik - yimsak	to grab (s.th.)	*mitwājid*	very common
al-muhimm	the important thing	*nagaḏ - yingiḏ*	to rescue (s.o.)
našīd pl. *anāšīd*	song m.	*nḏug*	throw m.s.!
rāḥ - yirūḥ	to go	*ramaḏ̣ān*	Ramadan m.
rijim - yurjum / yirjim	to throw (s.th.)	*rtāḥ - yirtāḥ (bi)*	to be happy (with)
ṣāḥub pl. *aṣḥāb*	friend; mate m.	*ṣāḥub al-bayt*	houseowner m.

šalīyih	confusion f.	*šarṭ* pl. *šurūṭ*	condition m.
ṣayyaḥ - yiṣayyuḥ	to sing; shout	*šibiḥ - yišbaḥ*	to take hold of; grasp (s.th.)
simiᶜ - yismaᶜ	to hear (s.th.)	*staᶜmal - yistaᶜmil*	to use (s.th.)
ṭabīᶜah	s.th. natural f.	*ṭalab*	call; demand m.
ṭarīguh	way f.	*ṭufl* pl. *aṭfāl*	child m.
txaṣṣaṣ - yitxaṣṣaṣ (bi)	to specialise (in)	*uslūb* pl. *asālīb*	method m.
wagt pl. *awgāt*	time m.	*xarā*	faeces m.
xaṣm pl. *xuṣūm*	opponent m.	*xirī - yixrā*	to defaecate
xuṭṭ / xaṭṭ pl. *xuṭūṭ*	line; stripe m.		

Grammar

1. *Pronunciation: emphatic consonants and the vowel u*[1]

In Ṣanᶜānī Arabic, the vowel *u* is pronounced in place of short *i* when it is preceded by an emphatic consonant in the word. The feminine ending *-ih* is pronounced as *-ih* (unless the final consonant of the word is a pharyngeal ᶜ or *ḥ*, in which case it is pronounced as *-ah* cf. Lesson 3), or one of the consonants in the word is *ṣ*, *ṭ*, or *ḏ̣*, in which case it is pronounced as *-uh*:

*ṭawīl**uh***	'tall f.'
*tafruṭ**uh***	'women's party f.'
*mistaṭīl**uh***	'long f.'
*guṣṣ**uh***	'story f.'
*riyāḏ̣**uh***	'sport f.'
*ᶜuṭl**uh***	'holiday f.'
*ᶜuṣab**uh***	'neck ache f.'

Similarly, the third masculine singular object pronoun *-ih* is pronounced as *-uh* and the third feminine plural pronoun *-hin* as *-hun* in a word which has at least one emphatic consonant:

*guṣṣ**uh***	'he cut it m.'
*bayn-agḏ̣īh**un***	'I spend them f.'

The plural of many words of the pattern KaTīB such as *šarīṭ* 'cassette', *ṭarīg* 'road; path', *šarīm* 'scythe' and *ṣafīf* 'shelf' is KiTwaB; however, where the first consonant is emphatic, the first vowel in the plural is not *i* but *u* (cf. *Syntax* p. 433):

*š**i**rwaṭ*	'cassettes'

[1] The relationship between emphatic consonants and *u* is not described or transcribed in *Syntax*.

*š**ir**wam*	'scythes'
*ṭ**ur**wag*	'roads'
*ṣ**uf**waf*	'shelves'

In nouns of the pattern KāTiB the vowel *i* will be pronounced as *u* after emphatic consonants:

*fāṭ**u**muh*	'Fatima [female name]'
*ṣāl**uḥ***	'Salih [male name]'
*ṭāl**ub***	'student m.'
*ṣāḥ**ub***	'friend m.'

Verbs with emphatic consonants either take the vowels *a-a* or *u-u* in the perfect aspect, even though *u-u* is the least common vocalism for verbs:

*ṭ**u**ḥ**us***	'to fall'
*w**u**ṣ**ul***	'to arrive'
*f**u**ṭ**um***	'to wean'
*ḍ**u**ḥ**uk***	'to laugh'

In the imperfect aspect, the final vowel of derived verbs is *u* rather than *i* after an emphatic consonant:

*yiṣall**uḥ***	'he fixes'
*yiṣayy**uḥ***	'he shouts'
*yiṭaww**ul***	'he takes a long time'
*yiṭamb**u**layn*	'they f. drum'

Finally, when a verb or an active participle takes a prepositional phrase with *lā/li* (lit: 'to') as in *raḥ lih* 'he went' and *štarā lih* 'he bought himself', the vowel *i* in the prepositional phrase is pronounced as *u* when the verb contains an emphatic consonant:

*yuḍwī **luh***	'he is going home'
*ḥāfiḍ **luh***	'he recalls, knows'

2. *Coordination: 'or'*

Or can be expressed in one of four ways in Ṣanᶜānī Arabic: *aw, awlā, wallā* (cf. *Syntax* pp. 292-298) or by asyndetic linkage - that is to say, by nothing at all (cf. *Syntax* pp. 312). Asyndetic linkage is used in particular when numbers are being discussed:

gad yijaw ṯalāṯih arbaᶜah	'three or four may come'
law-mā yijtamaᶜū jihhāl xamsih arbaᶜah	'when four or five children get together'
gālū bi-ᶜašarih bi-ᶜišrīn	'they m. said for ten or twenty'

3. *Repetition: 'one-by-one'*

Repetition is used far more in Arabic than in English. It is used in a few set adverbial phrases: the English phrase 'one-by-one', for example, is translated as:

ᶜalā wāḥid wāḥid	'one-by-one'

The English phrase 'bit-by-bit' or 'little-by-little' can be translated as:

šwayyih šwayyih	'bit-by-bit'

And the English phrase 'slowly, [slowly]' can be translated as:

dala' dala'	'slowly, slowly'

Repetition is also used when the speaker wants to emphasise a number of small things:

baᶜdā tūgaᶜ muxazzigih ṯugūg ṯugūg	'then it becomes split up in lots of small holes'

The adverb *gawī* 'very' can be repeated to emphasise intensity:

gāl aḥibbak gawī gawī	'he said, "I love you very much"'

Verbs are often repeated to emphasise intensity or that someone is continually doing something:

gad al-wāḥid bi-yākul bi-yākul bi-yākul al-gāt	'you are constantly eating *gāt*'

4. *Conjoining conditionals*

If two conditional clauses follow one another, the conditional particle does not need to be repeated.[2] When the conditional particle is not repeated the utterance is more concise, and often has a sense of urgency. Compare:

in yistarū rijiᶜū *mā yistarūš iḥtabasū*	'if they m. can they return, if not they are imprisoned'
in yistarū rijiᶜū *wa-'in mā yistarūš iḥtabasū*	'if they m. can they return, and if not, they are imprisoned'

5. *Repetition: subject pronoun before wa-*

When a verb has an initial pronoun subject and a following noun subject, the pronoun must be repeated after the verb, as in *anā* in the example below (cf. also dialogue in Lesson 7 for the first example of this type of sentence):

anā jī' anā wa-farīg	'I come, me and a team'

This contrasts with sentences in which a second noun is linked to the verb by *maᶜ* 'with'.[3] In this case the initial pronoun is not repeated:

anā jī maᶜ xabīratī	'I come with my friend'

When the speaker wants to say 'she and I came', however, where the subject of the verb is two *pronouns* the first pronoun comes both before the verb and after the verb, as in *anā jī'* ***anā*** *wa-farīg* 'I come, me and a team'. The second pronoun, however, is usually linked to the first by the phrase *w-iyyā*, and takes the form of a *possessive* pronoun. The second pronoun takes the form for possessive pronouns which are suffixed to a preposition or noun ending in a vowel (cf. Lesson 5). Examples:

anā jī' anā w-iyyāh	'I come with him'
anā jī' anā w-iyyāhā	'I come with her'
anā jī' anā w-iyyāhum	'I come with them m.'
anā jī' anā w-iyyāhin	'I come with them f.'
anā jī' anā w-iyyāk	'I come with you m.s.'
anā jī' anā w-iyyāš	'I come with you f.s.'
anā jī' anā w-iyyākum	'I come with you m.pl.'
anā jī' anā w-iyyākin	'I come with you f.pl.'

[2] This is not possible in English, where both conditional statements must be introduced by a conditional particle, see translations below.

[3] Note, however, that *anā jī'anā wa-xabīratī* is the most common way of translating 'I come/am coming *with* my friend'.

An interesting variant on *anā w-iyyāh* cconstructions is the use of the pronoun *hū* 'he' in place of *anā* 'I' where it is clear that *hū* refers to the first person:

jīnā hū w-iyyāhum	'we came, he [i.e. I] and them'
gad wṣulnā hū w-iyyāhā	'we arrived, he [i.e. I] and her'

6. *Verbal nouns: 'after going out ...'*

As we have seen earlier, Arabic does not have the concept of an infinitive. It does, however, have verbal nouns (cf. Lesson 11). These nouns are often used as the object of a preposition in place of a verb in much the same way as *gerunds* (words which end in '-ing', such as 'bathing', 'singing') can be used in English in place of a subject - verb phrase. Compare:

	preposition	verb
	baᶜd-mā 'after'	*akal* 'he ate'
versus		
	preposition	verbal noun
	baᶜd 'after'	*al-lakl* 'eating...'

When a verbal noun is used in place of a verb the verbal noun is *definite* - either by taking the definite article, as in the example above, or by being the first term in a definite annexion phrase:

baᶜd 'after'	*xurūj al-bayt* 'going out of the house'

7. *Verbs: 'to begin to do ...'*

To say 'begin to do s.th.' the verb *bida'(bada') - yibda'* is followed by a verb in the imperfect aspect, for example:

bida'ū yixazzinū	'they m. began to chew'

Alternatively, *bida'* can be followed by a definite verbal noun (cf. 6. above) to give the same meaning:

bida'ū l-xazzān	'they m. began to chew'

In both cases, the second element - the verb or the definite verbal noun - can be described as the *object* of the verb *bida'*.

The full paradigm of *bida'* in the perfect aspect is as follows:

	singular	plural
1.	*bida't*	*bida'nā*
2. m.	*bida't*	*bida'tū*
2. f.	*bida'tī*	*bida'tayn*
3. m.	*bida'*	*bida'ū*
3. f.	*bida'at*	*bida'ayn*

The full paradigm of *yibda'* in the imperfect aspect is as follows:

	singular	plural
1.	*abda'*	*nibda'*
2. m.	*tibda'*	*tibda'ū*
2. f.	*tibda'ī*	*tibda'ayn*
3. m.	*yibda'*	*yibda'ū*
3. f.	*tibda'*	*yibda'ayn*

8. *'To begin to be no longer...'*

In order to say that something has begun to disappear, no longer be around, or no longer be played, Ṣanᶜānī Arabic uses the verb *bida'* followed by the phrase *mā ᶜād fīš* (as in the second dialogue in this lesson) or *mā ᶜād biš*. The literal translation of this phrase would be 'has begun to be no longer'. The verb agrees in gender and number with the subject, even if the subject is not actually expressed:

gad bida'at mā ᶜād fīš	'[this game] has begun to no longer be [played]'
at-taglīd bida' mā ᶜād biš	'[this custom] has begun to no longer [be around]'

9. *Transitive verbs: verb objects*

In 7. above we have seen that the verb *bida'* can take either a definite verbal noun as an object or a verb as an object. There are a number of other verbs in San^c^ānī Arabic which can take both nouns and verbs as objects. These include verbs which we have already encountered such as *yištī* 'to want', *gidir/yigdir* and *satar/yistir* 'to be able; can' (cf. Lesson 13), and *jarrab/yijarrib* 'to try' (cf. *Syntax,* Chapter 5). For example:

noun	*yištī gāt*	'he wants *gāt*'
verbal noun	*yištī l-xazzān*	'he wants to chew'
verb	*yištī yixazzin*	'he wants to chew'

Another common verb which takes both noun and verb objects is *zād/yizīd* 'to do again'. It terms of its meaning, this verb behaves very much like its particle cognate, *zid* (cf. Lesson 12):

noun	*zīdī lī sukkar*	'give f.s. me more sugar!'
verbal noun	*azīd al-xazzān*	'I will chew again'
verb (phrase)	*azīd askub lak*	'I will pour you m.s. more [eg. tea]'

Verbs which mean 'to enable/let s.o. do s.th.' also take verbs as objects, but the verb object takes a different subject to the subject of the first verb (the 'enable' verb). The subject of the second verb is often the object pronoun of the first verb:

verb 1	verb 2	gloss
axallīhā 'I-let-her'	*tsāfir* 'she-goes'	'I will let her go'
makkinīhā 'help f.s.-her'	*tišrab* 'she-drinks'	'help f.s. her to drink!'

Verbs which mean 'to see' and 'to want' also take verb objects. The object pronoun is optional and the first verb may simply take the second verb as object, as in (cf. also *Syntax* p. 164, Lesson 18):

wa-ba^cdā tibsirī yilabbisūhā gamīṣ	'then you f.s. see them dress her in a dress from the museum'
mā tištay ništarī liš	'what do you f.s. want us to buy you?'

10. *Complements*

A number of verbs require complements (words or phrases which complete the sense of a verb phrase or clause, cf. *Syntax* p. 135). Complements can be adjectives, nouns, prepositional phrases or verbs. Verbs which require complements include *kān* 'to be', *wuga*^{c} 'to become', *ṣār* 'to become', *jalas* 'to keep doing; continue', *jā'* 'to turn out', *bigī* 'to become', *zād* 'to do again' (cf. 9. above) and *gām* 'to start doing; [and often not translated cf. *Syntax* p. 157]' (cf. *Syntax* pp. 154-160). For example:

adj.	*kān ḥālī*	'it was nice'
	bigī ḥālī	'it became nice'
noun	*kān mudīr*	'he was manager'
	bigī mudīr	'he became a manager'
verb	*kān yištaġil*	'he used to work'
	gām yištaġil	'he began to work'
prep. phrase	*as-sayyārih mā kānš lahā brayk*	'the car had no brake [lit: the car, there was not to it a brake'
	law-mā yūga^c *liš ḥājih*	'when something happens to you'

11. *Negation: verb strings*

When a sentence involves a combination of two or more verbs, the sentence is negated by negating the first verb only (as in English):

mā yištīš yixazzin	'he doesn't want to chew'
mā yištīš yijlis yiz^c*ij*	'he does not want to continue to be annoying'
mā zidš askub lak	'I will not pour you more [eg. tea]'
mā kānš yištaġil	'he did not use to work'

mā yijlisš yizᶜij	'he did not continue to be annoying'
lā tmakkinīhāš tišrab	'don't help f.s. her to drink!'
mā tibsiriš yilabbisūhā	'you f.s. don't see them dress her'

12. *'That'*

'That' in the sense of 'he said *that* he would go' is usually translated by nothing at all in Sanᶜānī Arabic[4] :

gāl ar-rajjāl ᶜa-ysāfir	'he said that the man would be travelling'
gāl ᶜa-ysāfir	'he said that he would be travelling'
lāzim aḏākir	'I must study [lit: it is necessary [that] I study]'

It can, however, be translated by the word *inn*, particularly when the speaker wants to emphasise a point:

gāl inn ar-rajjāl ᶜa-ysāfir	'he said that the man would be travelling'
gāl innū ᶜa-ysāfir	'he said that he would be travelling'
lāzim innī aḏākir	'I must study [lit: it is necessary that I study]'
bi-šarṭ innū ma yxrujš min al-ḥabs	'on condition that he does not leave the prison'

When *inn* is not followed immediately by a noun it usually takes a pronoun suffix, as in the last three examples above. This pronoun suffix is identical to the independent pronouns for third masculine singular and plural (i.e. 'he' and 'they') and for third feminine plural:

innū	'that he'
innum / innahum	'that they m.'
innin / innahin	'that they f.'

[4] Particularly when direct speech is involved (*Syntax* p. 165).

For all other persons (i.e. first and second persons and third feminine singular 'she') *inn* takes a form which is identical to the corresponding possessive pronoun:

	singular	plural
1.	*innī*	*innanā* or *innā*
2. m.	*innak*	*innakum*
2. f.	*inniš*	*innakin*
3. f.	*innahā*	

inn can also, but far less commonly, be followed by a verb:

al-muhimm inn agassim al-murabba^{c} lā 'agsām mitsāwī	'the important thing is for me to divide the square into equal parts'

13. *Far presentational particles: 'there he is!'*

In Lesson 15 we looked at the near presentational particles. In the first dialogue in this lesson the far presentational particle *(gadū) ḏakka* 'he's there!' is used. As with the demonstrative pronouns, the far presentational particles differ from the near presentational particles in taking final *-k*. In addition, the far presentational particles distinguish between feminine and masculine in the singular:

masculine	feminine
ḏāk	*ḏīk*
ḏakka	*ḏikki*

To say 'there s/he is!' the pronoun *hū/hī* usually comes before the presentational particle:

(gad)hū ḏāk	'there he is!
(gad)hū ḏakka	'there he is!'
(gad)hī ḏīk	'there she is!
(gad)hī ḏikki	'there she is!'

The plural far presentational particle does not distinguish between masculine and feminine plural (as with the demonstrative pronouns):

	hunḏālaka	'there they are!'
or		
	anḏālaka	'there they are!'

For further examples cf. *Syntax* pp. 423-425.

Thematic Vocabulary

Yemeni games

amān	den m.
banādig	pop guns
bayt aš-šayṭān	'safe place' in hopscotch or touch m.
ḏarab al-ḥidwī	[type of cricket] m.
dawr pl. *adwār*	turn m.
dāyirih	circle f.
fāyiz pl. *-īn*	winner m.
fil(i)s dāyir	heads or tails
gandal - yigandil	to flick
gandalih	flick [game] f.
gaws pl. *agwās*	catapult m.
ġummāḏuh	blind man's buff f.
al-ġurag	the pits [game] f.
gurnih pl. *guran*	corner f.
ḥabl	skipping rope; skipping m.
ḥabs wa-l-lamān	prison and safety [game] m.
ḥuṣam	counters [really small pebbles]
lāᶜib pl. *-īn*	player m.
lāḥigih	catch f.
liᶜbat al-lazrār	the button game f.
liᶜbat az-zanb	date-stone game f.
liᶜib - yilᶜab	to play (s.th.)
murabbaᶜ pl. *-āt*	square m.
ṣayd as-samak	fishing m.
wagal	hopscotch m.
warag al-gumār	cards
xāsir pl. *-īn*	loser m.
xaṣm pl. *xuṣūm*	opponent m.
xāṣum pl. *-īn*	opponent m.
zaggīnī ... zaggaytak	pass to me and I'll pass to you! [name of a game]
zanbih pl. *zanb*	date stone f.
zawjīyih pl. *-āt*	pair f.

Exercises

1. *Greetings*

Give appropriate greetings to which the following are replies:

i. ____________ *allāh yiḥayyīk!*

ii. ____________ *al-ḥamdu li-llāh ^{c}ala l-^{c}āfiyih mā lī šī!*

iii. ____________ *w-antū min ahl al-xayr!*

iv. ____________ *liš ḥayāt ad-dunyā!*

v. ____________ *^{c}alaykum as-salām!*

vi. ____________ *massākum allāh bi-l-xayr!*

vii. ____________ *allāh yisallimiš!*

2. *Negation*

Negate the following sentences:

Example: *nif^{c}al xuṭṭ min al-gurnih hāḏā* ——> *mā nif^{c}alš xuṭṭ min al-gurnih hāḏā*

i. *al-^{c}iyyāl yijarribū yilḏa^{c}ū yadih.* ____________

ii. *zid xaraj min al-ḥabs.* ____________

iii. *tištī tibda' tilaḥḥigiš min jadīd.* ____________

iv. *kān yištī yištarī gāt ḥālī.* ____________

v. *hāḏi l-li^{c}bih ismahā lāḥigih.* ____________

vi. *lāzim tijī til^{c}ab marrih ṯānī.* ____________

3. *Sentence formation*

Use each of the following words in an appropriate sentence. Where verbs are involved provide the correct inflections:

Example: *inn* ———> *gālat lī innahā ᶜa-tsīr ġudwuh ṣubḥ*

i. *yišti* ____________________

ii. *lāzim* ____________________

iii. *kān* ____________________

iv. *yigdar* ____________________

v. *yijarrib* ____________________

vi. *yištarī* ____________________

vii. *yibda'* ____________________

4. *Verb inflection*

Complete the table below by inflecting the verbs in the imperfect. The top left-hand corner has been completed by way of example:

	yijī	*yugūm*	*yizīd*	*yibda'*	*yixallī*	*yugūl*
anā	*ajī*					
iḥna						
antayn						
antū						
hin						
hum						

5. *Imperatives!*

Complete the table below by providing the correct imperative forms for the verbs in the imperfect. The top left-hand corner has been completed by way of example:

	yijī	*yugūm*	*yizīd*	*yibda'*	*yixallī*	*yugūl*
ant	*jī*					
antī						
antū						
antayn						

6. *Question formation*

Say that you want the following objects and ask if they are available:

Example: tea ———> *aštī šahay, šī šahay?*

i. coffee ______________________

ii. bread ______________________

iii. a newspaper ______________________

iv. sugar ______________________

v. juice ______________________

7. *Word stress*

Put the word-stress mark * before the stressed syllable in the following words.

Example: *murabba*^{c} —–> *mu*rabba*^{c}

i. *gurnih* ii. *makālif* iii. *xāsir* iv. *lā*^{c}*ibīn* v. *lāḥigih* vi. *banādig*

vii. *zaggaytak* viii. *murabba*^{c}*āt* ix. *ḥabl* x. *w-iyyāhum*

8. *Translation*

Translate the following groups of sentences into Ṣanᶜānī Arabic:

A. Use *inn*

i. I said that I wanted to chew *gāt*.

ii. My brother said that he wanted to buy a newspaper.

iii. They m. said that they wanted to have lunch.

B. Numbers

i. Four or five children came.

ii. The sugar is twenty or thirty riyals a kilo.

iii. They m. are at the age of six or seven.

C. Conditional sentences

i. If they m. can go they m. will be captured.

ii. If he comes here he will be imprisoned.

iii. If he were in Yemen he would play in the alley.

D. Relative clauses

i. This is the most expensive *gāt* I have chewed.

ii. This is the cheapest *saltih* I have eaten.

iii. These are the most beautiful clothes she has bought.

E. Arithmetic

i. Two and two equals four.

ii. Six divided by three equals two.

iii. Ten times ten equals a hundred.

LESSON 17

Aš-šikmih

Dialogue 1 *aš-šikmih*

Halima: *ḥayyā!*

Shelagh: *allāh yiḥayyīš yā ḥalīmih, kayfīš?*

Halima: *bi-xayrih wa-l-ḥamdu li-llāh, kayfīš antī?*

Shelagh: *al-ḥamdu li-llāh. ṭawwal* ^{c}*umriš, gulī lī yā ḥalīmih, mā hī š-šikmih?*

Halima: *nāhī sma*^{c}*ī, aš-šikmih hī ba*^{c}*d yawm as-sābi*^{c}*, yawm as-sābi*^{c} *ba*^{c}*d az-zifāf allaḏī yjaw fīh bayt al-ḥarīwih, maṯalan ummī wa-xawātī wa-*^{c}*ammatī yitġaddaw* ^{c}*indī fī bayt al-ḥarīw wa-y*^{c}*aṣṣubū l-*^{c}*uṣbuh, wa-bih šwayyat ma*^{c}*āzīm wa-ba*^{c}*dā ba*^{c}*d al-ġadā, yijayn nisā wa-nxazzin wa-hāḏā. ba*^{c}*dā l-ḥarīwih tijiss šwayyih* ^{c}*ind ahlahā wa-yšillūhā* ^{c}*ind al-ḥarīw, hāḏā yawm as-sābi*^{c}*. wa-ba*^{c}*d yawm as-sābi*^{c} *gadū yawm aš-šikmih. ahlī yjaw yitġaddaw fī bayt al-ḥarīw yawm as-sābi*^{c} *wa-l-ahl, ahlī 'anā sa*^{c}*am, yiriddu l-*^{c}*azūmih yawm aš-šikmih.*

Shelagh: *wa-man yiḥaddid al-maw*^{c}*id, man yiḥaddid maw*^{c}*id aš-šikmih?*

Halima: *al-ahl hum allaḏī yiḥaddidūh.*

Shelagh: *ahl al-ḥarīwih sa*^{c}*am?*

Halima: *nāhī. ya*^{c}*nī hū miš maw*^{c}*id muḥaddid, ayy maw*^{c}*id. al-muhimm innahum yirajji*^{c}*u l-ġadā yiġaddīhum. maṯalan lā jaw min ahlī xamsih lā* ^{c}*ind bayt al-ḥarīw yawm as-sābi*^{c} *yiriddū* ^{c}*ašarih ma*^{c}*āzīm yawm aš-šikmih w-iḏā jaw* ^{c}*ašarih yiddaw* ^{c}*išrīn. ya*^{c}*nī zāyid ḍa*^{c}*f al-kammīyih.*

Shelagh: *lāzim yizayyidū l-kammīyih?*

Halima: *aywih, hāḏā lāzim fī yawm aš-šikmih. fa-š-šikmih gadī 'āxir šī fī l-*^{c}*iris. yawm aš-šikmih bi-sammaw al-ḥarīwih šākimih. wa-bih ḥarāwī mā yuxrujanš min bayt zawjahā, mā yuxrujanš lā xārij wa-lā yuxrujayn dawrih illā law-mā škumūhā.*

Shelagh: *wa-*^{c}*ād bih nās yixallaw al-ḥarīwih šahr mā?*

Halima: *aywih, bih nās* ^{c}*ala t-taglīd al-lawwal yixallawhā ġarr šahr kāmil fī bayt zawjahā wa-mā gadīš lā ᶜindahum law-ma tsīr titġaddā ᶜindahum wa-baᶜdā ᶜa-tuxruj ᶜādī. yaᶜnī dalḥīn bih ḥarāwī ᶜādin zawwajayn wa-ᶜādin mā yuxrujanš maṯalan anā gul lahin jay lā ᶜindanā tugūl mā gad škumūnī law-mā yškimūnī w-anā šā-jī.*

Shelagh: *wa-l-yawm gad bih nās bi-škumū fī-sāᶜ mā?*

Halima: *ṣaḥḥ, ḏalḥīn bih nās bi-škumū fī-sāᶜ ᶜašān tuxruj, maṯalan yawm al-xamīs yūgaᶜ as-sābiᶜ yawm al-xamīs aṯ-ṯānī tūgaᶜ aš-šikmih yugūlū ᶜalā sibb tistir tuxruj. wa-ᶜād bih nās yištaw sāᶜ awwal šahr kāmil sāᶜ al-wālidih. al-wālidih mā tuxrujš illā baᶜd-ma tkammil al-arbaᶜīn yawm. hāḏā ḥaggana š-šikmih.*

Dialogue 2 *al-farḥah*

law-mā fī l-wilād, law-mā nsīr nifraḥ li-l-wālidih, nisammīhā ṭabᶜan al-farḥah, wa-nsīr niddī lahā miyih aw xamsīn, yaᶜnī kull wāḥid ᶜalā-mā yištī, ᶜalā kayfih. lāzim innū yiddī lhā farḥah yimmā zalaṭ aw hadīyih la-n-nīnī. niddī lahā šāl aw baṭṭāniyuh aw ayy ḥājih min hāḏi l-ḥājāt. w-iḏā hī bint niddī lhā xrāṣ aw xāṭam. wallā niddī zinnih la-l-lumm. al-muhimm inn iḥna lāzim inn iḥna nddī lahā ḥājih. nisammī hāḏa l-farḥah. fa-law-ma tkammil al-larbaᶜīn yawm ḥīn tūlad wāḥidih ṯāniyih min allaḏī ddaw lahā, lāzim innī tiridd lahā l-farḥah. iḏā jābat lahā miyih tiridd lahā miyih, w-iḏā jābat lahā zinnih tiddī lahā zinnih, w-iḏā ddit lā bint axrāṣ tirajjiᶜ lā bint axrāṣ. lāzim al-hadīyih lāzim tirajjiᶜhā fī wilād aṯ-ṯāniyih. maṯalan ana ddī liš hadīyih wa-law-mā ntī tkammilī w-ana wham w-awlad intī trajjiᶜī nafs al-hadīyih.

Vocabulary [1]

ᶜalā kayfih	as he likes	*ᶜamm* pl. *aᶜmūm*	paternal uncle; father-in-law m.
ᶜammih pl. *-āt*	paternal aunt; mother-in-law f.	*ᶜašān*	so that; because
		ᶜaṣṣab - yiᶜaṣṣub	to put on a head-band

[1] Revise also thematic vocabulary in Lesson 9.

^{c}azūmih	invitation f.	*baṭṭāniyuh* pl. *-āt*	blanket f.
ḏa^{c}f pl. *aḏ^{c}āf*	double m.	*fī-sā^c*	quickly
ġaddā - yiġaddī	to give (s.o.) lunch	*ġarr / ġayr*	only
ḥaddad - yiḥaddid	to establish; determine	*hadīyih* pl. *hadāyā*	present f.
ḥīn	when adjt.	*kāmil*	whole
kammīyih	amount f.	*ma^{c}zūm* pl. *ma^{c}āzīm*	guest m.
muḥaddid	determined; certain	*radd - yiridd*	to return (s.th.)
sā^c awwal	as before	*šākimih* pl. *-āt*	parturient; newly married woman on day of *šikmih*
šikmih	day bride's family invites groom's family after the wedding		
šakkam - yišakkim	to perform the *šikmih* (for s.o.)	*taglīd* pl. *tagālīd*	tradition m.
aṯ-ṯānī	the next	*wālidih* pl. *-āt*	parturient f.
xarṣ pl. *axrāṣ*	earring m.	*yā 'immā / yimmā… aw*	either … or
zawwaj - yizawwij	to get married	*zāyid*	increase
zayyid - yizayyid	to increase (s.th.)		

Grammar

1. *Pronunciation: contraction of words*

A common feature of Ṣan^{c}ānī Arabic is the contraction of words in rapid speech, particularly when the sound *š* is in the word. Thus form II verbs in the imperfect may be contracted in such a way as they sound like form I verbs:

^{c}a-yišakkimūnī — 'they will give me a *šikmih* party'

is contracted to

^{c}a-yškimūnī or *yškumūnī* — 'they will give me a *šikmih* party'

The verb 'to make *šfūṭ*' (cf. Lesson 20) is *šaffaṭ - yišaffiṭ*. In rapid speech the imperfect is contracted to:

^{c}a-yšfiṭ or ^{c}a-yšfuṭ — 'he will make *šfūṭ*'

Nouns of the pattern KVTBih may be contracted to KTBih (cf. Lesson 7). Thus:

šikmih — '*šikmih* party'

is contracted to

škmih	'*šikmih* party'

Nouns of the pattern KVTih may be contracted to KTih:

marih 'woman'

is contracted to

mrih 'woman'

Nouns of the pattern KVTVB may be contracted to KTVB:

xašab 'wood'

is contracted to

xšab 'wood'

2. *Greetings*

Two common variants of *kayf ḥālak* 'how are you?', etc. involve either suffixing the pronoun suffix to *kayf*, as in the dialogue in this lesson:

kayf + iš	*kayfiš*
'how' 'you f.s.'	'how are you f.s.?'

Or simply adding the independent pronoun to *kayf*, as in:

kayf + ant	*kayf ant*
'how' 'you m.s.'	'how are you m.s.?

When the speaker wants to emphasize *you* in the replying greeting, the independent pronoun follows the initial greeting, and receives most sentence stress. This is most common when *kayf* takes the pronoun suffix, as in:

kayfak ant 'how are *you* m.s.?'

3. '*Well*'

The phrase *bi-xayr* 'well' can function both as a prepositional phrase and as an adjective. When it functions as a prepositional phrase it does not inflect for gender or number:

gadanā bi-xayr	'I am well'
gadī bi-xayr	'she is well'
gadiḥna bi-xayr	'we are well'

gadin bi-xayr	'they f. are well'

When *bi-xayr* functions as if it is no longer a prepositional phrase, rather a single-word adjective, it takes the full range of inflectional endings:

gadanā bixayr	'I am well'
*gadī bixayr**rih***	'she is well'
*gadiḥna bixayr**rīn***	'we are well'
*gadin bixayr**rāt***	'they f. are well'

As an adjective, *bixayr* has the elative cognate *abxar* 'better' (*Syntax* pp. 32-33):

hāḏā 'abxar mimmā kān	'this m. is better than it was'
iddī lī 'abxar ṭāyur	'give m.s. me the best bird'

4. *'A little...' 'A few ...'*

The idea of 'a little', or 'few' of something is conveyed by the word *šwayyih* + *min* + *definite* noun, or by *šwayyat* plus an *indefinite* noun annex. When the noun is a *count* noun - that is to say, the noun describes something which can be counted, such as 'guests', 'animals', 'tyres', 'pens', etc. - the noun annex or the noun following *min* is in the plural:

šwayyih min al-ma^{c}āzīm	'a few of the guests'
šwayyat ma^{c}āzīm	'a few guests'

When the noun is a *non-count* noun - that is to say, the noun describes a collective (cf. Lesson 18), or something which cannot be counted, such as 'cattle', 'flour', 'food', etc. - the noun annex or the noun following *min* is in the singular:

iddī lī šwayyih min ad-dagīg	'give m.s. me a little of the flour!'
iddī lī šwayyat dagīg	'give m.s. me a little flour!'

5. *Tag clauses: '... and the like', '... and so on'*

In colloquial English, we often use tag clauses at the end of a sentence to prevent the sentence from ending abruptly. These tag clauses include '...and the like', '...and so on', '...and all', and '...or whatever'. Tag clauses are also common in colloquial Arabic. One such tag clause is used in the dialogue in this lesson, *wa-*

hāḏā 'lit: and this'. Other common tag clauses include *wa-hākaḏā* 'and the like', *wa-l-kull* 'and all', and *aw šī* 'lit: or (some)thing' (for other examples, cf. *Syntax* pp. 384-385). For example:

lā sabbarat al-ġadā wa-l-kull	'if she made lunch and all'
iḏā xarajat rijliš aw šī	'if your leg went out or whatever'
nisīr nitfarraṭ wa-hāḏā	'we go to a party and the like'

6. *Verbal nouns of form V, VIII and X verbs*

6.1. Verbal nouns of form V verbs

There are a number of patterns for the verbal noun of form V verbs. Four common patterns are:

pattern	verbal noun	verb	gloss
taKaTTāB	*ta*^{c}*akkāl*	*t*^{c}*akkal*	hopping
	ta^{c}*allām*	*t*^{c}*allam*	learning
tiKiTTāB	*tigillāb*	*tgallab*	inversion; upturning
	tibinnān	*tbannan*	eating well
taKaTTuB	*ta*^{c}*akkul*	*t*^{c}*akkal*	hopping
KiTTāBih	*ġissālih*	*tġassal*	act of washing

Other patterns include KaTTāB (cf. Lesson 12) and KaTTāBih.

6.2. Verbal nouns of form VIII verbs

There is one common verbal noun pattern for form VIII verbs, KtiTāB; however, form VIII verbs often take the same verbal noun as the corresponding form I verb:

pattern	verbal noun	verb	gloss
KtiTāB	*xtiyār*	*xtār*	choice
or	*xīrih*		
KtiTāB	*ltibāj*	*ltabaj*	striking; hitting
or	*labj*		
	ḥabs	*ḥtabas*	prison

6.3. Verbal nouns of form X verbs

There is one common verbal noun pattern for form X verbs, stiKTāB:

pattern	verbal noun	verb	gloss
stiKTāB	*stikbār*	*stakbar*	arrogance
	stiġrāb	*staġrab*	surprise

7. *Negation: 'neither ... nor'*

'Neither ... nor' is translated as *miš/mā/lā ... wa-lā*. 'Neither' translates as *mā* or *lā*, and also as *miš* before prepositional phrases with a noun annex, independent pronouns, nouns or adjectives; 'nor' translates as *wa-lā* (cf. *Syntax* pp. 259-260, cf. also Lesson 14). When 'neither' is translated as *mā* or *lā*, the negative suffix *-š* is optional when the word following *mā* is a pronoun, a verb or a prepositional phrase with a pronominal suffix. An example of *mā ... wa-lā* in the first dialogue in this lesson is:

mā yuxrujanš lā xārij wa-lā yuxrujayn dawrih	'they f. neither go outside nor do they go on a trip'
al-mafrūḏ mā yitkallimanš wa-lā yitḥākayn	'they f. should neither talk nor chat'

Other examples include:

al-bint mā tākul wa-lā tišrab	'the girl doesn't eat or drink'
mā ᶜādant fi l-bayt wa-lā fi s-sūg	'you m.s. are no longer in the house, nor in the market place'
lā samn fīhā wa-lā birr	'there is no butter in it and no wheat'

Examples of *miš ... wa-lā* include:

al-bint mišī kisilih wa-lā tāᶜibih	'the girl isn't lazy or tired'
hū miš yamanī wa-lā sūrī	'he is neither Yemeni nor Syrian'

mišū fī l-bayt wa-lā fī s-sūg	'he is neither in the house nor in the market'

8. *'Rather than ...'*

Wa-lā 'and not' is not only used in the sense of 'nor' but can also mean 'rather than' (cf. *Syntax* p. 260). This is particularly the case in proverbs. Two (usually indefinite) nouns joined by *wa-lā* means that the thing described by the first noun or noun phrase is better than that described by the second noun. For example:

ᶜirsayn	*wa-la*	*wlād*	'two marriages rather than children'
'two-marriages'	'and-not'	'children'	

In other words, two marriages are better than (less expensive than) children. Other examples include:

ramlih ġāliyih wa-lā zawj raxīṣ	'an expensive widow rather than a cheap husband'
ḍarbuh min usṭā wa-lā ᶜašar min mitᶜallim	'one strike from a master is better than ten from an apprentice'

9. *Adverbs: more on 'only'*

In Lesson 12, we considered two ways of expressing 'only': *bass* and *mā bi-lā*. In Lesson 14, we considered a third way, *mā ... illā*, also more literally translated as 'not ... unless/until'. The dialogue in this lesson has yet another way of expressing the sense of 'only'. This involves the word *ġarr* or *ġayr*; *ġarr* or *ġayr* is similar to the phrase *mā bi-lā* in that it comes before the term which is limited:

	gāl yištī ġarr hāḏā	'he said he wants only that'
compare		
	gāl yištī mā bi-lā hāḏā	'he said he wants nothing but that'

The example in the dialogue in this lesson is:

yixallawhā ġarr šahr kāmil	'they can only leave her for a whole month'

10. *Number phrases: 'the forty days'*

In a definite noun phrase in Arabic it is usual for both the noun and the adjective to take the definite article (cf. Lesson 4):

al-bayt *al-kabīr* 'the-house' 'the-big'	'the big house'

When a definite noun phrase involves an initial number from eleven upwards, however, only the number takes the definite article, as in:

*al-arba*ᶜ*īn yawm* 'the-forty' 'day'	'the forty days'

In addition, while the numbers from three to ten take a following *plural* noun:

aṯ-ṯalāṯ *al-banāt* 'the-three' 'the-girls'	'the three girls'
sittih xuṭūṭ 'six' 'lines'	'six lines'

the numbers from eleven upwards[2] take a following *singular* noun:

*al-ḥid*ᶜ*ašar* *jāhil* 'the-eleven' 'child'	'the eleven children'
*al-xamsat*ᶜ*ašar* *bint* 'the-fifteen' 'girl'	'the fifteen girls'
al-miyat *alf* 'the-hundred' 'thousand'	'the hundred thousand'
al-miyat *yawm* 'the-hundred' 'day'	'the hundred days'

11. *'One of my friends'*

Phrases such as 'one of my friends', 'one of my colleagues', 'one of my brothers' (or 'a friend [/brother/colleague] of mine') are translated into Ṣanᶜānī Arabic by

[2] The numbers in the phrases 'twelve girls', 'thirteen stairs' and 'fourteen bunches (of *gāt*)' are incorrectly given as ending in *-āš* befor e the noun rather than *-ašar* on p. 248 of *Syntax*.

wāḥid(ih) + zamīl(at)ī with the word for 'friends', 'colleagues', 'brothers' in the *singular* (cf. *Syntax* p. 175). The word *wāḥid* is masculine (i.e. *wāḥid*) when the following noun is masculine:

wāḥid	*ṣāḥubī*	'one f. of my friends f.'
'one m.'	'friend m.-my'	

and feminine (i.e. *wāḥidih*) when the following noun is feminine:

wāḥidih	*zamīlatī*	'one f. of my friends f.'
'one f.'	'friend f.-my'	

In order to say 'a Sudanese (/Yemeni) friend of mine' ('one of my Sudanese friends'), for example, the adjective is indefinite and follows the second noun:

wāḥidih zamīlatī sūdānīyih	'a Sudanese friend f. of mine'
wāḥid ṣāḥubī yamanī	'a Yemeni friend m. of mine'

Exercises

1. *Comprehension*

A. Re-read the first dialogue of this lesson and answer the following questions in English:

i. When does the bride's family have lunch with the family of the groom?

ii. Who comes to have lunch with the bride?

iii. What do they wear?

iv. What happens on the day of the *šikmih*?

v. Who decides what day the *šikmih* will be?

vi. How many people does the bride's family invite back?

vii. What may the bride do after the *šikmih*?

viii. How long do some people leave the bride until the *šikmih*?

B. Re-read the second dialogue of this lesson and answer the following questions in English:

i. How much money do people give the new mother?

ii. What else may people give to the new mother?

iii. What would they give to a new-born girl?

iv. What happens when someone who has given the mother a present then has a baby herself?

2. *Phrase identification*

A. Identify the Arabic for the following phrases in the text *aš-šikmih*. The phrases are given in the order in which they occur in the text.

i. There are a few guests.

ii. After the seventh day it is the day of *šikmih*.

iii. It isn't a definite time.

iv. The important thing is that they return the lunch and have them for lunch.

v. The *šikmih* is the last thing in a wedding.

vi. There are [some] brides who don't go outside or go on a trip.

vii. She doesn't go to them until she goes to have lunch with them.

B. Identify the Arabic for the following phrases in the text *al-farḥah*. The phrases are given in the order in which they occur in the text.

i. We go to give her 100 or 50.

ii. We give her a present - either money or a present for the baby.

iii. The important thing is that we give her something.

iv. She has to give back the present.

v. When you finish and I get pregnant and give birth you give back the same present.

3. *Greetings*

Give appropriate replies to the following greetings:

i. *msaytū!* ____________________

ii. *mā lukum šī!* ____________________

iii. *kaṯṯar allāh min xayrukum!* ____________________

iv. *tiṣbaḥū ᶜala l-xayr!* ____________________

v. *maᶜa s-salāmih!* ____________________

vi. *ṣbaḥtū!* ____________________

4. *Possession*

Replace the noun - possessive pronoun phrase in the following sentences with noun + a phrase involving *ḥagg*:

Example: *tannūrkin min ḥadīd maṣnūᶜ* ———> *at-tannūr* ***ḥaggakin*** *min ḥadīd maṣnūᶜ*

i. *waynū zawjiš?* ____________________

ii. *bayn-asīr baytak.* ____________________

iii. *aglāmih ᶜādhin fi l-faṣl* [= classroom]. ____________________

iv. *sirwāliš ḥālī marrih.* ____________________

v. *nixazzin fi makānkum.* ____________________

vi. *al-maṣriyīn madāᶜathum maṣnūᶜah min az-zujāj* [= glass]. __

____

5. *Negation*

Negate the following sentences:

Example: *hum fi l-bayt jālisīn* ———> *mišum fi l-bayt jālisīn*

i. *ašti bsiriš ġudwuh.* ____________________

ii. *jamīlih ᶜādī fī l-ḥawī.* ____________________

iii. *al-bint gadī ᶜāṭušuh gawī.* ____________________

iv. *ddī lī šwayyat dagīg.* ____________________

v. *al-makālif gad xarajayn dawrih.* ____________________

6. *'Neither ... nor'*

Answer the following questions negatively using *mā/lā/miš ... wa-lā*:

Example: *ᶜa-tsīr tištarī lak gāt wa-ḥilbih ——> mā šā-sirš aštarī lī gāt wa-lā ḥilbih*

i. *tisīrayn titfarraṭayn wa-txazzinayn? māšī,* ____________________

ii. *antī dārī kayf tsawwī saltih wa-tuxbuzī? māšī,* ____________________

____

iii. *as-sūg baᶜīdih min hānā wa-ġālī? māšī,* ____________________

____

iv. *šī mšakkal wa-līm? māšī,* ____________________

v. *šī bih saltih wa-ruzz? māšī,* ____________________

vi. *al-jaᶜālih fīhā zabīb wa-lawz? māšī,* ____________________

7. *'Only ...'*

Answer the following questions using the information in brackets and saying there is only ....

Example: *šī ġadā (saltih) ——> aywih, bass mā bi-lā saltih*

i. *šī malūj?* (one). *aywih, bass* ____________________

ii. *šī dafātir?* (three). *aywih,* ____________________

iii. *šī bih zalaṭ?* (ten *riyāls*). *aywih,* ____________________

iv. *šī madāᶜah?* (in the *mafraj*). ____________________

v. *šī bih širki l-yawm?* (beef). ____________________

vi. *šī ja^{c}ālih?* (raisins). ______________________

8. *'There's no lunch at all!'*

Answer the questions in 5. above negatively using the phrase *wa-lā*:

Example: *šī ġadā?* ————> *mā biš (ma^{c}ānā) ġadā wa-lā!*

9. *Translation*

Translate the following groups of sentences into Ṣan^{c}ānī Arabic:

A. Use *lā/mā … wa-lā*

i. Salih has not gone to the market, nor is he still in the house.

ii. We have not bought *gāt* or *saltih*.

iii. There is neither flour in it nor eggs.

iv. The tobacco in the waterpipe is neither wet nor dry.

B. Use *wa-lā!*

i. This m. isn't expensive at all!

ii. I haven't got a *riyāl*!

iii. He doesn't speak Yemeni at all!

C. Number phrases

i. She has finished the forty days.

ii. Where are the fifteen boys?

iii. The eighteen girls went out yesterday.

D. Relative clauses

i. Who is the girl who visited you f.s.?

ii. What is the food which we ate yesterday?

iii. What is the present which I have to return to her?

LESSON 18

Al-gāt fī l-yaman

Dialogue 1 *al-gāt*

b-ism illāh ar-raḥmān ar-raḥīm. ana šā-tkallim ^{c}an al-gāt. al-gāt hāḏā hū bi-zra^c fī l-yaman, w-hū ^{c}ayyinih min al-ašjār al-xaḏrā. wuṣul ilā l-yaman hānā a^{c}tagid ^{c}an ṭarīg al-ḥabaših, miš ^{c}ārif matā wuṣul yimkin fī ^{c}ahd abrahā. al-muhimm u-gad ista^{c}malih abrahā l-ḥabašī hāḏā fī zamān. jā' al-yaman ^{c}an ṭarīg iṯiyūbīyā wa-ziri^{c}at šijarāt al-gāt, māniš ^{c}ārif matā ya^{c}nī ziri^{c}at, lākin hū šijar xaḏrā bi-zra^c hānā fī l-yaman. hū ^{c}ayyināt kaṯīrih u-bih lih 'asāmī allī ysammīh as-sawtī w-allī ysammīh al-baladī w-allī ysammīh al-ḥamdānī. ya^{c}nī kull ^{c}ayyinih min al-gāt lahā 'ism. wa-lammā tgul lih ḥamdānī wallā ḥagg al-gariyih hāḏā gadū al-gāt al-bāhir wallā ḏulā^{c}ī. hāḏā gadū al-gāt al-ḥālī llī bi-^{c}jib an-nās kulluhum al-bāhir. fa-bī-jī ^{c}alā šakl ^{c}īdān ṭawīluh. ya^{c}nī hī bi-tizra^c ka-'ašjār. maṯalan miṯl al-gāt al-baladī hāḏā hū bī-jī ṭawīl zayy aš-šajarih al-kabīrih, wa-ba^{c}dā yigaṭṭufūh, ya^{c}nī yigaṭṭu^{c}ū š-šijar. iḥna ngūl yigaṭṭufu š-šijar. yigaṭṭu^{c}ū minhā al-^{c}īdān ḥagg al-gāt ya^{c}nī aš-šijni l-wāḥid hāḏā bī-jī fīh ^{c}īdān kaṯīrih. wa-ṭab^{c}an al-gāt hāḏā bī-jī lih ar-rās ḥaggih bī-jī gadū mizhir waragih. gad al-mugawwit hū aš-šaxṣ allī bi-zri^{c}ih, gadū dārī bih. al-gabīlī gadū dārī 'ayyin allī yigba^{c}ūh wa-yigaṭṭufūh fī ṣ-ṣabāḥ al-bākir, ya^{c}nī min aṣ-ṣabāḥ yibakkirū yigaṭṭu^{c}ūh, yigaṭṭufūh. wa-yijī l-mugawwit yštī yštarī min al-gabīlī, yištarī b-rxīṣ, wa-yiwaṣṣul lā s-sūg. akṯarat al-mugawwitīn gadum m^{c}arrafīn ^{c}ind an-nās. maṯalan gad al-wāḥid yit^{c}āmal ^{c}alā mgawwit mi^{c}ayyan. gadū yi^{c}rifih, yisīr ḏayyak al-wagt aḏ-ḏuhr yisīr yištarī l-gāt min ^{c}indih. wa-l-gāt hāḏā bī-xazzinūh al-yamanīyīn yimkin ṯamānīn fī l-miyih aw akṯar. kull al-yamanīyīn aṣbaḥ innum bi-yākulū l-gāt lannum bī-gul lak mā biš ma f^{c}al ajiss axazzin. kull wāḥid bī-gul lak mā biš ma f^{c}al li'annū mā bi-štaġil illā ṣ-ṣabāḥ, w-ba^{c}d aḏ-ḏuhr hāḏā gadū muhtamm bi-l-gāt. f-kull wāḥid ^{c}ind aḏ-ḏuhr hāḏā bī-sīr yištarī l-gāt ḥaggih, allī bi-štarī l-baladī w-allī bi-štarī s-sawtī w-allī bi-štarī l-^{c}ānisī w-allī bi-štarī l-

ġaylī. gad bih asmā' kaṯīrih. mā kān minn awwal mā ni^{c}raf illā sawtī wa-baladī, lākin ma^{c} kuṯrat allī bī-xazzinū l-mixazzinīn uṣbaḥ al-gāt yizra^{c} fī kull bug^{c}ah. wallā mā minn awwal allī ^{c}a-yxazzin mā yxazzin illā bih gāt sawā, māšī tibsirī 'ahl ṣan^{c}ā hāḏā lā gad al-gāt bāyit mā raḏawš yištaraw. al-mugawwit yiddaw li-man yibī^{c}. yifalliṭuh wa-yiftaja^{c} lā gad al-gāt ^{c}aybāt ^{c}alayh wa-yidawwir man yjī yištarī min ^{c}indih bi-kam-mā kān, ya^{c}nī yibi^{c} lak bi-z-zalaṭ allī yištī hū, bi-s-si^{c}r allī yišti l-mgawwit, māšī mā ^{c}ād yibi^{c}š fa-gadū yirkan ann iḏā ma štaraytš ana yjī ^{c}ind wāḥid ṯānī yištarī minnih. iḏā gal lak bi-miyatayn girš w-ant mā ^{c}a-tsīr tidfa^{c} illā xamsīn girš mā yirḏāš li'annum bī-jaw li-nās ma^{c}āhum zalaṭ hāḏawlāk at-tujjār allī bī-jaw yidfa^{c}ū flūs allī kam-mā gāl al-mugawwit. al-gāt hū miškilih hānā fī l-yaman li'ann al-insān iḏā hū mwaḏḏaf mā mi^{c}ih illā l-ma^{c}āš mā yiddī. yiṭuffī gāt awlā yiṭuffī fī 'akl wa-šarbih wa-ḏay illī lā jahhālih. gad al-maṯal bī-gūl kam ad-dīk wa-kam al-marag. hāḏā maṯal yamanī yigul lak kam ad-dīk wa-kam allī marag. ya^{c}nī ma^{c}ak dīk wa-ma^{c}ak ^{c}išrīn wāḥid. kam ^{c}a-yākulū min ad-dīk wa-kam ^{c}a-yšrabū l-marag ḥaggih. kam ad-dīk wa-kam maragih.

Dialogue 2 ***al-jalsih wa-l-xazzān***

al-yamanīyīn w-allāh kulluhum bī-xazzinū. ya^{c}nī māhūš innū wāḥid awla ṯnayn. al-muhimm innū kull wāḥid bī-sīr yštarī fī ḏ-ḏuhr hāḏā fī 'awgāt aḏ-ḏuhr. aswāg al-gāt gadī kaṯīrih ḏalḥīnih minn awwal mā kān biš illā galīlih yā sawtī yā baladī. tijī li-l-gāt wa-txazzin gadak tittafig ^{c}ind aṣḥābak. tugul lhum w-allāh al-yawm nixazzin jam^{c}ah, aw yigul lak wāḥid aṣḥābak ^{c}a-tjī l-yawm tixazzin ^{c}indī wa-gad ^{c}a-yjaw ^{c}indī flān wa-flān wa-^{c}a-yjī ḏayyā, ya^{c}nī l-xubrih. gadum ujtama^{c}ū fī bayt wāḥid hāḏawlāk allī njiss nixazzin iḥna w-iyyāhum, wallā ^{c}ind wāḥid gadum yijtami^{c}ū kull yawm gad kull wāḥid yidrā 'innū ^{c}a-yxazzin fī l-bayt al-flānī. gad kull wāḥid yiddī gātih, wa-nsīr ^{c}ind ḏayyā llī ^{c}azzam ann nixazzin ^{c}indih. zārathīn tilgā ḏayyā llī ^{c}a-txazzin ^{c}indih gadū yiddī ṯalājāt ḥagg al-mā', yimillīhin bi-l-mā', wa-yiṭraḥ al-barādig wa-ygaddim aṭ-ṭufāyāt ya^{c}nī ḥājāt allī ^{c}a-yitgahwaw allī ^{c}a-yxazzinū ^{c}indih kulluhum. lākin hāḏi l-iyyām gad tigtalib al-

lumūr mā ^{c}ād yif^{c}alūš fī hāda l-wagt. lā bih wāḥid bi-xazzin ^{c}ind an-nās kull yawm kull yawm kull yawm gadū zabal. gadū ma^{c} hādā bi-ji bi-ftaḥ baytih ahla wa-sahla bass ġarr inn mā gad kull wāḥid ya^{c}nī yiddī gātih wa-yddi l-gāt ḥaggih wa-yddī l-mā ḥaggih wa-yddī ḥājātih ma^{c}ih, lannū dā 'ant bi-txazzin fī l-bayt hādā yawmīyih kam jā li-ṣāḥub al-bayt yiddī lak mā' wa-yiddī lak bibs wa-hāda llī yštī madā^{c}ah wa-hādā šuġlih. ya^{c}nī l-madā^{c}ah tištī nār. wa-n-nār tištī man yigūm ywahhif lhā wa-yiṣalluḥū hādā. inna 'ašyā gadī ṣa^{c}buh. al-ān gadū kull wāḥid yiddī gāt u-māhuh, wa-ṣāḥub al-bayt mā bī-gaṣṣarš illī bi-txazzin ^{c}indih mā bī-gaṣṣarš, yiddī kull šī. hādā min nāḥiyih. ba^{c}dā mujtama^{c}īn mixazzinīn fī bayt wāḥid, nijiss nitjābar. kull wāḥid ġarr bi-ddī ya^{c}nī kull wāḥid yištī yitḥākā ^{c}ādū fāriġ mā gad xazzanš kull wāḥid bi-tḥākā: dayyā bi-ddī guṣṣuh wa-dayyā bi-ddī s-syāsih wa-dayyā bi-yitḥākā, wa-dayyā bi-yizbij. al-muhimm kull wāḥid bi-tkallim tijī an-nušṭuh la s-sā^{c}ah ka-dayyāhā xams. mā tibsir law gad al-makān dayyā kān hādawlā llī gad ṣayyaḥū mā ^{c}ād biš. gad kulluhum ġarr sākitīn gadū yiṭannunū ma^{c} al-gāt. allī bi-ḥsub bi-kam ištara l-gāt al-yawm; w-allī bi-yiḥsub ġudwuh minayn ^{c}a-yjī gīmat al-gāt; w-allī bī-fakkir fī mašākilih; gad al-wāḥid ġayr muṭannun bī-fakkir wa-dayyā gadū law-mā mā bih ḥadd yitḥākā gadū ġarr bī-xaddir wa-bī-fakkir fī mašākilih fī 'umūrih mā ma^{c}ih ġudwuh min ^{c}amal mā ^{c}a-ysabbir min ġudwuh wallā ba^{c}d ġudwuh. wa-ṭūl al-wagt al-wāḥid ġarr fī lugfih hādā bi-yākul bi-yākul bi-yu^{c}raṭ al-gāt sā^{c}atayn ṯalāṯ wa-bi-yu^{c}raṭ al-gāt. gadak ġarr tisma^{c} min as-sā^{c}ah xams zārat wāḥid yiddī kalimih gadū yitḥākā min mawḍū^{c} - fī s-syāsih aw igtiṣād ḥagg al-bilād aw ayy xabar yiṭla^{c} fī rās al-wāḥid. wa-ba^{c}dā min ba^{c}d al-maġrib hādakā gad kull wāḥid yigūm yiriḥ lih. kull wāḥid yiriḥ lih ayyaḥīn-ma štā ya^{c}nī allī bī-riḥ lih s-sā^{c}ah sitt wa-nuṣṣ w-allī bī-riḥ lih sab^{c} w-allī m^{c}ih ^{c}amal bī-gūm baḥīn w-allī mā biš ma^{c}ih ^{c}amal yštī yijiss yiġinn ya^{c}nī yijiss yiftahin mā gadūš ^{c}a-yriḥ lih awlā šī iḥna ngūl yiġinn. hādā yijlis lā ṯamān lā tis^{c}, wa-gadū wagt mḥaddad gad kull wāḥid ma^{c}ih wagt mḥaddad yigūm yiriḥ lih la-l-bayt ba^{c}d al-gāt. wa-hādā ḥagg al-gāt, wa-yawmīyih hākadā min yawm lā yawm.

Vocabulary

abrahā	Abraha [male name]	^{c}*ahd* pl. ^{c}*uhūd*	time; era m.
ahla wa-sahla	welcome!	*akṯarat al-…*	most of the …
al-ān	now	^{c}*alā šakl*	in the form of
amr pl. *umūr*	matter; thing f.	^{c}*an ṭarīg*	via
^{c}*araṭ - yu*^{c}*raṭ*	to gnaw (s.th.)	*aṣbaḥ*	to become
^{c}*aybih* pl. *-āt*	defect f.	*ayyin*	which
^{c}*ayyinih* pl. *-āt*	type f.	^{c}*azzam - yi*^{c}*azzim*	to invite (s.o.)
bahār pl. *-āt*	worry f.	*bāhir*	very good
bakkar - yibakkir	to do (s.th.) early	*bākir*	early
baladī	local	*bardag* pl. *barādig*	glass; cup m.
bāyit	bad; corrupt	*bug*^{c}*ah* pl. *buga*^{c}	place; spot f.
dawwar - yidawwir	to look for (s.th.)	*dīk* pl. *adyāk*	cockeral m.
ḍulā^{c}*ī*	from Dulā^{c} [famous *gāt*-growing area in Hamdān]	*fakkar - yifakkir*	to think
fallaṭ - yifalliṭ	to leave (s.th.)	*fāriġ* pl. *furġān*	empty; free
flūs	money m.	*ftahan - ftahin*	to relax
ftaja^{c} *- yiftaja*^{c}	to be surprised	*gā*^{c} pl. *gi*^{c}*ān*	ground; floor m.
gaba^{c} *- yigba*^{c}	to take (s.th.)	*gabīlī* pl. *gabāyil*	tribesman m.
gaddam - yigaddim	to give; offer (s.o., s.th.)	*ġann - yiġinn*	to relax
gaṣṣar - yigaṣṣar	to skimp	*gaṭṭaf - yigaṭṭuf*	to cut *gāt*
gīmih pl. *giyam*	price; cost f.	*gtalab - yigtalib*	to turn around; change
guṣṣuh pl. *guṣuṣ*	story f.	*ḥabašī*	Ethiopian
ḥabaših	Ethiopia f.	*ḥasab - yiḥsub*	to work (s.th.) out
igtiṣād pl. *-āt*	economy m.	*iṯiyūbīyā*	Ethiopia f.
jam^{c}*ah*	together	*ka-*	like prep.
kuṯrih	many; large number f.	*ma*^{c}*āš* pl. *-āt*	salary m.
m^{c}*arraf*	well-known	*matā*	when
maṯal pl. *amṯāl*	proverb m.	*mawḍū*^{c} pl. *mawāḍī*^{c}	matter m.
mi^{c}*ayyan / m*^{c}*ayyin*	particular; certain	*min nāḥiyih*	on the one hand
miškilih pl. *mašākil*	problem f.	*mixaddir*	narcotic; doped-up
mizhir	in flower; blooming	*muhtamm (bi-)*	concerned (with)
mujtama^{c} *[-īn]*	gathered, collected [usually in plural]	*mwaḍḍaf*	employed

nušṭuh	activity f.	*raḍī - yirḍā*	to want
raḥ (li-) - yiriḥ (li-)	to go	*rikin - yirkan*	to think
rxīṣ / raxīṣ	cheap	*sākit*	silent; quiet
šaxṣ pl. *ašxāṣ*	person m.	*šijnī* pl. *ašjān*	branch m.
si^{c}*r* pl. *as*^{c}*ār*	price m.	*šuġlih*	hard work f.
syāsih / siyāsih	politics f.	*ṭaffā - yiṭuffī*	to do without (s.th.)
tājir pl. *tujjār*	trader; merchant m.	*ṯalājih* pl. *-āt*	thermos f.
t^{c}*āmal - yit*^{c}*āmal (*^{c}*alā)*	to deal (with s.o.)	*tanak* pl. *atnāk*	water tank m.
ṭannan - yiṭannun	to be distracted	*tkallam - yitkallim (*^{c}*an)*	to talk (about s.th.)
ṭufāyuh pl. *-āt*	ash-tray f.	*ṭūl al-wagt*	the whole time
ṭunnānuh	wonder; distraction f.	^{c}*ūdī* pl. ^{c}*īdān*	twig m.
wahhaf - yiwahhif	to fan [a fire]	*waragih*	leaf f.
waṣṣal - yiwaṣṣul (lā)	to take (s.th., to)	*xabīr* pl. *xubrih*	mate, friend m.
xaddar - yixaddir	to be doped up	*xizānih* pl. *xazāyin*	cistern; tank f.
zabaj - yizbij	to jest, joke	*zabal*	weariness; badness m.
zara^{c} *- yizra*^{c}	to cultivate	*ziri*^{c} *- yizra*^{c}	to be cultivated

Grammar

1. *Greetings: at a gāt chew*

Specific greetings are used on specific occasions. At a *gāt* chew people entering will often not greet everyone, but will give a general greeting. The people sitting will then all reply. The following greetings and replies are common at men's *gāt* chews. In the reply to the first and second greetings *hū* is used in place of *ant* 'you m.s.' or *antū* 'you m.pl.' to mean 'you'. In the second greeting *hum* is used in place of *kum*:

	greeting	reply
1.	*rīḥkum* 'may you be contented!'	*wa-hū wa-l-kull* 'and you too!'
2.	*rīḥhum* 'may you be contented!'	*wa-hū* 'and you too!'

3.	*salām tḥiyyih* 'greeting of welcome!'	*ablaġt* 'you m.s. have conveyed [it]!'

On leaving a *gāt* chew a man will again give a general greeting to which the people sitting will reply:

greeting	reply
annas allāh bi-ḥayātkum 'may God give you pleasure in your lives'	*w-antū al-uns* 'you m.pl. are the pleasure [i.e. you are the one who has given pleasure.]

At a wedding, the person entering will use one of the greetings given above, but will add the phrase *mā ᶜad al-ḥarīw* 'except for the groom' and will greet the groom separately. The reply will remain the same.

2. *Collective nouns and unit nouns*

In Ṣanᶜānī Arabic there are a number of nouns which have the pattern of singular nouns but which in fact refer to a collective. A few collectives are found in English: for example, *cattle* [cp. *cow, cows*]. Collective nouns in Ṣanᶜānī Arabic include (cf. Rossi 1939:14 for additional examples):

collective	gloss
bagar	cattle
šijar	trees
ḥajar	stones
xubz	bread
šawṣar	cockroach
ġurrāb	crows
gummal	fleas

To talk about a unit of X, or a single X, the ending *-ih* or *-ī*, depending on the particular noun, is added to the collective. Where the ending is *-ih* the singular is feminine, where the ending is *-ī* the singular is masculine:

collective	unit	gloss
bagar	*bagarih*	cow f.
šijar	*šijarih*	tree f.
ḥajar	*ḥajarih*	stone f.
ṯawm	*ṯawmih*	garlic f.
baṭāṭ	*baṭāṭuh*	potato f.
jawz (al-hind)	*jawzih*	coconut f.
warag	*waragih*	paper; leaf f.
bayḏ	*bayḏuh*	egg f.
xubz	*xubzih*	piece of bread f.
šawṣar	*šawṣarī*	cockroach m.
ġurrāb	*ġurrābī*	crow m.
gummal	*gummalī*	flea m.

Other unit nouns ending in *-ī* but which have a corresponding *plural* rather than a collective form include (cf. Rossi 1939:15 for additional examples):

unit	plural	gloss
ḏubbī	*ḏubbān*	fly
šijnī	*ašjān*	branch
bilzigī	*blāzig*	bracelet
ᶜūdī	*ᶜīdān*	twig
xuzgī	*xizgān*	hole

Certain collective nouns do not have a unit form. These nouns include:

collective	gloss
ruzz	rice m.
mā'	water m.
gāt	*gāt* m.
dagīg	white flour m.
ṭaḥīn	flour m.
xašab	wood m.
akl	food m.
ḥilbih	fenugreek f.

In order to talk about 'a bit of flour' or 'a piece of *gāt*' a noun is put in annexion (cf. Lesson 9) with the collective noun. Typical nouns which are put in annexion with these collectives include *ḥabbih (ḥabbat)* 'piece; bit', *šwayyih (šwayyat)* 'little', *galīl* 'little', *bardag* 'cup', *mal^{c}agih* 'spoon', *^{c}ūdī* 'twig', and *rubṭuh (rubṭat)* 'bunch':

collective	unit	gloss
ruzz	*ḥabbat ruzz*	a piece of rice
dagīg	*šwayyat dagīg*	a little flour
gāt	*rubṭat gāt*	a bunch of *gāt*
gāt	*^{c}ūdī gāt*	a twig of *gāt*
mā'	*bardag mā'*	a cup of water
mā'	*mal^{c}agat mā'*	a spoon of water
ḥilbih	*galīl ḥilbih*	a little fenugreek

3. *Complementation: 'in terms of...'*

To express the sense of 'in terms of...', 'by way of...' or, in some cases, 'of' an indefinite noun follows an adjective (cf. *Syntax* pp. 144-145). For example:

gadū + mizhir + waragih 'it-is' 'blossomed' 'leaf'	*gadū mizhir waragih* 'it m. is blossomed in leaf [i.e. it has small flowers on its leaf]'
gadū + malān + šijar 'it-is' 'full' 'trees'	*gadū malān šijar* 'it is full of trees'
gadū + malān + jahhāl 'it-is' 'full' 'children'	*gadū malān jahhāl* 'it is full of children'
bī-kūn + axḏar + lawn 'will-be' 'green' 'colour'	*bī-kūn axḏar lawn* 'it will be green in colour'

4. *Verbs: 'to do ... early'*

In order to express 'to do something early' the verb *bakkar - yibakkir* is put before a main verb in the imperfect and takes the same subject as the main verb. When an event in the past is discussed the verb *bakkar* is in the perfect, as in:

bakkar + yigaṭṭuf 'did-early' 'pick-*gāt*'	*bakkar yigaṭṭuf* 'he picked *gāt* early'

Where an event in the present or future is discussed the verb *bakkar* is in the imperfect (*yibakkir)*, as in:

yibakkir + *yigaṭṭuf* 'do-early' 'pick-*gāt*'	*yibakkir yigaṭṭuf* 'he picks *gāt* early'

5. *Verbs: 'to turn out', 'to become'*

The verb *aṣbaḥ* is sometimes used before *inn* (cf. Lesson 16) or before a verb in the imperfect to express the sense of 'to turn out' or 'to become':

aṣbaḥ innum bi-yākulū l-gāt	'it turned out that they eat *gāt*'
aṣbaḥ al-gāt yizraᶜ fī kull bugᶜah	'*gāt* has come to be cultivated everywhere'

6. *'To buy cheaply'*

To say that you buy or sell something cheaply the prepositional phrase *bi-rxīṣ* is used after the verb:

ništarī l-gāt bi-rxīṣ	'we buy *gāt* cheaply'
al-mugawwit yištarī bi-rxīṣ	'the *gāt* seller buys cheaply'

7. *Verbs: 'to need'*

The verb *yištī* 'to want' can be used not only when the subject is animate, but also when the subject is inanimate in the sense of 'to need'. The examples in the second text in this lesson are:

al-madāᶜah tištī nār	'the waterpipe needs fire'
wa-n-nār tištī man yigūm yiwahhif lhā	'the fire needs whoever/someone to get up and fan it'

Other examples include:

al-gāt yištī wagt	'*gāt* needs time'

'Need' can also be translated by the word *lāzim*:

al-gāt lāzim wagt	'*gāt* needs time'

8. *Verbs: 'to want'*

There are two verbs which express the sense of 'to want'. The most common verb *yištī* we have encountered in previous lessons. The second verb is *raḍī* - *yirḍā*. The full paradigm of *raḍī* in the perfect is as follows:

	singular	plural
1.	*raḍīt*	*raḍīnā*
2. m.	*raḍīt*	*raḍītū*
2. f.	*raḍītī*	*raḍītayn*
3. m.	*raḍī*	*raḍyū*
3. f.	*raḍat*	*raḍyayn*

The full paradigm of *yirḍā* in the imperfect is as follows:

	singular	plural
1.	*arḍā*	*narḍā*
2. m.	*tarḍā*	*tarḍaw*
2. f.	*tarḍay*	*tarḍayn*
3. m.	*yirḍā*	*yirḍaw*
3. f.	*tarḍā*	*yirḍayn*

One of the main differences between *raḍī* and *yištī* is that *raḍī* can be used in the perfect and can therefore refer to past events without needing an initial verb *kān*. Compare:

raḍīnī	'he wanted me'
kān yištīnī	'he wanted me'

This verb can be used on its own in the sense of 'didn't/doesn't want to!':

gāl mā yirḍāš	'he said he didn't want to!'
bass mā raḍītš	'but I didn't want to!'

It can also be used with a following imperfect verb in the sense of 'to want to do something':

mā raḍīš yibī^c	'he didn't want to sell'

9. *'I want you to...'*

Usually when *yištī* takes a following imperfect verb the subject of the imperfect verb is the same as the subject of *yištī*. The verb *yištī* can, however, also be used with an imperfect verb which takes a different subject to *yištī* (cf. also Lesson 16). In this way the speaker can produce sentences of the type 'X wants Y to do...'. In this case *yištī* can either take an object pronoun before the imperfect verb to give the sense of 'X wants Y, Y does...', or *yištī* can be directly followed by the imperfect verb (the verb object, cf. Lesson 16, 9.) to give the sense of 'X wants, Y does...'. Compare the two ways to say i. 'I want you to give me water', ii. 'I want her to give me water', and iii. 'I want them m. to give me water':

	'X wants Y, Y does...'	'X wants, Y does...'
i.	*ašti**k** **tiddīnī** mā'*	*aštī **tiddīnī** mā'*
ii.	*ašti**hā** **tiddīnī** mā'*	*aštī **tiddīnī** mā'*
iii.	*ašti**hum** **yiddawnī** mā'*	*aštī **yiddawnī** mā'*

10. *Numbers: percentage*

Percentage is expressed by the appropriate cardinal number followed by the phrase *fi l-miyih* 'lit: in the hundred'. Where the percentage is less than ten the count form of the number is given (cf. Lesson 6):

ṯalāṯih fi l-miyih	'three percent'
sittih fi l-miyih	'six percent'
^{c}ašarih fi l-miyih	'ten percent'
^{c}išrīn fi l-miyih	'twenty percent'
xamsih wa-ṯalāṯīn fi l-miyih	'thirty-five percent'
sittih wa-xamsīn fi l-miyih	'fifty-six percent'
miyih fi l-miyih	'one hundred percent'

11. *'Otherwise...'*

The sense of 'otherwise' in sentences such as 'do X, otherwise Y will happen' is most commonly expressed by the word *māšī* (= 'no') followed by a verb either in the perfect or the imperfect. This type of sentence often carries a sense of threat:

wāḥid wa-ts^{c}īn fi l-miyih	'91% increase otherwise you m.s.

ziyādih, māšī faraġt al-bayt	can leave the house!'
jissī liš ḏalḥīnih, māšī ša-ḍrubiš ḍarb	'sit f.s. down now, otherwise I will really hit you!'
yibi^c lak bi-z-zalaṭ allī yištī hū, māšī yigul lak ^cayb ^calayk	'he sells to you for the amount he wants, otherwise he says, 'Shame on you!'

12. *Coordination: 'either ... or...'*

'Either ... or...' is expressed by *yā ... yā*, by *yā 'immā ... yā 'immā*, by *yimmā ... yimmā*, by *yimmā ... wallā,* or by *yimmā ... aw* (cf. *Syntax* pp. 303-304, cf. Lesson 16). Compare:

yā sawtī yā baladī	'either *sawtī* or local *gāt*'
yimmā sawtī yimmā baladī	'either *sawtī* or local *gāt*'
yā 'immā l-yawm yā' immā ġudwuh	'either today of tomorrow'

13. *'I have nothing to do'*

To convey the sense of 'I have nothing to do' the phrase *mā biš* 'there is not' is used followed by *mā f^cal* 'what I do':

mā biš ma f^cal	'I have nothing to do'
mā biš ma yif^cal	'he nothing to do'
mā biš ma tif^cal	'she has nothing to do'
mā biš ma yif^calū	'they m. have nothing to do'

14. *Adjunctions: 'when', whenever', 'wherever', 'however much'*

In order to say 'whenever', 'when', 'wherever' or 'however much' in Ṣan^cānī Arabic the question word *ayyaḥīn* 'when?', *ayn* 'where?' or *kam* 'how much?' takes *-mā*[1] followed by a verb in the perfect (less commonly by a verb in the imperfect). These conditional-like constructions tend to follow questions. Note that it is only after conditional-like constructions that the verb *yištī* 'to want' can be

[1] By contrast, in 'whoever' and 'whatever', the question words *man* and *mā* do not take following -*mā* (Lesson 19).

used in the perfect. Consider the following examples:

kam at-taman?	'how much is the fare?
kam-mā štayt	However much you want.'
kam addī lak ḥagg at-tilifūn?	'how much should I give you for the phone?
kam-mā štaytī	However much you f.s. want.'
kull wāḥid yiriḥ lih ayyaḥīn-ma štā	'everyone goes when they like.'
gadū yisīr ilayn-ma štā	'he will go wherever he wants.'

15. *Pronouns: 'one'*

al-wāḥid 'lit: the one' is commonly used in the same way as 'one' in certain dialects of British English (or as 'you' in most modern dialects of English). Consider the following examples:

gad al-wāḥid ġayr mutannun	'one is just distracted'
matalan gad al-wāḥid yit^{c}āmal ^{c}alā mgawwit m^{c}ayyan	'for example, you will deal with one particular *gāt* trader'
ṭūl al-wagt al-wāḥid bi-yākul	'the whole time you are eating…'

16. *Numbers: more on wāḥid*

Another common use of *wāḥid* is after a cardinal number when the noun is not expressed (i.e. when in talking about 20 *people*, for example, the word *people* is not expressed). In English, *wāḥid* is either not translated at all or is translated as 'people', 'men', 'children', etc. depending on the actual context:

w-ant ma^{c}ak ^{c}išrīn wāḥid	'and you have twenty with you'
hādī gad ma^{c}āhā talātīn wāḥid	'this one f. has thirty'

Exercises

1. *Comprehension*

A. Re-read the text entitled *al-gāt* and answer the following questions in English:

i. Compile a list of types of *gāt* mentioned in the text.

ii. Write down three facts about *gāt* which are mentioned in the text.

iii. What is the role of the *mugawwit*?

iv. What percentage of Yemenis are said to chew *gāt*?

v. Why do Yemenis chew *gāt* according to the speaker?

B. Re-read the text entitled *al-jalsih wa-l-xazzān* and answer the following questions in English:

i. When do Yemenis buy their *gāt*?

ii. What three things may be prepared by the person in whose house the *gāt* chew takes place?

iii. Why does the speaker say that the waterpipe is hard work?

iv. What do people say and talk about before they have really started chewing *gāt*?

v. What happens after 5 p.m.?

vi. What does the *gāt* chewer think about at this time?

vii. When do people leave the *gāt* chew?

2. *Summary*

A. In your own words, summarise the text entitled *al-gāt* in Ṣanᶜānī Arabic.

B. In your own words, summarise the text entitled *al-jalsih* in Ṣanᶜānī Arabic.

3. *Word stress*

Put in the word-stress mark * before the stressed syllable in the following words.

Example: *lāẓim* ——> **lāẓim*

i. *naššād* ii. *miškilih* iii. *miyih* iv. *al-ġadā* v. *šaḏarawān* vi. *šaḏarawānāt*

4. *Percentage*

Read the following percentages out loud in Ṣanᶜānī Arabic:

i. 23% ii. 40% iii. 55% iv. 92% v. 100% vi. 13% vii. 18% viii. 36% ix. 80%

5. *Substitution: 'and' > 'either ... or'*

Change the following sentences from '... and...' to 'either...or' by substituting *wa-* for either *yimmā ... yimmā/wallā/aw* or *yā...yā:*

Example: *aštī s-sawtī wa-l-baladī* ——> *aštī* ***yā*** *s-sawtī* ***yā*** *l-baladī*

i. *gāl yisāfir al-yaman wa-s-saᶜūdī.* ______________________________

ii. *aštī štarī lī mā' wa-bibs.* ______________________________

iii. *nitġaddā wa-nitᶜaššā.* ______________________________

iv. *ᶜa-yštaġil fī l-bank wa-fī l-wiẓārih.* ______________________________

v. *gad bazz al-awwal wa-ṯ-ṯānī.* ______________________________

6. *Substitution: 'and' > 'neither ... nor'*

Change the following sentences from '... and...' to 'neither...nor' by substituting *wa-* for *mā/lā/miš ... wa-lā:*

Example: *aštī s-sawtī wa-l-baladī* ——> ***mā*** *štīš as-sawtī* ***wa-lā*** *l-baladī*

i. *yisāfir al-yaman wa-s-saᶜūdī.* ______________________________

ii. *aštī štarī lī mā' wa-bibs.* ______________________________

iii. *nitġaddā wa-nit^caššā.* ______________________________

iv. *^ca-yštaġil fī l-bank wa-fī l-wizārih.* ______________________________

____

v. *gad bazz al-awwal wa-t-tānī.* ______________________________

7. *Question and answer*

Answer the following questions using one of the conditional adjunctions described in section 14 above.

Example: *kam addī lih?* ——> *kam-ma štayt*

i. *ayyaḥīn nisāfir?* ______________________________

ii. *ilayn nisīr?* ______________________________

iii. *kam adfa^c lih?* ______________________________

iv. *ayyaḥīn ajī liš?* ______________________________

8. *Translation*

Translate the following groups of sentences into Ṣan^cānī Arabic:

A. Use *aštī*

i. I want him to buy *gāt*.

ii. I want them f. to buy *gāt*.

iii. I want you m.pl. to buy *gāt*.

iv. I want her to buy *gāt*.

B. Use a form of *bakkar*

i. She prepared breakfast early.

ii. She prepared lunch early.

iii. She picked *gāt* early.

iv. She went to the market early.

C. Use a form of *yibakkir*

i. They m. pick *gāt* early.

ii. They m. go to the market early.

iii. They f. chew *gāt* early.

iv. They f. fill the thermos flasks early.

D. Use *māšī*

i. Sit down m.s., otherwise we will hit you!

ii. Write properly, otherwise the teacher will say, 'Shame on you!'

iii. 50% more, otherwise leave f.s. the house!

iv. He will sell [it] to you m.pl. for a lot, otherwise he will go to those who have money.

LESSON 19

Al-madīni l-gadīmih

Dialogue 1 *al-biyūt*

ṣan^{c}ā l-gadīmih hāḏā, ṭab^{c}an intī gad ^{c}iriftī ṣan^{c}ā l-gadīmih wa-jamīlih fī hāḏi l-iyyām jamīlih mā biš ajmal minnahā. biyūt ḥālī biyūt, al-biyūt tibsirīhā ġarr bayt jamb bayt jamb bayt jamb bayt jamb bayt, mā biš innū fāṣul aw ayy ḥājih ḏayyā bayt ḥagg flān fi^{c}il lih fāṣul w-gad ḏayyā bayt ḥagg fulān wa-fi^{c}il lih fāṣul. mā biš hāḏā. al-bayt min jadr ^{c}arḏ. aywih al-jadr ^{c}arḏ al-jadr ^{c}arḏ al-jadr. wa-l-ḥājih allī fīhā llī yi^{c}jibnī nā yimkin inn antī gad lāḥaḏtī hāḏā šūfi l-lašbīh ḥagg kull bayt. mā biš jūb^{w}ā mā bi-dxulhāš aš-šams, min al-biyūt kullhā bi-raġm annahā mašbūkih min hānā w-min hānā w-min hānā mā biš jūb^{w}ā mā bi-dxulhāš aš-šams. tibsirī iḏā l-bayt hāḏā fī hāḏa l-juhah hū yimmā yikūn wāṭī wallā ykūn ^{c}ālī min šān hāḏāk yidxulih aš-šams wa-hāḏāk yidxulih aš-šams. aw aṯ-ṯānī jambī yikūn a^{c}lā wa-hākaḏā. fī l-māḏī allī bida' fīhā aw ^{c}amalhā min al-bidāyih kān yifakkir ašyā ḥālī gawī.

Dialogue 2 *as-sūg ḥagg ṣan^{c}ā*

as-sūg ḥagg ṣan^{c}ā. as-sūg hāḏāk sūg bāhir ya^{c}nī yudxul wāḥid hākaḏāhā yiḥiss innahū fī balad ^{c}ādī ṭabī^{c}ī ^{c}ād an-nās ^{c}alā-mā hum. tudxulī hānā sūg al-milḥ wa-hānā sūg al-ḥabb wa-hānā sūg al-gišr wa-hānā sūg al-bazz ya^{c}nī aswāg kaṯīrih, wa-sūg aṭ-ṭīsān, sūg al-ḥadīd, sūg an-naḥḥās. ya^{c}nī li-kull ḥājih yištī l-insān yilgāhā fī s-sūg hāḏā, wa-kull šī mawjūd ma^{c}ih sūg maxṣūṣ bih. fa-^{c}alā-mā gult liš sūg al-bazz, sūg aṭ-ṭaḥīn, sūg al-gišr, sūg al-ḥadīd, sūg al-xšab, sūg al-^{c}irj. antī dārī māhū sūg al-^{c}irj hāḏā? sūg al-^{c}irj ḥagg al-laḥmirih, hāḏā l-laḥmirih al-miksirih allī mā ^{c}ād tuxṭāš. hāḏā lā bih wāḥid ma^{c}ih ḥimir gadū a^{c}raj wallā šī yisīr yiṭruḥuh hinīyih fī l-bug^{c}ah hāḏī yisammūh sūg al-^{c}irj ḥagg al-laḥmirih. aywih al-^{c}arjih wa-hāḏā yiṭraḥūhin hinīyih li-ḥadd yištaw yistaxdimū minnahin.

wa-bih sūg al-bagar, la-l-bagar sūg. wa-bih sūg an-naḥḥās allī gult liš awwal, sūg al-^{c}inab. wa-bih sūg az-zabīb. bih sūg at-titin, sūg al-muxlāṣ. hāḏa l-muxlāṣ al-yamanī l-ḥālī 'allī bī-jaw ajānib kaṯīr yištaraw minnih. lākin ba^{c}ḍ an-nās mā humš dārī yigūlū mā lak ant wa-hāḏā tištarī min ḥagg al-gabāyil. ^{c}indanā hānā yigūlū hāḏā min ḥagg al-gabāyil ^{c}a-tištarī min hāḏā! bi-ḏāt an-niswān ḥagganā mā ^{c}a-yštayn illā ḏ-ḏahab. al-balāzig al-ḥālī wa-l-ġālī, al-ašyā l-jamīlih mā yištanš yigūlayn ḥayyā ^{c}a-tddī lī min ḥagg al-gabāyil mā biš ma^{c}ī mihrih. hāḏa n-niswān ḥagganā yigūlayn hākaḏā. aswāg ṣan^{c}ā jamīlih gawī gawī, iḥna nsammīhā sūg al-milḥ.

Dialogue 3 *al-ḥammāmāt fi ṣan^{c}ā*

Abd al-Salam: *antī dārī fī ṣan^{c}ā bih ḥammāmāt kaṯīrih. al-ḥammāmāt hāḏā 'a^{c}tagid innahā min ^{c}ahd at-turk, yimkin. lākin ṣan^{c}ā kullahā malān ḥammāmāt. fī kull ḥārah ḥammām yimkin. iḥna ^{c}indanā hānā fī l-bawmiyih bih ḥammām al-bawmiyih, wa-jambanā hānā ḥammām ^{c}alī, wa-fī l-gā^{c} hānakā ḥammām al-fayš, wa-bih arba^{c} ḥammāmāt ma^{c}ānā wlā xams ḥammāmāt ġarr hinīyih: ḥammām al-fayš, wa-ḥammām al-… šūfī hāḏā b-ismih hāḏā allī fī bāb al-gā^{c}. w-allāh mā 'anā dārī b-ismahin. kān bih ḥammām al-ḥamdānī. hāḏa l-ḥammāmāt ḥālī gawī. bih ya^{c}nī baladī yidxul fīha l-wāḥid. kān minn awwal hāḏa l-ḥammāmāt ya^{c}nī ṭabī^{c}at al-ḥammām min nafsih hū ma^{c}mūl sā^{c} al-gubab, bass hū taḥt al-gā^{c}, ya^{c}nī taḥt al-larḍ, mabnī taḥt al-larḍ. ṭab^{c}an bi-yibnaw zayy al-ġuraf hākaḏā'. yidxul wāḥid lā ġurfih tūga^{c} ḥāmī gawī. hāḏā yisammūhā sadr.*

Louise: *sadr?*

Abd al-Salam: *as-sadr, aywih. zayy as-sadr hāḏā, nafs al-ism. yisammūhā s-sadr. as-sadr gadī al-ḥāmīyih fi l-ḥammām al-gawī. hāḏā yidxul al-wāḥid awwal-mā yidxul yidxul yijiss fīhā yiḥmī, law-mā gadū bi-yi^{c}rig šwayyih. wa-bih al-xizānih jambahā. tūga^{c} ṯintayn xazāyin: xizānih bi-magṭaṣ. al-magṭaṣ ya^{c}nī l-barik hāḏā 'allī ykūn fīhā mā' allī bī-jī lahā l-mā'. wa-xizānih munfalliṯ li-ḥālhā min al-xizāni ṯ-ṯānīyih. hī ^{c}alā sās innū fīhā maḥwaḍ. ba^{c}dayn tilgay fī kull ġurfih* *min hāḏa l-ġuraf allī hin ḥagg al-ḥammām. kull wāḥidih fīhā ḥawḍ, fīhā ṯnayn ṯalāṯi ḥwāḍ. aḥwāḍ hāḏā zayy at-tanak. ḥawḍ hū miṯl at-tanak wa-hū ḥajar. u-bih al-mā' bī-jī min xārij ḥāmī w-bārid. al-ḥāmī hāḏā bī-jī min as-sadr lā wasṭ al-ḥawḍ hāḏā. yimtili l-ḥawḍ w-ant tġarraf minnahā, titḥammam. aw tixallī l-ḥammāmīn, bih wāḥid fī l-ḥammām gadū yijirr ad-dalw. ad-dalw hāḏā hū al-maġrafih. aywih yijirrū yibizzū yiddaw bih al-mā'. w-ya^{c}nī llī bi-tḥammam gad bih wāḥid hānā fī l-ḥammām yisannib yijī yirāg mā'. gad kull wāḥid yid^{c}ā yā barrād gāl yā barrād!*

Louise: *yā barrād!*

Abd al-Salam: *yā barrād ya^{c}nī innū ḏayyā llī bi-sayyib al-mā'. ddī lanā dalw mā'! mā ^{c}ād biš mā'! hāḏāk yijī yddī l-mā' yiskub lih al-mā'. hāḏā fī ḥammām ar-rijāl, mā an-niswān ṯānī hum yiftaḥū lahin ḥanafī lā ^{c}indahin, mā r-rijāl mā bi-lā yida^{cc}aw, wa-ya^{c}nī ḍarūrī wāḥid yisīr yijī b-dalw wa-yuskub lih mā', yimillī lih al-ḥawḍ wa-yitġassal. wa-law-mā yitimm yitġassal yida^{cc}ī l-bārid hāḏā yā bārid gāl māhū gāl iṣfinī! ya^{c}nī yiġassilih gabl-mā yuxruj. hāḏā ḥagg al-ḥammām ṭab^{c}an fī l-ḥammām ḥagg ar-rijāl hāḏā ṯalāṯ arba^{c} min al-ḥammāmīn yijaw yikayyisūk al-kīs, al-kīs al-laswad. gadum muxtaṣṣīn ant ^{c}a-tijlis wa-hum yikayyisūk. wa-ba^{c}d-mā titimm tiddī lum šagāhum ḥagg al-kīs hāḏāk. ya^{c}nī yikayyisūk ya^{c}nī nnahum yiġassilūk hum. ar-rajjāl nafsih yijī yikayyisak yiġassilak ant w-ant gadak al-jālis. wa-'iḏā tštī tkayyis nafsak jarrayt al-kīs ḥaggak lā šī ma^{c}ak kīs, jarraytih wa-tkayyast. wa-kayyast nafsak, wa-ba^{c}d at-tuṣfī tuxruj xārij. zārathīn yijī wāḥid m^{c}aḏḏal hānā fī ragabatih, yisīr yiḥammim. yigūl asīr aḥammim yisīr yidfī ma^{c} ad-dif' min al-bard wallā šī, yisīr yiḥammim yidfī'. wa-^{c}ād al-ḥammāmī ygūm yidfā ḥālih, yidfī lih al-^{c}aṣab lā šī ^{c}aṣabuh.*

Louise: *māhī l-^{c}aṣabuh?*

Abd al-Salam: *al-^{c}aṣabuh ^{c}ind-mā yūja^{c}iš ḍahruš hānā min al-bard. māniš dārī mā tgūlū lih antū. ^{c}ind-mā yūja^{c}iš ḍahruš hānāhā aw ragabatiš: aywih fī ḍahruš intī ma tisturīš tḥarrikī ḍahruš wallā šay hākaḏā, bass iḥna nsammīh min al-bard hāḏā, min sabab al-bard. al-ḥammāmī gad ^{c}indih xibrih. an-nās al-muxtaṣṣīn gad ^{c}indahum xibrih hānā ^{c}ārif wāḥid asīr lā ^{c}indih. asīr lā ^{c}indih* *wa-ḍahrī b-yūja^{c}nī agūl lih yūja^{c}nī hānā fī ḏahrī mā stirš aḥarrikih wallā šī. yigūl lī hānā, yigūl lī bi-yūja^{c} lak hānāhā? agūl aywih! yigūl lī mtadd! w-anā sir amtadd, amtadd hinayk bi-l-ḥammām. wa-hū ġarr yijī yiḥarrik ḏahrī bi-rijlih yigūl lī hnayih! agūl lih aywih! gadū dārī gad ^{c}indih xibrih. wa-hū yif^{c}al hākaḏā bi-rijlih. axruj w-anā bi-xayr. hāḏā fī l-ḥammām, aw an-nās muxtaṣṣīn bi-hāḏā š-šay. wa-hāḏā fī l-ḥammām wa-ba^{c}dā, ba^{c}da-mā ytimm, agūm ġarr albas al-ladah ḥaggī w-addī lih ḥagg al-ḥammām. addī li-l-ḥammāmī ḥaggī ḥagg al-ḥammām kam-mā kānat, ^{c}išrīn wallā ṯalāṯīn riyāl. zārathīn xamsīn girš. w-addī lih iḏā tkayyast fī l-ḥammām iḏā jā' al-ḥammāmī yikayyisnī gadanā ddī lih miyat girš wallā ṯamānīn girš. wa-ḏayyik allī bi-ddī mā' bārid gadiḥna nddī lih ^{c}ašarih ^{c}išrīn, ^{c}ašarih gadī mā lahā šī. gad kull wāḥid yiddī lih ^{c}ašarih ^{c}ašarih wa-hū ġarr ḥagg man yisayyib luhum al-mā'. hāḏā šī ḥālī fī ṣan^{c}ā. anā ḏalḥīn bayn-asīr yimkin kull yawm gabl-mā xazzin. bi-y^{c}jibnī l-ḥammām ḥagg al-gāt, yigūlū ḥammām gāt. mā yisbur al-ḥammām ḥagg al-gāt illā ba^{c}d al-ġadā. titimm ġarr titġaddā wa-tsīr tif^{c}al lak ḥammām. wa-tjī txazzin tjī ti^{c}mal al-^{c}ūdī l-gāt sawā. ba^{c}d-mā titḥammam. anā gadanā bayn-asīr yimkin yawmīyih: yawm fī l-bawmīyih, wa-yawm fī ^{c}alī lannū hānā yawm rijāl wa-yawm niswān: yawm fī l-bawmiyih wa-yawm fī ^{c}alī. wa-hāḏā fī ṣan^{c}ā hākaḏā mā biš ma^{c}ānā hānā zayy-mā hāḏā ḥagg hāḏi l-iyyām as-sūna wa-midrī māhū.*

Dialogue 4 *binā l-ḥammāmāt*

Abd al-Salam: *ba^{c}ḍ an-nās daxxalū luhum as-sūna lākin mā yi^{c}jibhumš, lākin w-allāh gad bih nās ḏalḥīn gadum bi-bnaw luhum ḥammāmāt. tibsirī ḏalḥīnih gad bada'at al-ḥammāmāt tuksar fī ṣan^{c}ā. gad bih nās yibnaw ḥammāmāt min hāḏā l-gadīmih wa-bi-tkallaf mabāliġ. anā ^{c}ārif wāḥid gāl 'innū bada' yi^{c}mal lih ḥammām wa-^{c}a-ykallafih fī ḥawālī ṯamantašar milīyūn li'annī hī tštī tšūf al-ḥammāmāt hāḏā hī mā tištiš ayy ḥijarih wallā ayy šay. ḍarūrī 'innū min ḥajar ḥabaš.*

Louise: *al-ḥajar al-ḥabaš hāḏā māhū?*

Abd al-Salam: *al-ḥajar al-ḥabaš hād̲ā hū l-ḥajar as-sawdā. hāk al-ḥajar al-ḥabaš. wa-ṭab^{c}an ^{c}ādī ḍarūrī tkūn mwaggaṣuh. mwaggaṣuh ya^{c}nī ma^{c}mūlih aw mṣallaḥah mxalfa^{c}ah. yixalfa^{c}ūhā law-mā yixallawhā bi-šakl rubā^{c}ī wa-mwaggaṣuh, ya^{c}nī hākad̲ā bi-tūga^{c} samḥ. fa-hād̲awlā yiwagguṣūhā bi-l-frās wa-l-maṭraguh law-mā yixallawhā samḥ. hākad̲ā ḥabaš, wa-gaḍāḍ.*

Louise: *māhū l-gaḍāḍ?*

Abd al-Salam: *al-gaḍāḍ hād̲ā hū mā kān biš ^{c}indanā hānā s-simint. mā kān ^{c}indanā llā l-gaḍāḍ. wa-l-gaḍāḍ hā hād̲ā hū min an-nūrih. hād̲ā an-nūrih hād̲ā hī māddih yimkin hī ḥagg al-kibrīt. hād̲ā an-nūrih. aywih. yiḥammawhā gawī an-nūrih, wa-law-mā tiḥmā yidiggūhā, wa-ba^{c}dayn tibsirīhā sā^{c} al-^{c}ajīn, wa-tṭraḥḥā ġarr ^{c}ala l-jidār. lākin law tizgamīhā fī yadiš hād̲ā an-nūrih bāridih yif^{c}alūhā lā hānā w-yif^{c}alūhā lā hānā wa-hī fī yadiš yimkin tiḥrig yadiš.*

Louise: *ṣudg?*

Abd al-Salam: *aywih, hād̲ā an-nūrih. tibsirī l-barik hād̲ā fīhā hād̲ā ḥaggahā l-lawwal mā kān biš as-simint hād̲ā abadan, lākin fī gā^{c} al-ḥammām yif^{c}alū fīh al-ḥajar al-ḥabaš. wa-d̲alḥīn ba^{c}ḍuhum gadum kulluhum ġarr ḥabaš. bi-l-ḥabaš hū 'afḍal. yimsak al-ḥarārih, yixzin ḥarārih al-ḥabaš al-laswad, wa-bass. wa-hād̲ā ḥagg al-ḥammāmāt fī ṣan^{c}ā.*

Vocabulary[1]

abadan	ever [in neg.]	*^{c}ad̲alih*	neck-ache f.
a^{c}jam pl. *^{c}ijmān*	dumb m.	*ajmal*	more beautiful
^{c}ajīn	dough m.	*a^{c}lā*	higher
^{c}alā sās	so that	*^{c}ālī*	high
^{c}aṣab	neck/back-ache m.	*^{c}aṣabuh*	a neck or back-ache f.
ašbīh	similarity m.	*aswad* f. *sawdā*	black
ba^{c}ḍ	some	*bard*	cold m.
barrād pl. *-īn*	cold-water bringer m.	*bayya^{c} - yibayya^{c}*	to sell
bazz	cloth m.	*bi-d̲āt*	especially
bidāyih pl. *-āt*	beginning f.	*bilzigī* pl. *balāzig*	bracelet m.
bi-raġm ann...	despite the fact that...	*da^{c}ā - yid^{c}ā*	to call

[1] Revise also thematic vocabulary in Lesson 5.

da^{cc}ā - yida^{cc}ā	to call	*ḏahab*	gold m.
dalw pl. *adliyih*	bucket m.	*dif'*	warmth m.
difī - yidfī	to become warm	*fāṣul*	gap m.
frās pl. *-āt*	chisel m.	*gaḏāḏ*	native cement to plaster containers m.
ġarraf - yġarraf	to scoop up (s.th.)	*gubbih* pl. *gubab*	arch; vaulted building f.
ḥabaš	black [type of stone]	*ḥajar*	stone coll. f.
hāk	that is	*ḥāmī*	hot
ḥamī - yiḥmī	to become hot	*ḥammām* pl. *-āt*	bath; Turkish bath m.
ḥammāmī pl. *-īn*	man who works in Turkish bath m.		
ḥarag - yiḥrig	to burn (s.th.)	*ḥarārih*	heat f.
ḥarrak - yiḥarrik	to move (s.th.)	*ḥass - yiḥiss*	to feel (s.th.)
ḥawḏ pl. *aḥwāḏ*	bath tub m	*ḥimir / ḥimār* pl. *aḥmirih*	donkey m.
^{c}irig - yi^{c}rig	to sweat	*^{c}irj*	lameness m.
jadr pl. *jidār*	wall m.	*jamb*	beside, next to
jamīl	beautiful	*juhah*	direction f.
kallaf - yikallaf	to cost (s.th.)	*kayyas - yikayyis*	to wash with a *kīs*
kibrīt	matches m.	*kīs* pl. *akyās*	wash bag, mit m.
kisir - yuksar	to break	*ladah*	clothes
lāḥaḏ - yilāḥiḏ	to observe (s.th.)	*ligī - yilgā*	to find (s.th.)
li-ḥadd	until	*mabnī*	built m.
māddih	material; substance f.	*māḏī*	past
magṭaṣ pl. *magāṭiṣ*	bath; Jewish ritual bath m.		
maġrafih pl. *maġārif*	scoop f.	*maḥwaḏ* pl. *maḥāwiḏ*	trough m.
mallā - yimillī	to fill (s.th.)	*ma^{c}mūl*	made
mašbūk	interlinked	*maṭraguh* pl. *maṭārug*	hammer f.
maxṣūṣ (bi-)	specially (for s.th.); specialised (in s.th.)	*mihrih*	price f.
miksir	broken down	*mṣallaḥ*	made
mtadd - yimtadd	to lie down; stretch out	*mtilī - yimtilī*	to fill up; become full
mu^{c}aḏḏal	having neck-ache	*munfalliṭ*	left; isolated

muxtaṣṣ	experienced	*mwaggaṣ*	trimmed [stone]
mxalfa^c	worn; trimmed [stone]	*naḥḥās*	copper; brass m.
nūrih	slaked lime f.	*rubā*^{c}*ī*	four sided
rāg - yirīg / yirāg	to pour (s.th.)	*sabab* pl. *asbāb*	reason m.
sabar - yisbur	[in neg.] can't be, do	*sadr*	hot room in Turk. bath m.
šāf - yišūf	to see (s.th.)	*ṣaffā / ṣfā - yuṣaffī / yuṣfī*	to bathe; wash trns.
šagā - yišgā	to work	*šagā*	work; wage m.
samḥ	straight	*sannab - yisannib*	to stand up
sayyab - yisayyib	to carry (s.th.)	*ṣudg*	really!
sūna	sauna f.	*simint*	cement m.
ṭaḥīn	flour m.	*taḥt*	below, beneath
tkayyas - yitkayyas	to wash o.s. with a *kīs*	*at-turk*	the Turks
waggaṣ - yiwaggaṣ	to trim [stone]	*wāṭī*	low
wa^c*y*	awareness m.	*xalfa*^{c} *- yixalfa*^{c}	to trim [stone]
xazan - yixzin	to hold [e.g. heat]	*xibrih*	experience f.
zāratḥīn	sometimes	*zigim - yizgam*	to take; grab (s.th.)

Grammar

1. *Pronunciation*

1.1. Hollow verbs + *li-*

When a hollow verb takes the preposition *li-/lā* + pronoun the long vowel on the verb reduces to a short vowel and the final syllable of the verb is stressed. The verbs which are most commonly affected by this are *gāl* 'to say' and *rāḥ li-* 'to go':

*lāzim yi*riḥ lih*	'he must go'
*gad *raḥ lih*	'he has gone'
*gad *gal lī jī*	'he told me to come'
*yi*gul lak bass*	'he tells you enough!'

1.2. Final weak verbs

Final weak verbs (cf. Lesson 7) which have an emphatic consonant in the root take *u* as the vowel of the imperfect prefix:

emphatic		non-emphatic	
yuxṭā	'he walks'	*yid^{c}ā*	'he calls'
yuḏ̣wī	'he goes home'	*yimšī*	'he walks'
yuṣfī	'he cleans'	*yilgā*	'he finds'

2. *Diminutive*

The diminutive is not very common in Ṣan^{c}ānī Arabic, but is found as a variant of some adjectives, in particular *zġīr* 'small' and *gadīm* 'old'. It is formed on the patterns *zuġayrī* and *zuġayyirī*. The diminutive probably does not have a large effect on the meaning; in some contexts, however, it could be interpreted as having a similar effect to adding '-ish' to an adjective in English ('oldish', 'smallish'). When the adjective agrees with a feminine noun the final *-ī* is replaced by *-ih*:

makān zuġayrī	'a small room'
makān gudaymī	'an old room'
walad zuġayyirī	'a small boy'
bint zuġayrih	'a small girl'

A double diminutive also exists, of the pattern *...annanī*, as in *zuġannanī*. It is used in the word for 'draft' (*šannanī*) when, during a *gāt* chew, a man may call out:

ġallig al-bāb šannanī!	'Shut the door, [there's] a draft!'

3. *Word order: split adjective from adverb*

Just as a noun can be split from its adjective by a filler word such as *ka-ḏayyā, hākaḏā, ya^{c}nī* or by a prepositional phrase (cf. Lesson 15), so an adjective can be split from its adverb by a prepositional phrase, as in the example in the dialogue in this lesson:

gadī l-ḥāmiyih *fi l-ḥammām al-gawī*	'it is the very hot [one] in the Turkish bath'

where *fi l-ḥammām* 'in the bath' separates *al-ḥāmiyih* 'the hot' from *al-gawī* 'very'.

4. *'I don't know its name'*

To say to know or not know something, the object of the verb *dirī - yidrā* (or its active participle *dārī*) may alternatively be the object of the preposition *b(i)*:

mā 'anā dārī ***b****-ismahā*	'I don't know its name'
gadak dārī ***bi****-l-gabr*	'do you know about the grave?'

5. *Reflexive verbs: 'to wash oneself'*

There are two ways of expressing 'to do something to oneself' in Ṣanᶜānī Arabic. The first way we have seen in Lesson 13 is by using a reflexive verb: a verb which takes initial *t-* and which then turns a verb from 'to do X to someone' to 'to do X to oneself':

transitive		reflexive	
ġassal	to wash	*tġassal*	to wash o.s.
kayyas	to wash with *kīs*	*tkayyas*	to wash o.s. with *kīs*
ḥammam	to bath	*tḥammam*	to bathe
naggaš	to tatoo s.o.	*tnaggaš*	to tatoo o.s.

The second way is by using the transitive verb and adding *nafs* + pronoun:

transitive + *nafs*	reflexive	gloss
ġassal nafsih	*tġassal*	'he washed himself'
kayyast nafsak	*tkayyast*	'you washed y.s. with a *kīs*'
ḥammam nafsih	*tḥammam*	'he bathed'

When there is a plural subject, *nafs* is in the plural form *anfus* or *anfās*:

transitive + *nafs*	reflexive	gloss
ḥammamū anfushum	*tḥammamū*	'they m. bathed'

6. *Expression of pain or illness*

Pain is most commonly expressed by the verb *waja^c - yūja^c* 'to hurt' + object pronoun. To say 'I have a headache' in Ṣan^{c}ānī Arabic a structure equivalent to 'my head is hurting me' is used:

subject	verb	gloss
rāsī 'head-my'	*bi-yūja^{c}nī* 'hurts-me'	'my head is hurting me'

Similarly, 'my eye is hurting', and 'my leg is hurting' are expressed by:

subject	verb	gloss
^{c}aynī 'eye-my'	*bi-tūja^{c}nī* 'hurts-me'	'my eye is hurting me'
rijlī 'leg-my'	*bi-tūja^{c}nī* 'hurts-me'	'my leg is hurting me'

Two slight variants on this structure are found in the second text in this lesson: namely *bi-yūja^c* + pronoun followed by *fī* + noun:

verb	prep. phrase	gloss
bi-yūja^{c}nī 'hurts-me'	*fī ḍahrī* 'in back-my'	'my back is hurting me'

or *bi-yūja^c* + *li-* + pronoun followed by *fī* + noun:

verb phrase	prep. phrase	gloss
bi-yūja^c lih 'hurts' 'to-him'	*fī ragabatih* 'in neck-his'	'his neck is hurting him'

To ask whether someone has a pain in a particular place the question is *bi-yūja^c* +

li- + pronoun followed by *hānā:*

bi-yūja^c lak	*hānā*	'does it hurt here?'
'hurts' 'to-you'	'here'	

To say 'I have a headache' or 'I have a cough' the structure used is *fī* 'in' + pronoun + noun (lit: 'in me is a headache'):

prep. phrase	noun	gloss
fīnī	*ṣudā^c*	'I have a headache'
'in-me'	'headache'	
fīnī	*kuḥḥah*	'I have a cough'
'in-me'	'cough'	
fīnī	*^caṣabuh*	'I have a neckache'
'in-me'	'neckache'	
fīnī	*ishāl*	'I have a diarrheoa'
'in-me'	'diarrheoa'	

7. *'To pay s.o. for s.th.': more on ḥagg*

As we have seen in earlier lessons, *ḥagg* can be used to translate a number of different types of sentences. One common use of *ḥagg* is in paying for something. In a sentence like 'I will pay you for the telephone', 'for the telephone' is translated by *ḥagg* + *at-tilifūn*:

šā-ddī lak ḥagg at-tilifūn	'I will give you for the telephone'

Similarly, in the texts in this lesson:

addī lih ḥagg al-ḥammām	'I pay him for the bath'
tiddī lhum šagāhum ḥagg al-kīs	'you give them their wage for the *kīs'*

ḥagg + pronoun is also used to express the sense of 'owing':

addī lih ḥaggī (ḥagg al-ḥammām)	'I shall give him what I owe (for the bath'

8. *'Whoever'*

'Whoever' is expressed by the word *man* (cf. Lesson 18, for additional examples cf. *Syntax* pp. 352-353):

ḥagg man yisayyib luhum al-mā'	'for whoever brings them water'
addī li-man yibī^c	'I give to whoever will sell'
hāḏā ḥagg man yijī	'this is for whoever will come'

9. *'Whatever'*

'Whatever' is expressed by the word *mā*. On its own (i.e. without a preceding word such as *ka-*, *kull-* or *kam-*), it is less common in everyday conversations than *man* (8. above), but is common in proverbs (for additional examples cf. *Syntax* p. 353):

šā-ddī lih mā yištī minnī	'I shall give him what he wants from me'
in xarrajtih, šallayt lak mā štayt	'if you can get it out I'll give you whatever you want'

'Whatever' can also be expressed by the word *mahmā* (*Syntax* p. 351), which usually comes at the beginning of a sentence:

mahmā sawwaytī lāzim saltih	'whatever you f.s. do, you must have *saltih*'

10. *'Despite the fact that…'*

'Despite the fact that…' is expressed in Ṣan^cānī by *bi-raġm ann …*:

bi-raġm annahā mašbūkih min hānā w min hānā	'Despite the fact that they are inter-linked here and here'
bi-raġm ann al-bayt ba^cīd šā-jī liš	'Despite the fact that the house is far away I will come to you f.s.'

11. *The perfect aspect: 'if X, then do Y!'*

The perfect tense is most commonly used to express the past tense (Lesson 4, 8.). It also may be used in conditional clauses as discussed in Lesson 11. When a conditional clause is followed by a command in the main clause - that is to say, a clause which says 'if X, *do Y!*' - the verb in the main clause is in the perfect aspect in Ṣanᶜānī Arabic (cf. *Syntax* pp. 65-66):

conditional clause	main clause
iḏā tštī tkayyis nafsak 'if you want to wash y.s.'	*jarrayt al-kīs wa-tkayyast* 'take the *kīs* and wash y.s.!'
iḏā tštī tsāfir 'if you want to travel'	*sāfart* 'travel!'

12. *'So-and-so'*

'So-and-so' is expressed by the word *fulān* or *flān*:

bayt fulān	'so-and-so's house'
marat fulān	'so-and-so's wife'
yigūl lih fulān māt al-yawm	'he tells him so-and-so died today'

An adjective ('such-and-such') is made from *fulān* by adding *-ī*:

fī l-bayt al-fulānī	'in such-and-such a house'

Thematic Vocabulary

Sickness and health

ᶜālaj - yiᶜālij	to treat (s.o.)
ᶜamalīyih pl. *-āt*	operation f.
ᶜazīmih pl. *ᶜazāyim*	amulet f.
dawā	medicine; liquid medicine m.
duktūr pl. *dakātirih*	doctor m.
ġurfat al-inᶜās	hospice f.
ḥabbih pl. *ḥubūb*	tablet m.

ḥakīm	practitioner of traditional medicine m.
ḥaṣbuh	measles f.
ḥirz pl. *aḥrāz*	amulet m.
ḥummih	fever f.
ibrih pl. *ibar*	needle f.
^{c}ilāj pl. *-āt*	treatment m.
ishāl	diarrhoea m.
jafāf	dehydration m.
jarrāḥ pl. *-īn*	surgeon m.
kawā - yikwī	to cauterise
makwih pl. *makāwī*	cauterisation f.
malāriyā	malaria m.
maraḍ pl. *amrāḍ*	sickness; illness m.
marīḍ pl. *-īn / amrāḍ*	patient; sick person m.
mazkūm	having a cold
mijabbir pl. *-īn*	traditional bone setter m.
mumarriḍ pl.*-īn*	nurse m.
muruḍ - yimraḍ	to become ill
mushil	laxative m.
mustašfā pl. *-yāt*	hospital m.
mustawṣaf pl. *-āt*	clinic m.
sa^{c}ālih	a cough f.
šafā - yišfī	to make (s.o.) well
ṣaḥḥ - yiṣuḥḥ	to get well
ṣaḥḥah	health f.
sayyārat is^{c}āf	ambulance f.
si^{c}il - yis^{c}al	to have a cough
ṣudā^{c}	headache m.
tā^{c}ib	unwell; tired
t^{c}ālaj - yit^{c}ālij	to be treated
talgīḥ pl. *-āt*	vaccination m.
tbaxxar - yitbaxxar	to recover
tsa^{cc}al - yitsa^{cc}al	to cough
waja^{c}	pain m.
waja^{c} - yūja^{c}	to hurt (s.o.)
zukkām / zukām	cold; flu m.

Exercises

1. *Comprehension*

A. Re-read the dialogue entitled *al-biyūt* and answer the following questions in English:

i. How are the houses arranged in the old city?

ii. What does the speaker like about the houses in the old city?

B. Re-read the dialogue entitled *as-sūg ḥagg ṣan^c^ā* and answer the following questions in English:

i. Name five of the markets mentioned by the speaker.

ii. What is *sūg al-^c^irj?*

iii. Who likes the silver sold in the silver market?

iv. What do Yemeni women think about silver today?

C. Re-read the dialogue entitled *al-ḥammāmāt* and answer the following questions in English:

i. When do the Turkish baths date back to?

ii. Where are the baths in Ṣan^c^ā'?

iii. What is the *sadr*?

iv. How many *xazāyin* are there?

v. What is found in every room of the bath?

vi. What is this made of?

vii. What does the *barrād* do?

viii. What does the *ḥammāmī* do?

ix. When would a man have a *gāt* bath?

D. Re-read the dialogue entitled *binā l-ḥammāmāt* and answer the following questions in English:

i. What has begun to happen to the Turkish baths in Ṣan^c^ā'?

ii. What does it cost to build a traditional bath?

iii. What type of stone is used to build a bath?

iv. How is this stone smoothed?

v. What is used as cement?

vi. What would happen if you put this 'cement' in your hand?

2. *Phrase identification*

Identify the Arabic for the following English phrases. The phrases are given in the order in which they appear in the dialogues in this lesson:

A. *al-biyūt*

i. There is nothing more beautiful than it.

ii. The wall is the breadth of the wall.

iii. Look at the similarities of every house.

iv. It is either low or high.

B. *as-sūg ḥagg ṣan^{c}ā*

i. As I told you, the cloth market.

ii. The broken-down donkeys which can no longer walk.

iii. They put them there until they want to make use of them.

C. *al-ḥammāmāt fī ṣan^{c}ā*

i. There are a lot of Turkish baths in Ṣan^{c}ā'.

ii. The whole of Ṣan^{c}ā' is full of Turkish baths.

iii. One goes into a room which is very hot.

iv. There are two cisterns.

v. Each one has a trough.

vi. Three or four of the *ḥammāmī*s come to wash you with a *kīs*.

vii. The *ḥammāmī* is experienced.

viii. I go to him when my back hurts.

ix. The *gāt* bath can only be after lunch.

D. *binā l-ḥammāmāt*

i. Some people have had a sauna put in.

ii. The Turkish baths have begun to break in Ṣan^{c}ā'.

iii. They heat the slaked lime up a lot.

iv. You put it straight on the walls.

3. *Give the plural*

Give the plural form of the following words:

i. *maṭbax* ii. *ḥammām* iii. *sūg* iv. *jūb^{w}ā* v. *daymih* vi. *ġurfih* vii. *xizānih* viii. *bīr* ix. *makān* xi. *^{c}ūdī*

4. *Word stress*

Put the word-stress mark * before the stressed syllable in the following words:

Example: *maṭbax* —> **maṭbax*

i. *ḥammām* ii. *ḥanafī* iii. *yiġassilih* iv. *ragabih* v. *aḥwāḏ̣* vi. *maṭraguh* vii. *ṭab^{c}an* viii. *zārathḥīn* ix. *minnahā* x. *rubṭuh*

5. *Declarative > conditional*

Change the following declarative sentences into conditional clauses. Make the clause in brackets into the main clause:

Example: *tštay tisāfiri l-bilād (tisāfirī)* —> *lā tštay tisāfiri l-bilād, sāfartī*

i. *tštī tištari l-gāt (tištarī lak)* ______________________________

ii. *tštaw tisīru s-sūg (tisīrū).* ______________________________

iii. *tštayn titfarraṭayn (titfarraṭayn).* ______________________________

iv. *tštī tijiss li-waḥdak (tijiss).* ______________________________

v. *tštay titġaddaw (titġaddaw).* ____________________

6. *Imperfect > perfect*

Put the following sentences into the past by changing the appropriate verb from imperfect to perfect.

Example: *al-barrād yisayyib al-mā'* ——> *al-barrād [gad] sayyab al-mā'*

i. *hāḏāk yiskub lih al-mā'.* ____________________

ii. *wāḥid yiḥiss innahū fī balad* ^{c}*ādī.* ____________________

iii. *law-mā bi-yi*^{c}*rig šwayyih.* ____________________

iv. *wa-ba*^{c}*d at-tuṣfī tuxruj xārij.* ____________________

v. *ṯalāṯ arba*^{c} *min al-ḥammāmīn yijaw yikayyisūk.* ____________________

____

7. *Translation*

Translate the following groups of sentences into Ṣan^{c}ānī Arabic:

A. Use *dārī bi-*

i. He doesn't know the Turkish baths.

ii. I know the University.

iii. She knows the town.

B. Use verb + *nafs*

i. You m. wash yourself.

ii. My daughter has hennaed herself.

iii. I have tatooed myself.

C. Use *fulān*

i. They f. are in such-and-such a house.

ii. So-and-so's wife gave birth today.

iii. He said so-and-so died yesterday.

D. Use *ḥagg*

i. I want to pay you for the telephone.

ii. I gave the teacher what I owed for the teaching.

iii. Pay the *ḥammāmī* for the bath.

E. Use *mā bih ḥadd*

i. I came and Muhammad wasn't in.

ii. You m.pl. came and I wasn't in.

iii. The teacher will arrive and the students won't be there.

LESSON 20

Al-mawt wa-l-^{c}azzā

Dialogue 1 *al-^{c}azzā*

Janet: *yā karīmih, gulī lī fi l-mawt lāzim tiddaw zalaṭ wa-l-kull, mā?*

Karima: *mā, fi l-mawt al-filūs hāḏā māšī, ^{c}ādī, bass al-kaṯīr ḥāl mā ysīrayn an-nisā yi^{c}azzayn yisammawh ṭab^{c}an al-^{c}azzā. awwal yawm ṯānī yawm ṯāliṯ yawm rābi^{c} yawm yawmī al-^{c}azzā lā yawm al-ḥid^{c}āš. yawm al-ḥid^{c}āš ya^{c}nī gadū 'āxir yawm. bih an-nās al-kaṯīr allaḏī bī-jaw fi l-mawt fī yawm ṯāliṯ al-mawt wa-sābi^{c} al-mawt wa-'āxir al-mawt, ya^{c}nī al-ḥid^{c}āš.*

Janet: *yawm aṯ-ṯāliṯ wa-s-sābi^{c} wa-l-ḥid^{c}āš.*

Karima: *aywih, wa-l-ḥid^{c}āš. ya^{c}nī an-nās yikṯarū fi hāḏi l-iyyām. wa-bī-kūn an-našīd ya^{c}nī bi-nšidū la-l-mayyit, ba^{c}ḍuhum yigraw yāsīn mubārak, wa-bih nās ya^{c}nī al-kaṯīr allaḏī bī-jaw fi l-mawt bī-jībū aš-šfūṭ. aš-šfūṭ ya^{c}nī bih nās law-mā yisīr yi^{c}azzī yigūl al-yawm ^{c}a-nšfiṭ lā bayt filān ma^{c}āhum mawt. ^{c}a-nšaffiṭ. hāḏā dāyiman awwal mā kān yif^{c}alū llā š-šfūṭ, mā ḏalḥīnih bih nās bi-f^{c}alū al-gahwih, hāḏa l-gahwih gadī m'akkadih aw ar-rawānī al-ḥalāwā. ya^{c}nī nafs al-kīkih bass fīhā mā wa-ya^{c}nī nsammīhā šrub.*

Janet: *māhū šrub?*

Karima: *aš-šrub min mā' wa-sukkar ziyādih wa-zirr wa-hayl, wa-ba^{c}dā yiskubū š-šrub fawg al-kīkih. nisammīh rawānī 'aw ḥalāwā. ya^{c}nī hāḏā lā bayt al-mawt yisabbirū lhum. ašraḥ liš innī nafs al-kīkih bass ^{c}alayhā š-šrub, wa-nisammīhā rawānī ḏā fīhā šrub.*

ṭab^{c}an al-^{c}azzā gadū yawmīyih. bih nās ya^{c}nī bī-sīr ṯānī yawm ya^{c}nī ḥasb al-garābih allaḏī baynuhum. wa-maṯalan an-nās allī ^{c}irifūnī aw jīrānī maṯalan wa-tmūt xālatī hākaḏā lāzim al-jīrān yijaw yisīr yi^{c}azzaw bayt al-mawt wa-hū ba^{c}īd minnahum yigūlū ^{c}ašān karīmih, hī jāratnā. hāḏā lāzim ya^{c}nī fi l-mawt lāzim yisīrayn. aw al-jīrān yidrayn wa-yigūlayn yisīrayn ^{c}alā mayyit fulānih wa-hū yugrub lahā. yisīrayn ḥattā wa-hū ba^{c}īd yisīrayn. hānā l-kaṯīr yisīrayn fī bayt al-

mawt. wa-ṭab^{c}an bayt al-mawt yijlisū, maṯalan fī l-makān hāḏā kullih, bayt al-mawt lāzim yijlisayn jamb jamb. ya^{c}nī al-usrih lāzim tikūn fī juhah wāḥidih hāḏā lāzim. yijayn maṯalan an-nisā yibsirayn aynī bayt al-mawt ba^{c}d libsahin ya^{c}nī gadin kullahin aswad bass bayt al-mawt tlaṯṯamayn ba^{c}d yikftayn yikftayn aṣ-ṣarmiyuh yikftayn ^{c}alā sibb yi^{c}rafayn innahin bayt al-mawt. ^{c}ašān fī l-mawt mā ysallimūš ^{c}alā n-nās kulluhum zayy al-^{c}iris wa-hāḏā bass mā ydxul yisallimū ^{c}alā bayt al-mawt wa-yigūlayn luhum ^{c}aḏḏam allāh lakum al-lajr. yigūlayn niḥmad allāh wa-nuškurih. aywih ya^{c}nī l-ḥamdu li-llāh w-iḥna šākirīn. wa-ba^{c}dā yijlisayn an-nisā šwayyih ^{c}indahin ba^{c}dā lammā yisīrayn yigūlayn maṯalan ^{c}a-yṣabbir allāh galbiš aw gulūbakin lā hin majmū^{c}ah. ya^{c}nī yigūlayn niḥmad allāh wa-nuškurih wa-yigūlayn lahin aššar allāh xuṭākum. ya^{c}nī 'inn allāh yi^{c}lam innahin gad jayn yi^{c}azzayn lahin. wa-ba^{c}dā yisīrayn.

awwal al-mawt ya^{c}nī ḏā maṯalan mātat garībatī mātat as-sā^{c}ah wāḥidih wa-nuṣṣ. ya^{c}nī n-nās yidraw ^{c}alā ṭūl lāzim inn ahl al-mawt hāḏā lāzim yiballiġū l-ahl ^{c}agb al-mawt mubāširih. fa-fī l-mawt ^{c}alā ṭūl ya^{c}nī s-sā^{c}ah ṯintayn yikūn al-bayt imtilī, mā biš nuṣṣ sā^{c}ah law gad an-nās kulluhum ^{c}induhum ya^{c}nī yiġaṭṭaw al-mayyitih yixallawhā fī makān li-waḥdahā, wa-yijayn yibsirayn usrat al-mayyit. ya^{c}nī nās yidawwax nās yibkī nās yiṣīḥ. ba^{c}dayn ṭab^{c}an al-mayyitih yixallawhā fī makān law-mā tjī wāḥidih mxaṣṣaṣuh tixalliṣ al-ladah allaḏī fawgahā wa-tġassilhā wa-tkaffinhā wa-tḥuṭṭ ^{c}alayhā rīḥān wa-l-^{c}uṭūrāt wa-r-rayāḥīn ya^{c}nī hāḏā tḥuṭṭhā fī l-kafan ḥagg al-mayyitih.

ba^{c}dā law-mā yikammilū yixarrijūhā, yixarrijū l-mayyitih. ṭab^{c}an yisammaw allaḏī yiġassilū l-mayyitih fawgih yisammawh al-muġtsal. yijī xašabih kabīrih maftūḥah fataḥ zġīrih min an-nuṣṣ ^{c}asibb al-mā yinzil. wa-yḥuṭṭūhā fawgih wa-yġassilūhā.

Janet: *fī 'ayy makān yiġassilūhā?*

Karima: *fī makān wāsi^{c} maṯalan fī l-ḥijrih aw fī d-dihlīz, al-makān al-wāsi^{c} allaḏī tudxul fīh al-jināzih li'annī kabīrih. drītī? ba^{c}dā ka-mā gult liš yikammilū yiġassilūhā fawg al-muġtsal. wa-ba^{c}dayn yikaffinūhā wa-ba^{c}dā law-mā yikammilū yikaffinūhā yijirrūhā yiḥuṭṭūhā fawg al-jināzih. wa-hāḏa l-jināzih nafs* *aš-šī. tijī xašab min xārij wa-ḥabl min dāxil. wa-ṭab^{c}an yiḥuṭṭū ^{c}alayhā l-frāš yiḥuṭṭūhā fawghā wa-ḏā kānat marih ya^{c}nī lāzim yi^{c}rafu n-nās hī marih aw rajjāl. al-marih yiḥuṭṭū ^{c}alayhā sitārih zayy-mā ḥna nilbas sitārih, bass as-sitārih jadīdih, yiġaṭṭawhā bihā. w-iḏā kān rajjāl yiḥuṭṭū ^{c}alayh šāl hāḏāk aš-šāl allaḏī yḥuṭṭū fawgih.*

Janet: *aš-šāl allī kabīr yijī?*

Karima: *aywih yiḥuṭṭū ^{c}alayh šāl ^{c}ašān yi^{c}rafū an-nās innahū rajjāl. ba^{c}dā yisīrū yigbirūh fī l-magbirih.*

Janet: *yigbirūh bi-yawmahā?*

Karima: *ṭab^{c}an bi-yawmahā. ṭab^{c}an lā mātat as-sā^{c}ah wāḥidih wa-nuṣṣ aw ṯintayn, mā yislaḥš yixarrijūhā ba^{c}d al-ġadā. ^{c}indanā māšī. ya^{c}nī fī l-ḥudaydih aw fī ti^{c}izz iḏā māt al-mayyit yixarrijūh ^{c}alā ṭūl sawā 'ann al-^{c}ašīyih aw aṣ-ṣubḥ aw ba^{c}d al-ġadā yixarrijūh ^{c}alā ṭūl. amm iḥna mā yislaḥš iḏā mātat aṣ-ṣubḥ yixarrijūhā ^{c}alā ṭūl, mā yigbirū ^{c}indanā llā ṣ-ṣubḥ bass. ammā ba^{c}d al-ġadā l-^{c}ašī mā biš.*

Janet: *aṣ-ṣubḥ bass?*

Karima: *aywih, lāzim yikūn as-sā^{c}ah sab^{c} wa-nuṣṣ yišillūhā l-jāmi^{c} yiṣallaw ^{c}alayhā ṣalāt al-mayyit wa-ba^{c}dayn minnahā yixarrijūhā yigbirūhā. fa-^{c}indanā hānā magbirat xuzaymih. ya^{c}nī ḥna lammā wāḥid yišġalnā nigul lih lā xuzaymih. agul lih sīr xuzaymih! y-allāh lā xuzaymih! wallā w-anā tā^{c}ibih agūl šā-sīr xuzaymih, gadanā štī mūt ma štīš ḥājih y-allāh xuzaymih! wa-gad ma^{c}ānā magbirat šu^{c}ūb hānā šigganā jīrān. dirītī.*

fa-ba^{c}d yigbirūhā ṭab^{c}an ba^{c}d-mā ṣallaw ^{c}alayhā yišillūhā yigbirūhā, bi-yirja^{c}ū r-rijāl maṯalan al-agārib yijaw yitġaddaw fī l-bayt. bih ba^{c}ḏ an-nās iḏā mātat ka-mā gult liš iḏā mātat aṣ-ṣubḥ aw ba^{c}d al-ġadā bayt al-mawt fa-bi-yi^{c}malū ^{c}ašā. bayt al-mayyit lāzim yi^{c}malū ^{c}ašā. f-iḏā mātat aṣ-ṣubḥ wa-gabarūhā ṣ-ṣubḥ lāzim yi^{c}malū ġadā.

Janet: *hāḏā miš ta^{c}b ^{c}alā bayt al-mayyit?*

Karima: *aywih hāḏā ta^{c}b ya^{c}nī ḥarām hāḏā lākin iḥna yigūlū ^{c}indanā lammā yinšaġilū 'ahl al-mayyit bi-l-ġadā wa-bi-l-midrī mā yinsaw šwayyih. lākin mā*

hāḏā ṣaḥḥ lākin bī-kūn ta^{c}b. an-nās tā^{c}ibīn wa-bi-yibkaw wa-hāḏā ba^{c}dā yijaw yis'alūhum aynī kaḏā aynī kaḏā. ṭab^{c}an mišum allaḏī bi-^{c}malayn hāḏā mā bi-^{c}malanš min al-lakl wa-l-ġadā wa-hāḏā. ṭab^{c}an bi-jlisayn wa-l-jīrān wa-l-lahl ya^{c}nī llī ^{c}āduhum mā luhum šī yijayn yisabbirayn. bass hin mišin dāriyāt bi-l-bayt wallā aynī hāḏā wallā aynī hāḏā. dāyiman yijayn yis'alayn bayt al-mawt aynī kaḏā aynī kaḏā. ṭab^{c}an hāḏā ^{c}ādih mišī ḥāliyih.

Dialogue 2 *al-migbār wa-l-mijābirih*

al-mawt, ^{c}ind-mā yimūt ayy wāḥid hānā ^{c}indanā fi l-yaman fi l-ḥārah aw min ma^{c}ārifnā aw min agāribnā, ahlih bī-nabbaw aṣḥābuhum u-ma^{c}ārifhum u-kull wāḥid bī-nabbī ṣāḥubuh. yugul lih fulān māt al-yawm, wa-^{c}a-ygbirūh maṯalan ġudwuh aṣ-ṣabāḥ, li'annū ^{c}ādatan akṯarat-mā yugburū hū aṣ-ṣabāḥ, aw iḏā māt aṣ-ṣabāḥ yigbirūh fi ḏ-ḏuhr. fa-kull wāḥid bī-nabbī ṣāḥubuh allī yi^{c}raf aš-šaxṣ al-mayyit. yawm al-migbār bī-sīrū an-nās lā bayt hāḏa š-šaxṣ allī māt, wa-yūṣalū la l-bayt. iḏā ^{c}ādū fi l-bayt mā gad xarrajūš bī-rayya^{c}ū law-mā yxarrijūh bi-l-jināzih. wa-ḏā gadū fi l-bāb xārijī gadum ġarr yizgamu l-jināzih wa-yxrujū ma^{c} an-nās. kull wāḥid yibuzz al-jināzih. yibuzzhā ya^{c}nī yimskū ma^{c}āhum yitsā^{c}adū min wāḥid lā wāḥid ^{c}alā sās mā ykunš ta^{c}b ^{c}ala n-nās allī bi-ḥmalūhā. wa-ba^{c}dayn bī-xarrijūh min al-bayt bī-šillūh ilā l-jāmi^{c}, yiṣallaw ^{c}alayh ṣalāṭ al-mayyit, wa-min al-jāmi^{c} bi-yuxrujū wa-yšillūh al-magbirih, lā xuzaymih, ^{c}alā sās inn gad al-gabr ḥaggih jāhiz gad jahhazūh ahlih. yūṣalū hānāk lā fawg al-gabr ḥayṯ-mā ^{c}a-ydfinūh, yibda'ū yinazzilūh min fawg al-jināzih ḥaggih, yidaxxilūh al-gabr iṯnā-mā yiṭraḥūh, an-nās kulluhum al-mawjūdīn yibda'ū bi-dirāsat ba^{c}ḍ al-gur'ān yāsīn tabārak āyāt min al-gur'ān wa-l-ašxāṣ allī hum bī-yidfinūh aw ^{c}alayhum hāḏa l-^{c}amal hum allī bī-gūmū bi-^{c}malū d-dafn ma^{c} wāḥid min agāribih - sawā 'ann ibnih, aw axūh, aw zawjih iḏā hī marih zawjahā aw ayy wāḥid, al-muhimm min ahlahā. ba^{c}d-mā ytimmū yigbirūh wa-gad tammū darīs al-gur'ān hāḏāk, kull wāḥid min an-nās al-mawjūdīn yirmī šwayyih min at-turāb ṯalāṯ ṯalāṯ ḥufan min at-turāb yirmawhin lā fawg al-gabr wa-ygūlū minhā wa-

'ilayhā - minhā xalagnākum wa-'ilayhā niᶜīdukum - bi-hāḏa l-maᶜnā. yaᶜnī l-muhimm innum yiddaw ṯalāṯ kalimāt min kalām. wa-baᶜdayn bī-gūm wāḥid hānāk gadū yigūl la-n-nās al-mawjūdīn maᶜānā darīs fī l-jāmiᶜ al-flānī ṯalāṯ iyyām wa-l-mijābirih fī bayt al-mayyit maṯalan aw fī bayt jār al-mayyit. al-muhimm fī bayt gadum yiᶜrafūh an-nās kulluhum. an-nās hāḏawlāk bi-yixṭaw w-aṣḥāb al-mayyit allaḏī hum min ahlih bi-ṣṭaffū fī ṣaff wāḥid, wa-kull wāḥid min hāḏawl allī jaw yigbirūh bī-sīr yisallimū ᶜalayhum wa-ygūlū luhum ᶜaḏḏam allāh lakum al-ajr wa-hāḏāk yigūl ajrak karīm wallā yigūl lih al-ḥamdu li-llāh, wallā ygūl lih aššar allāh xuṭākum. hāḏāk bī-gūl raḥim allāh mayyitkum wa-hāḏāk yigul lih aḥsan allāh saᶜyakum. al-muhimm, min hāḏā yiddaw hāḏa l-kalimāt. kull wāḥid bī-traḥḥam ᶜala l-mayyit wa-hāḏāk yiridd lih šukrih lih saᶜyih innū bī-jī yigbirih maᶜih law-ma ytimmū kull n-nās yisallimū ᶜalayhum bī-jirrū ahl al-mayyit yirawwaḥu l-bayt. ṭabᶜan hum ḥazīnīn wa-zaᶜlānīn ᶜala llī māt ᶜalayhum. baᶜd al-ġadā hāḏāk allī yjaw yigbirūh aw an-nās al-maᶜārif allī yiᶜrafū innū māt mastaṭaᶜūš yisīrū yigbirūh aw ayy ḥājih bī-sīrū yjābirū baᶜd al-ġadā fī bayt al-mayyit, yijābirū hlih aw-yjissū maᶜāhum yixazzinū. bī-jī naššād yitraḥḥam ᶜalayh wa-ygrā ᶜalayh al-fātiḥah wa-ḏayyā law-mā yi'aḏḏin maġrib. bi-yxrijū yisīrū al-jāmiᶜ yiṣallaw ᶜalayh wa-yidrisū lih āyāt min al-gur'ān gadī 'āyāt mḥaddadih maṯalan lā wagt al-ᶜišā. yigūmū yiṣallaw ᶜišā wa-kull wāḥid yiriḥ lih. wa-tibgā hāḏā ṯalāṯ iyyām: mijābirih baᶜd al-ġadā wa-darīs al-ᶜašiyih, fa-maṯalan iḏā ma stirš asīr ajābirhum al-yawm šā-sīr ajābirhum ġudwuh. iḏā ma stirš asīr ajābirhum ġudwuh šā-sīr baᶜd ġudwuh. yaᶜnī fīh amāmī furṣuh ṯalāṯ iyyām. lākin al-ašxāṣ allī hum min ahlih gadum mā yūgaᶜ illā yisīrū yawmīyih. wa-law hum mašġūlīn ḍarūrī yifḍaw ᶜalā mayd yisīrū yijābirū min ajl yjābirhum. mā yistirš yifalliṭū al-bayt wa-ysīr yidawwirū w yixazzinū wlā šī. wa-hāḏā yaᶜnī ḥagg al-mayyit kayf bi-fᶜalū ḥagg al-mayyit, wa-bass.

Vocabulary

aᶜād - yiᶜīd	to make (s.o.) return	*ᶜādatan*	usually
aḏḏan - yi'aḏḏin	to call for prayer; to be called [prayer]	*ᶜagb*	after

akṯarat-mā + verb	most commonly	*^{c}alā mayd*	so that
^{c}alā ṭūl	straight away	*al-kaṯīr*	most (of them)
amām	in front of; before	*āyih* pl. *-āt*	verse f.
^{c}azzā	mourning m.	*^{c}azzā - yi^{c}azzī*	to mourn
bakā - yibkī	to cry	*ballaġ - yiballiġ*	to inform (s.o.)
bigī - yibgā	to last	*bi-yawmahā*	immediately
dafan - yidfin	to bury (s.o.)	*dafn*	burial m.
daras - yidris	to recite [the Qur'an]	*darīs*	reading of Qur'an m.
dawwar - yidawwir	to go round	*dawwax - yidawwax*	to faint
dāyiman	always	*dirāsih*	recitation [of Qur'an] f.
fatḥah pl. *fataḥ*	opening f.	*fātiḥah*	[opening chapter of Qur'an f.]
fiḏ̣ī - yifḏ̣ā	to make time	*frāš*	covering m.
furṣuh pl. *furaṣ*	chance f.	*gabar - yigbir*	to bury (s.o.)
gabr pl. *gubūr*	grave m.	*garab - yugrub (lā)*	to be related (to)
garābih	relationship f.	*garīb* pl. *agārib*	relation m.
garībih pl. *-āt*	relative f.	*ġaṭṭā - yiġaṭṭī*	to cover (s.th.)
girī - yigrā (^{c}alā)	to recite (for s.o.)	*ḥabl*	rope m.
ḥalāwā	sweetness f.	*ḥarām*	unlawful
hayl	cardamon m.	*ḥayṯ-mā*	where adjt.
ḥazīn	sad	*ḥimil - yiḥmal*	to carry (s.th.)
^{c}ilim - yi^{c}lam	to know	*^{c}išā*	evening prayer m.
iṯnā-mā	while adjt.	*jābar - yijābir*	to console; pay condolences
jahhaz - yijahhiz	to prepare (s.th.)	*jāhiz*	ready
jārih pl. *-āt*	neighbour f.	*jināzih* pl. *janāyiz*	funeral bier f.
kafan / kfan	shroud m.	*kafat - yikfit*	to bind; wear (s.th.)
kaffan - yikaffin	to put (s.o.) in a shroud		
kalimih pl. *-āt*	word f.	*ka-mā*	as adjt.
kīkih	cake f.	*kiṯir - yikṯar*	to be many
lammā	when adjt.	*libis - yilbas*	to put on; wear (s.th.)
libs	clothes m.	*maftūḥ*	open
magbirih pl. *magābir*	graveyard f.	*majmū^{c}ah*	group f.
m'akkad	certain	*man*	someone
mašġūl	busy	*māt - yimūt (^{c}alā)*	to die (on s.o.)
mawt pl. *amwāt*	death; funeral m.	*mayyit*	deceased m.

migbār	burial m.	*mijābirih*	consoling; mourning f.
min ajl	in order to; so that	*mubāširih*	immediately
muġtsal	washing slab m.	*muxaṣṣaṣ*	specialised
nabbā - yinabbī	to tell; inform (s.o.)	*našad - yinšid*	to sing songs [at funerals/ births]
naššād pl. *-īn*	singer m.	*nazzal - yinazzil*	to lower (s.th.)
nšaġal - yinšaġil	to be occupied	*raḥim - yirḥam*	to have pity
ramā - yirmī	to throw (s.th.)	*rawānī*	sweet cake
rayya^{c} - yirayya^{c}	to wait (for)	*rīḥān* pl. *rayāḥīn*	parsley m.
sa'al - yis'al	to ask (s.o.)	*ṣabbar - yiṣabbir*	[God] to grant forbearance
ṣaff pl. *ṣufūf*	line m.	*šaffaṭ - yišaffiṭ*	to make *šafūṭ*
šafūṭ	dish of sour pancake and yoghurt m.		
šaġal - yišġal	to bother; trouble (s.o)	*ṣāḥ - yiṣīḥ*	to shout; cry out
šākir pl. *-īn*	thankful m.	*ṣalaḥ - yiṣlaḥ*	to be right; to do
ṣalāh pl. *ṣalawāt*	prayer f.	*ṣallā - yiṣallī (^{c}alā)*	to pray (for s.o.)
sallam - yisallim (^{c}alā)	to greet (s.o.)		
šaraḥ - yišraḥ	to explain (s.th.)	*sawā ('ann) … aw*	whether … or
sa^{c}y	effort; endeavour m.	*šrub*	sugar syrup m.
ṣṭaff - yiṣṭaff	to be in line	*sṭaṭā^{c} - yisṭaṭī^{c}*	to be able
šukr	thanks m.	*ta^{c}b (^{c}alā)*	tiring (for s.o.)
tlaṯṯam - yitlaṯṯam	to wear a *liṯmih*	*traḥḥam - yitraḥḥam*	to pay respects
trawwaḥ - yitrawwaḥ	to go home	*tsā^{c}ad - yitsā^{c}ad*	to help o.a.
turāb	dust, soil m.	*^{c}uṭūr* pl. *-āt*	perfume m.
wāsi^{c}	wide, broad	*xalag - yuxlug*	to create (s.th.)
xallaṣ - yixalliṣ	to take off (s.th.)	*xāriji*	outside adj.
xašab	wood m.	*xašabih*	piece of wood f.
xuzaymih	[graveyard in Ṣan^{c}ā']	*y-allāh*	come on!
yawmī / yawmīyih	daily	*za^{c}lān (^{c}alā)*	sad; worried (about s.o.)
zirr	cloves coll. m.		

Grammar

1. *Pronunciation: contraction of words*

The word *ammā* 'as for', which is most commonly used to introduce a new topic, is frequently contracted to *mā*:

	mā ḏalḥīnih bih nās bi-f^{c}alū l-gahwih	'now there are people who make coffee'
compare		
	ammā ḏalḥīnih bih nās bi-f^{c}alū l-gahwih	'now there are people who make coffee'

Similarly, the words *lammā* and *law-mā* may be contracted to *mā*:

bass mā ydxul yisallimū ^{c}alā bayt al-mawt	'but when they come in they greet the bereaved family'

2. *Condolences*

Specific greetings and condolences are used at funerals. Importantly, this is the one time when you do not greet everyone present, but rather only members of the bereaved family. Typical condolences include:

^{c}aḏ̣ḏ̣am allāh ajrukum	'may God make your reward great'
^{c}aḏ̣ḏ̣am allāh lakum al-ajr	'ditto'

Replies to these condolences could be:

	^{c}aḏ̣ḏ̣am allāh al-jamī^c	'may God reward everyone'
or		
	al-ḥamdu li-llāh	'thanks be to God'
or		
	ajrak karīm	'your reward is noble'
or		
	niḥmad allāh wa-nuškurih	'we praise God and give him thanks'
or		
	aḥsan allāh sa^{c}yakum	'may God make your efforts worthwhile'

Other condolences include:

raḥim allāh mayyitkum	'may God have mercy on your deceased'
aššar allāh xuṭākum	'may God direct your steps well'

ᶜa-yṣabbir allāh galbak / iš	'may God grant your heart forbearance'

3. *'Some people'*

In earlier lessons we have seen the use of *zārat* and *baᶜḍ* to express 'some'. Another way to express 'some *people*' is to use the noun *nās* 'people' with the verb in the *singular*:

bih nās law-mā yisīr yiᶜazzī yigūl al-yawm ᶜa-nšfiṭ ...	'there are people, when they go to mourn, they say, 'Today I will make *šfūṭ* ...''
nās yidawwax nās yibkī nās yiṣīḥ	'some people faint; some cry; some shout'

4. *'Within half an hour'*

To express 'within' in the sense of 'within half an hour' Sanᶜānī Arabic uses *mā biš ... law,* literally 'there was not ... until':

mā biš nuṣṣ sāᶜah law gad an-nās kulluhum ᶜinduhum	'within half an hour everyone is with them'
mā biš nuṣṣ sāᶜah law gad al-bayt imtilī	'within half an hour the house was full'

5. *'It isn't allowed'*

'It isn't allowed...' or 'it can't be done to...' is expressed by *mā yiṣlaḥš* or *mā yisburš*:

mā yiṣlaḥš yixarrijūhā baᶜd al-ġadā	'it can't be done to take her out after lunch'
mā yisburš ḥammām al-gāt illā baᶜd al-ġadā	'it isn't done [to have a] *gāt* bath except after lunch'

6. *Coordination: 'whether ... or'*

'Whether ... or' or 'irrespective whether ... or' is expressed by *sawā ('ann) ...*

aw (cf. *Syntax* pp. 304-305):

sawā 'ann ibnih aw axūh — 'whether his son or his brother'

sawā l-ġadā aw al-^{c}ašā — 'irrespective whether it is lunch or supper'

tigūl ijlisū yā wald sawā la-l-^{c}ajūz aw la-š-šaybih — 'you m.s. say, 'Sit down, father' whether to an old woman or to an old man'

7. *'When'*

wa- in Arabic is far more flexible than 'and' in English, and is often used in the sense of 'when' in a subordinate clause:

maṯalan an-nās allī ^{c}irifūnī ***wa-****tmūt xālatī lāzim al-jīrān yijaw yisīr yi^{c}azzaw bayt al-mawt* — 'for example, the people who knew me when my Aunt died, the neighbours had to pay condolences to the bereaved'

This is particularly the case when the clause introduced by *wa-* describes a state or condition:

yisīrayn ḥattā wa-hū ba^{c}īd — 'they f. go even when it is far'

w-allāh w-anā tā^{c}ibih agūl šā-sīr xuzaymih — 'by God, when I am tired I say I'll go to Xuzaymih'

For a detailed discussion of this use of *wa-* and related constructions see *Syntax* pp. 373-379.

8. *The perfect: 'do you understand?'*

The perfect is usually used to express the past tense (Lesson 4, 8.). As seen in Lesson 19, however, the perfect can also be used to express the imperative in conditional sentences.[1] In addition, with verbs which describe understanding the perfect is used where we would use the present tense in English. These verbs include *dirī* 'to know', *^{c}irif* 'to know' and *fihim* 'to understand':

fhimtī — 'do you f.s. understand?'

[1] Also the optative and wonder (*Syntax* p. 66).

drītī	'do you f.s. understand?'
fhimt	'I understand'

9. *'The paper comes in large and small'*

The verb *jā' - yijī* 'to come' is very frequently used in the imperfect in the sense of 'to come in' or 'to be', as in 'this paper comes in large and small', and 'the dress which is black'. This is essentially the case when the subject of the verb is inanimate and is referred to in a general way. There are three examples of *yijī* used in the sense of 'to be' in the first dialogue in this lesson:

aš-šāl allī kabīr yijī	'the shawl which is large'
al-muġtsal yijī xašabih kabīrih	'the *muġtsal* is a large piece of wood'
wa-hāḏā l-jināzih nafs aš-šī tijī xašab min xārij wa-ḥabl min dāxil	'the funeral bier is the same thing: it is wood on the outside and rope in the middle'

10. *'With I-don't-know-what'*

Just as phrases such as 'I-don't-know-what' can be the object of a preposition in English as in 'he's occupied with I-don't-know-what', so *midrī mā* 'I don't know what' can be the object of the preposition *bi-* in Ṣan^{c}ānī Arabic. In contrast to the English 'I-don't-know-what', however, the phrase *midrī mā* takes the definite article as the object of a preposition:

law-mā yinšaġilū 'ahl al-mayyit bi-l-ġadā wa-bi-l-midrī mā	'when the family are occupied with the lunch and I-don't-know-what'

11. *Modal expressions: 'must'*

'Must' can be translated by *lāzim* as we have seen in earlier lessons. Another way of conveying the sense of 'must' is by using the phrase *mā yūga^{c} illā* '[lit: it cannot be except ...]' followed by a verb in the imperfect. *mā yūga^{c} illā* probably has more force than *lāzim*:

allī hum min ahlih gadum mā	'those from his family must go

yūga^{c} *illā yisīrū yawmīyih*	everyday'

12. *Lack of number agreement*

Where strings of verbs are involved and the subject is plural, the first verb (the modal verb) often lacks number agreement and is given in the third person singular. This is particularly, but not exclusively, the case in rapid speech:

yisīr yi^{c}*azzaw*	'they go to mourn'
mā yirḍāš yištaraw	'they don't want to buy'
mā yistirš yifalliṭū l-bayt	'they cannot leave the house'

13. *More adjunctions*

In the second dialogue in this lesson there are three more adjunctions which end in *-mā: ḥayṯ-mā* 'where; in the place where', *iṯnā-mā* 'while', and *akṯarat-mā* 'mostly; most of the time'. These adjunctions are followed by a verb:

yūṣalū lā fawg al-gabr ḥayṯ-mā yidfinūh	'they go to the top of the grave where they [will] bury him'
iṯnā-mā yiṭraḥūh, an-nās kulluhum al-mawjūdīn yibda'ū bi-dirāsat ba^{c}*ḍ al-gur'ān*	'while they are putting him [in the grave] everyone who is present begins to recite from the Qur'an'
akṯarat-mā yugburū hū aṣ-ṣabāḥ	'mostly they bury in the morning'

The adjunction *ḥayṯ-mā* may also be followed by an independent pronoun:

gad wuṣulū ḥayṯ-mā hū	'they m. arrived where he was'

Exercises

1. *Comprehension*

A. Re-read the dialogue *al-ᶜazzā* and answer the following questions in English:

i. How many days does mourning take place?
ii. On which days do most people give their condolences?
iii. What did women used to bring when they gave their condolences?
iv. What two things do women bring now?
v. Who should come to pay their condolences?
vi. How is the family of the deceased distinguished from the other mourners?
vii. How long do mourners sit with the bereaved family?
viii. When do people find out that someone has died?
ix. What is done to the body before it leaves the house?
x. What is used to cover the body if it is a woman?
xi. What is used to cover the body if it is a man?

B. Re-read the dialogue *al-migbār* and answer the following questions in English:

i. At what time of day does burial usually take place?
ii. Who bears the funeral bier?
iii. Where is the body taken first?
iv. Where is it then taken?
v. Who has prepared the grave?
vi. What do the mourners do while the body is being lowered into the grave?
vii. What is the importance of the number three during burial and during the mourning period?
viii. What happens on each day of the mourning period?
ix. Which people must attend every day of the mourning period?

2. *Greetings*

Give appropriate replies to the following greetings:

i. *ḥayy allāh man jā'!* ______________________________

ii. *^{c}aḏḏam allāh lakum al-ajr!* ______________________________

iii. *raḥim allāh mayyitkum!* ______________________________

iv. *al-ḥamdu li-llāh ^{c}ala s-salāmih!* ______________________________

v. *tiṣbaḥū ^{c}ala l-xayr!* ______________________________

3. *Substitution*

A. Replace *lāzim* with *mā yūga^{c} illā* in the following sentences.

Example: *lāzim tisāfir li-waḥdak* ——> ***mā yūga^{c}š illā*** *tisāfir li-waḥdak*

i. *lāzim yisāfir ^{c}adan kull sanih.* ______________________________

ii. *lāzim yiballiġū l-lahl ^{c}agb al-mawt mubāširih.* ______________

____

iii. *lāzim yijissū fī l-bayt ṯalāṯ iyyām.* ______________________________

B. Replace *mā yiṣlaḥš* by *mā yistirš* in the following sentences.

Example: *mā yiṣlaḥš tijiss li-waḥdak* ——> ***mā tistirš*** *tijiss li-waḥdak*

i. *mā yiṣlaḥš yigbirū l-mayyit ba^{c}d al-ġadā.* ______________________

____

ii. *mā yiṣlaḥš yifalliṭū l-bayt ba^{c}d al-mawt.* ______________________

____

iii. *mā yiṣlaḥš tuxruj al-bint ba^{c}d al-maġrib.* ______________________

____

4. *Gap filling*

In the following sentences insert the appropriate adjunction or conjunction from the list:

law-mā, ḥayṯ-mā, iṯnā-mā, tijāh-mā, ba^{c}d-mā, wa-, sā^{c}-mā, ka-mā

Example: *yidarrisū l-gur'ān* __________ *yi'aḏḏin maġrib* ——> *yidarrisū l-gur'ān* ***law-mā*** *yi'aḏḏin maġrib*

i. __________ *gabarūh, yisīrū l-bayt yitġaddaw.*

ii. *yuwaṣṣulūh lā l-gabr*__________ *yigbirūh.*

iii. *antī dārī, kūfiyih*__________ *iḥna nilbas kūfiyih.*

iv. __________ *ḏkur šī šā-gul liš.*

v. __________ *yixazzinū yiddaw kalām kaṯīr.*

vi. *mā yiṣlaḥš tijay ^{c}indī*__________ *anā mā bih ḥadd.*

vii. *yiġassilū l-mayyit*__________ *yixarrijūh min al-bayt.*

viii. __________ *gult lak.*

ix. __________ *txazzin tifakkir fī 'ašyā ḥāliyih.*

5. *Negation*

Negate the following sentences.

Example: *gad tammū ydarrisū l-gur'ān* ——> *mā gad tammūš yidarrisū l-gur'ān*

i. *iḏā ^{c}ādū fī l-bayt.* ____________________

ii. *allī ^{c}alayhum hāḏa l-^{c}amal.* ____________________

iii. *gad jahhazūh ahlih.* ____________________

iv. *an-nās yitimmū yitġaddaw.* ____________________

v. *gadū bi-xayr.* ____________________

7. *Translation*

Translate the following groups of sentences into Ṣanᶜānī Arabic:

A. Use *man*

i. They sell to whoever will buy.

ii. He is looking for whoever will help him.

iii. He wants someone who will give him money.

B. Use *law-mā*

i. When Abd al-Rahman comes I will come to you.

ii. Sit here until your father comes.

iii. They f. chew until the sunset [prayer] is called.

C. Use *bida'* + imperfect

i. They m. began to bury him in the graveyard.

ii. He began to recite the Qur'an.

iii. The people present began to throw dust onto the grave.

iv. *Saltih* has begun to no longer be [eaten].

D. Use *mā* or *mahmā*

i. Whatever we do we must make lunch.

ii. Whatever he says I must give him lunch.

iii. I will give him whatever he wants.

GLOSSARY

a^{c}ād - yi^{c}īd	to make (s.o.) return
abadan	ever [in neg.]
abrahā	Abraha [male name]
absar - yibsir	to see (s.th.)
abū šanab	satellite m.
^{c}adad pl. *a^{c}dād*	number m.
^{c}aḏalih	neck-ache f.
^{c}adan	Aden f.
^{c}adanī	Adeni m.
^{c}ādanī	I (am) still
^{c}ādatan	usually
aḏḏan - yi'aḏḏin	to call for prayer; to be called [prayer]
^{c}ādī	it f. (is) still
^{c}ādī	that's okay; normal
^{c}ādih pl. *-āt*	custom f.
^{c}ādiš	you f.s. are single
afḏal	preferable
^{c}afwan	sorry; excuse me
^{c}agb	after
^{c}agd pl. *^{c}ugūd*	upper arched window, now with coloured glass m.
ahamm	more important
^{c}ahd pl. *^{c}uhūd*	time; era m.
ahl pl. *ahālī*	family; people m.
ahla wa-sahla	welcome!
aḥmar	red
aḥsan šī	the best thing m.
a^{c}jab - yi^{c}jib	to please (s.o.)
a^{c}jam pl. *^{c}ijmān*	dumb m.
^{c}ajīn	dough m.
^{c}ajīnih	dough f.
ajmal	more beautiful
ajnabī pl. *ajānib*	foreigner m.
akṯarat al-…	most of the …
akṯarat-mā + verb	most commonly
ākul	I eat
al-	the [definite article]
a^{c}lā	higher
^{c}alā	on; against
^{c}alā ḥisāb(ak)	at (your m.s.) own expense
^{c}ālaj - yi^{c}ālij	to treat (s.o.)
^{c}alā kayfih	as he likes
^{c}ala l-asaf	unfortunately
^{c}alā-mā	as adjt.
^{c}alā mayd	so that
al-ān	now
^{c}alā šakl	in the form of
^{c}alā sās	so that
^{c}alā sibb / ^{c}asibb	for; because (of)
^{c}alaykum	lit: on you m.pl.
al-bāb	the gate [of old city]
al-baḥrayn	Bahrein f.
al-barīd	the post m.

al-bayḍā	al-Bayḍā [place in Yemen] f.
al-bunṣar	fourth finger f.
alf pl. *alāf*	one thousand m.
al-ax	the brother m.
al-ġurag	the pits [game] f.
al-gur'ān	the Qur'an m.
al-ḥāl	the state m.
al-ḥamd	thanks; praise m.
al-ḥudaydih	Hudayda [place in Yemen] f.
ᶜālī	high
ālif	experienced
al-ittiṣālāt	communications f.
ᶜāliyat sāᶜah	at the most an hour
al-jawāzāt	[term for ministry of the interior f.]
al-jazāyir	Algeria f.
al-kabīsih	index finger f.
al-kaṯīr	most (of them)
al-kuwayt	Kuwait f.
allaḏī	that; which
ᶜallāgīyih pl. *-āt*	bag; box f.
allāh	God m.
allāh yiḥayyīk	[reply to *ḥayyāk …]*
allāh yixallīhum liš	may God preserve them for you f.s.!
allāh yixallīk	may God preserve you! [i.e. thank you]
al-maġrib	Morocco m.
almānī	German m.
almāniyā	Germany f.
al-marih	the woman; wife f.
al-muhallilih	index finger f.
al-muhimm	the important thing
al-muxā	Mokha [place in Yemen] f.
al-urdunn	Jordan m.
al-wald	the boy m.
al-wusṭā	middle finger f.
al-yaman	Yemen m./f.
al-yawm	today
al-yūnān	Greece f.
ᶜamal - yiᶜmal	to do
ᶜamal	work m.
ᶜamalīyih pl. *-āt*	operation f.
amām	in front of; before
aman	security
amān	safety; den m.
āmīn	amen!
ᶜamm pl. *aᶜmūm*	paternal uncle; father-in-law m.
ammā / mā	as for
ᶜammal - yiᶜammil (lā)	to do (s.th., to s.o.)
ᶜammih pl. *-āt*	paternal aunt; mother-in-law f.
amr pl. *umūr*	matter; thing f.
ᶜamrān	Amran f.
ams	yesterday
ᶜan	about
anā	I
ᶜan ṭarīg	via

antī	you f.s.
ᶜaraṭ - yuᶜraṭ	to gnaw (s.th.)
ᶜarḍ	breadth m.
ᶜārif	knowing m.s.
ᶜarras - yiᶜarris (lā)	to marry (s.o.) off
ᶜašā	evening meal (often a snack)
ᶜaṣab	neck/back-ache m.
ᶜaṣabuh	a neck or back-ache f.
asᶜad	to make (s.o.) happy; to bless
ᶜašān	so that; because
asās pl. *usus*	basis m.
ᶜasb	money given as present m.
aṣbaḥ	to become
ašbīh	similarity m.
ashal	easier
ᶜašī / ᶜašīyih	evening
ᶜasīb pl. *ᶜuswab*	scabbard m.
ᶜasīd	porridge m.
āsif	sorry m.s.
ᶜaṣīr	juice m.
aṣl pl. *uṣūl*	origin m.
aṣlan	originally
ᶜaṣṣab - yiᶜaṣṣub	to put on a headband
aštarī (lī)	I buy
ᶜāṣumuh pl. *ᶜawāṣum*	capital f.
ᶜaswab - yiᶜaswib	to give *ᶜasb* as a present
aswad	black
aṯ-ṯānī	the next
at-turk	the Turks
ᶜāṭuš	thirsty
aw	or
awlā	or
awwal	first; at first
awwal-mā	when first adjt.
awwal šī	the first thing
ax pl. *axwih*	brother m.
axḍar	wet; green
axī	my brother m.
ᶜayb	shame m.
ᶜaybih pl. *-āt*	defect f.
āyih pl. *-āt*	verse f.
ayn	where
ᶜayn pl. *ᶜuyūn*	eye f.
ayy	any
ᶜayyāf	morning sickness in pregnancy m.
ayyaḥīn	when
ayyin	which
ᶜayyinih pl. *-āt*	type f.
aywih	yes
ᶜazīmih pl. *ᶜazāyim*	amulet f.
ᶜazūmih	invitation f.
ᶜazzā	mourning m.
ᶜazzā - yiᶜazzī	to mourn
ᶜazzam - yiᶜazzim	to invite (s.o.)

az-zġīrih	little finger f.
bā^c - yibī^c	to sell (s.th.)
bāb pl. *abwāb*	gate; door m.
ba^{c}d	after
ba^{c}ḍ	some
ba^{c}dā	then; afterwards
baddal - yibaddil	to change (s.th.)
badlih ḏahab	a wide gold collar f.
badrūm pl. *-āt*	cellar m.
bagar	cattle coll. m.
bagarih	cow f.
bāgī	remaining m.
bahār pl. *-āt*	worry f.
bahārāt	spices
baḥīn	early
bāhir	very good
ba^{c}īd	far
bakā - yibkī	to cry
bākir	early
bakkar - yibakkir	to do (s.th.) early
bāl - yibūl	to urinate
baladī	local
balāš	for nothing
ball - yibill	to wet (s.th.)
ballaġ - yiballiġ	to inform (s.o.)
bāmiyih	ladies' fingers f.
banādig	pop guns
bank pl. *bunūk*	bank m.
bard	cold m.
bardag pl. *barādig*	glass; cup m.
bardih pl. *baradāt*	curtain f.
bārid	cold; cold drink
barik pl. *birkān*	pool; pond f.
barrād pl. *-īn*	cold-water bringer m.
bāṣ pl. *bāṣāt*	bus m.
baṣal	large spring onions coll. m.
ba^{c}sas	to muck around
bass	but; only
baṭāṭ	potatoes coll. m.
baṭn pl. *buṭūn*	stomach f.
baṭṭāniyuh pl. *-āt*	blanket f.
bawl	urine m.
baxūr	incense m.
bayḍ	eggs coll. m.
bayḍānī	of/from al-Bayḍā m.
bāyit	bad; corrupt
bayn	between; in
baynih	in it m.
bayt pl. *biyūt*	house m.
bayt aš-šayṭān	'safe place' in hopscotch or touch m.
bayya^c - yibayya^c	to sell (s.th.)
bazz	cloth m.
bazz - yibuzz / yibizz	to take (s.th.)

bibs	Pepsi m.
bida' / bada' - yibda'	to begin
bi-ḏabṭ	exactly
bi-ḏāt	especially
bidāyih pl. *-āt*	beginning f.
bi-dūn	without
bigī - yibgā	to last
bih	there is
bījū pl. *-āt*	Peugot taxi f.
bilād pl. *balāyid*	village; home town f.
bilzigī pl. *balāzig*	bracelet m.
bi-nafar	by person [i.e. in a shared taxi]
bint pl. *banāt*	girl f.
bint aṣ-ṣaḥn	sweet dish of layered pastry with honey and black onion seed f.
bīr pl. *abwār*	well f.
bi-raġm ann…	despite the fact that…
birmih pl. *biram*	clay cooking pot f.
bisbās	chilli pepper m.
b-ismiš	what is your f.s. name?
bi-sur^{c}*ah*	quickly
bi-xayr	well
bi-yawmahā	immediately
brīṭānī	British m.
brīṭāniyā	Britain f.
bug^{c}*ah* pl. *buga*^{c}	place; spot f.
bulbul	fluently [lit: nightingale]
bunn	coffee m.
būrī pl. *-āt*	waterpipe top m.
burtagāl	oranges coll. m.
buṣṣālūh	round onions coll. m.
bustān pl. *basātīn*	garden m.
da^{c}*ā - yid*^{c}*ā*	to call
da^{cc}*ā - yida*^{cc}*ā*	to call
dabbāb pl. *-āt*	small bus m.
ḍabbat ġāz	gas cannister f.
ḍa^{c}*f* pl. *aḍ*^{c}*āf*	double m.
dafa^{c} *- yidfa*^{c}	to pay (s.o., s.th.)
dafan - yidfin	to bury (s.o.)
dafn	burial m.
daftar pl. *dafātir*	exercise book m.
dagdag - yidagdag	to knock
dagg - yidigg / yidugg	to knock, hit (s.th.)
ḍaġġāṭ pl. *-āt*	pressure cooker m.
dagīgih pl. *dagāyig*	minute f.
ḏahab	gold m.
ḍahr	back m.
ḍa^{c}*īf*	weak; thin
ḏakka	there he is!
ḏakkar - yiḏakkir	to remember (s.th.)
ḍalḥak	to laugh
ḏalḥīn	now
dalw pl. *adliyih*	bucket m.

da^{c}mam	to ignore
dār pl. *dūr*	house f.
ḍarab al-ḥidwī	[type of cricket] m.
darajih pl. *darājīn*	stair f.
dār al-ḥamd	[name of hotel f.]
daras - yudrus	to learn; study
daras - yidris	to recite [the Qur'an]
ḍarf pl. *ḍurūf*	envelope m.
darīs	reading of Qur'an m.
ḏarrā - yiḏarrī	to sprinkle (s.th.)
ḍars pl. *aḍrās*	molar tooth m.
ḍarūrī	essential
ḍawā - yuḍwī	to go home
dawā	medicine; liquid medicine m.
dawlih pl. *duwal*	state; country f.
dawr pl. *adwār*	floor [e.g. first floor]; turn, go m.
dawrih pl. *-āt*	trip f.
dawwar - yidawwir	to look for (s.th.); to go round
dawwax - yidawwax	to faint
daxal - yudxul	to enter; go into
dāxil	in; inside
dāyiman	always
dāyirih	circle f.
daymih pl. *diyam*	traditional kitchen f.
ḏayyā	this m.
dayyar - yidayyir	to have a turn
ddī	give m.s.!
dif'	warmth m.
difī - yidfī	to become warm
dihlīz pl. *dahālīz*	hall; place m.
dijāj	chicken coll. m.
dijājih	a chicken f.
dīk pl. *adyāk*	cockeral m.
dirāsih	learning; recitation [of Qur'an] f.
dīwān pl. *dawāwīn*	sitting room [often best room] m.
dixišš	roast chick peas m
ḍubbuh	pumpkin f.
dublih	gold wedding ring f.
ḍuhr	noon m.
duktūr pl. *dakātirih*	doctor m.
dūlāb pl. *dawālīb*	drawer m.
ḍulā^{c}ī	from Dulā^{c} [famous *gāt*-growing area in Hamdān]
dunyā	world f.
duwalī	international
fa-	so conj.
faḍḍal - yifaḍḍul	to prefer (s.th.)
fāḍī	free m.
fagaṭ	only
fagīr	poor
faḥḥ	hot and spicy
fajja^{c} - yifajji^{c}	to frighten; surprise (s.o.)
fakkar - yifakkir	to think
faks pl. *-āt*	fax m.

fallaṭ - yifalliṭ	to leave (s.th.)
fannān pl.*-īn*	artist; singer m.
faransā	France f.
faransāwī	French m.
fard pl. *afrād*	person m.
farḥah pl. *faraḥāt*	present given on birth of a child; joy, pleasure f.
farīg pl. *furūg*	team m.
fāriġ pl. *furġān*	empty; free
farrāših pl. *-āt*	cleaner f.
faṣl pl. *fuṣūl*	classroom m.
fāṣul	gap m.
fasūliyih	French beans f.
fataḥ - yiftaḥ	to open (s.th.)
fatḥah pl. *fataḥ*	opening f.
fātiḥah	[opening chapter of Qur'an f.]
fatrih pl. *-āt*	while; time span f.
fawg	on; on top of
fāyiz pl. *-īn*	winner m.
fī	in
fiḍī - yifḍā	to make time
fidiyū pl. *-āt*	video m.
figh	jurisprudence m.
fīh	there is
fi^{c}il - yif^{c}al	to do; make (s.th.)
fil(i)s dāyir	heads or tails
firiḥ - yifraḥ (lā)	to visit (a new mother)
firiš	furnishings m.
fi-sā^{c}	quickly
fī sinn …	(at) the age of …
flūs / filūs	money m.
frās pl. *-āt*	chisel m.
frāš	covering (e.g. carpet, blanket) m.
ftahan - yiftahin	to relax
ftaja^{c} - yiftaja^{c}	to be surprised
fūl	horse beans m.
fundug pl. *fanādig*	hotel m.
furn pl. *afrān*	modern oven with stove; baker's oven m.
furṣuh pl. *furaṣ*	chance f.
fustān zifāf	wedding dress m.
fustug	pestachios m.
fūṭuh pl. *fuwaṭ*	sarong f.
gā^{c} pl. *gi^{c}ān*	ground; floor m.
gaba^{c} - yigba^{c}	to take (s.th.)
gabar - yigbir	to bury (s.o.)
gabīlī pl. *gabāyil*	tribesman m.
gabl	before
gabl-mā	before adjt.
gabr pl. *gubūr*	grave m.
ġadā	lunch m.
gaḍā pl. *agḍiyuh*	sub-governorate; province m.
gaḍāḍ	native cement to plaster containers m.
gadanā	I (am)
ġaddā - yiġaddī	to give (s.o.) lunch

gaddam - yigaddim	to give; offer (s.o., s.th.)
gadiḥna	we (are)
gadīm	old
gādim	previous
gadū	he (is)
gafā	behind
gaḥš abyaḍ	grey mullet m.
gaḥš aḥmar	red mullet m.
gahwih	spicy coffee husk drink f.
gahwih pl. *gahāwih*	coffee shop f.
gāl - yugūl / yigūl	to say (s.th.)
galam pl. *aglām*	pen m.
galb pl. *gulūb*	heart m.
ġālī	expensive
galīl	little m.
gamarīyih / gamarī pl. *-āt*	top round window in alabaster f.
gambar	to sit
gamīṣ pl. *gumṣān*	loose dress; dress worn by a bride m.
gandal - yigandil	to flick
gandalih	flick [game] f.
ġanī	rich
ġann - yiġinn	to relax
garab - yugrub (lā)	to be related (to)
garābih	relationship f.
gargūš pl. *garāgīš*	square bonnet worn by babies and young girls m.
garīb pl. *agārib*	relation m.
garībih pl. *-āt*	relative f.
gariyih pl. *gurā*	village f.
ġarr / ġayr	only
garrā - yigarrī	to teach (s.o., to read)
ġarraf - yġarraf	to scoop up (s.th.)
gaṣabuh pl. *gaṣīb*	pipe f.
gaṣdī	I mean
gaṣgaṣ	to cut up
gasmak	since you m.s.
gaṣr pl. *guṣūr*	palace m.
ġassal - yiġassil	to wash (s.th./s.o.)
ġassāl pl. *-īn*	washer (of clothes) m.
ġassālih pl. *-āt*	laundry f.
gassam - yigassim	to divide out (s.th.)
gaššām pl. *-īn*	*gušmī*-patch worker
gaṣṣar - yigaṣṣar	to skimp
gaššār pl. *-īn*	coffee seller m.
ġaṭṭā - yiġaṭṭī	to cover (s.th.)
gaṭṭaf - yigaṭṭuf	to cut *gāt*
gawā	please
gawī	very; strong, thick
gaws pl. *agwās*	catapult m.
gawzab	to sit, squat
ġāz	gas m.
gidir - yigdir	to be able; can
ġimāg	black head covering of the *širšaf* which can be lowered over the face m.
gīmih pl. *giyam*	price; cost f.

ginā^c pl. *-āt*	veil m.
gindīl pl. *ganādīl*	lightbulb m.
girāyih	reading; learning f.
girī - yigrā (^{c}*alā)*	to recite (for s.o.)
girš pl. *gurūš*	Riyal m.
gišr	spicy coffee husk drink known as *gahwih* m.
giṭār pl. *-āt*	guitar m.
gtalab - yigtalib	to turn around; change
ġubār	dust m
gubbih pl. *gubab*	arch; vaulted building f.
ġudwuh	tomorrow
gumgumī pl. *gamāgim*	tin can m.
ġummāḏuh	blind man's buff f.
gunṭuruh pl. *ganāṭur*	shoe f.
ġurfat al-in^c*ās*	hospice f.
ġurfih pl. *ġuraf*	room f.
gurnih pl. *guran*	corner f.
guṣṣuh pl. *guṣuṣ*	story f.
guṭ^c*ah* pl. *guṭa*^{c}	piece f.
guwih	strength f.
ḥabaš	black [type of stone]
ḥabašī	Ethiopian
(al-)ḥabaših	Ethiopia f.
ḥabbih pl. *-āt*	a unit; one f.
ḥabbih pl. *ḥubūb*	tablet m.
ḥabbih sawdā	onion seed f.
ḥabl	skipping rope, skipping; rope m.
ḥabs	prison m.
ḥabs wa-l-lamān	prison and safety [game] m.
hāḏā	this m.
ḥadd	someone m.
ḥaddad - yiḥaddid	to establish; determine (s.th.)
ḥadīd	iron m.
ḥadīṯ pl. *aḥādīṯ*	Prophetic tradition m.
hadīyih pl. *hadāyā*	present f.
ḥafar - yiḥfar	to dig a hole; bore
ḥaflat ^{c}*iris*	wedding party f.
ḥagg	of; amounting to
ḥajar pl. *ḥijār*	stone; mortar f.
ḥājih pl. *-āt*	thing f.
hāk	that is
ḥākā - yiḥākī	to talk (to s.o.)
hākaḏā	like this
ḥakīm	practitioner of traditional medicine m.
ḥalāwā	sweetness f.
ḥālī	nice
ḥāliš	your f.s. state m.
ḥālukum	your m.pl. state m.
ḥāmī	hot
ḥamī - yiḥmī	to become hot
ḥāmil	pregnant
ḥammā - yiḥammī	to heat (s.th.)
ḥammām pl. *-āt*	modern-style bathroom; bath; Turkish bath m.

ḥammāmī pl. *-īn*	man who works in Turkish bath m.
hānā	here
ḥanafī pl. *-āt*	tap f.
ḥānūt pl. *ḥawānīt*	shop m.
ḥārah pl. *-āt*	area f.
ḥarām	unlawful
ḥarārih	heat f.
ḥarīw pl. *ḥarāwī*	bridegroom m.
ḥarīwih pl. *ḥarāwī*	bride f.
ḥārr	hot
ḥarrak - yiḥarrik	to move (s.th.)
ḥasab / ḥasb	according to
ḥasab - yiḥsub	to work (s.th.) out
ḥaṣbuh	measles f.
ḥass - yiḥiss	to feel (s.th.)
ḥaṭab	wood m.
ḥaṭṭ - yiḥuṭṭ	to put (s.th.)
ḥattā	until; up to; even
ḥawā - yiḥwī	to contain (s.th.)
ḥawḍ pl. *aḥwāḍ*	trough m.
ḥawā'ij	spices
ḥawālī	around; about
ḥawḍ pl. *aḥwāḍ*	bath tub m
ḥawī pl. *ḥwāyā*	yard m.
ḥayāh pl. *-āt*	life f.
hayl	cardamon coll. m.
ḥayṯ-mā	where adjt.
ḥayyā	come on! may God give you life!
ḥayyāk allāh	thank you! [lit: may God give you life!]
ḥazīn	sad
ḥijrih pl. *ḥijar*	hall f.
ḥilbih	fenugreek f.
ḥimil - yiḥmal	to carry (s.th.)
ḥimir / ḥimār pl. *aḥmirih*	donkey m.
ḥīn	when adjt.
ḥinnā	henna m.
hirib - yuhrub	to flee; escape
ḥirz pl. *aḥrāz*	amulet m.
ḥizām pl. *aḥzimih*	belt m.
ḥtabas - yiḥtabis	to be imprisoned
ḥummih	fever f.
ḥuṣam	counters [lit: small pebbles]
ibb	Ibb [place in Yemen] f.
ibn pl. *abnā*	son m.
ibrih pl. *ibar*	needle f.
ᶜīd pl. *aᶜyād*	festival; holiday m.
iḏā	if
igtiṣād pl. *-āt*	economy m.
ᶜilāj pl. *-āt*	treatment m.
ilayn	to where
ᶜilbih pl. *ᶜilab*	tin; box f.
ᶜilim - yiᶜlam	to know
illā	but yes!

^{c}*ilm*	knowledge m.
^{c}*ind*	with; at the house of
^{c}*ind-mā*	when adjt.
innamā	however adjt.
in šā' allāh	God willing; hopefully
insān pl. *nās*	person m.
^{c}*irif - yi*^{c}*raf*	to know (s.th.)
^{c}*irig - yi*^{c}*rig*	to sweat
^{c}*iris* pl. *a*^{c}*rās*	wedding m.
^{c}*irj*	lameness m.
^{c}*išā*	evening prayer m.
ishāl	diarrheoa m.
iṣlāḥ	making (e.g. bread) m.
ism pl. *asāmī/ asmā*	name m.
(i)smī	my name m.
^{c}*išrīn*	twenty
istirlīnī	Sterling
iṯiyūbīyā	Ethiopia f.
iṯnā-mā	while adjt.
iṯnayn	two m.
itṣal - yitṣal (bi)	to telephone; call (s.o.)
^{c}*iyyāl*	children
jā' - yijī	to come
ja^c*ālih*	sweets coll. f.
jāb - yijīb (lā)	to bring (to s.o.)
jābar - yijābir	to console; pay condolences
jadd pl. *ajdād*	mat. grandfather m.
jaddad - yijaddid	to renew (s.th.)
jaddih pl. *-āt*	mat. grandmother f.
jadīd pl. *judud*	new
jadr pl. *jidār*	wall m.
jafāf	dehydration m.
jahhaz - yijahhiz	to prepare (s.th.)
jāhil pl. *jahhāl*	child m.
jāhiz	ready
jalas - yijlis	to sit; stay
jālis	staying m.
jallās pl. *jalālīs*	waterpipe stand m.
jama^c *- yijma*^{c}	to gather, collect
jam^c*ah*	together
jamb	beside, next to
jambiyih pl. *janābī*	curved silver dagger f.
jāmi^c pl. *jawāmi*^{c}	mosque m.
jāmi^c*ah* pl. *-āt*	university f.
jamīl	beautiful
jār pl. *jīrān*	neighbour m.
jārih pl. *-āt*	neighbour f.
jarr - yijirr	to take (s.th.)
jarrab - yijarrib	to try (s.th.)
jarrāḥ pl. *-īn*	surgeon m.
jass - yijiss	to stay; keep doing (s.th.)
jāwab - yijāwab	to answer (s.o.)
jawāz pl. *-āt*	passport m.

jāwi^{c}	hungry
jaww	weather m.
jawz al-hind	coconut m.
jawzih	coconut f.
jazzār pl. *-īn*	butcher m.
jibnih	cheese f.
jibnih bayḏā	white cheese f.
jiddih pl. *-āt*	midwife f.
jīhān	Jihan [female name]
jiḥr	behind m.
jināzih pl. *janāyiz*	funeral bier f.
jtama^{c} - yijtama^{c}	to get together; meet
jūb^{w}ā pl. *ajbīyih*	roof f.
juhah	direction f.
ka-	like prep.
ka^{cc}ak - yika^{cc}ik	to make cake
kabīr pl. *kubār*	grown-up; adult m.
kaḏā	like that
ka-ḏayyā(hā)	like that
kafan / kfan	shroud m.
kafat - yikfit	to bind; wear (s.th.)
kaffā - yikaffī	to be enough
kaffan - yikaffin	to put (s.o.) in a shroud
ka^{c}k	[type of] cake m.
kalām	speech; s.th. said m.
kalimih pl. *-āt*	word f.
kallaf - yikallaf	to cost (s.th.)
kallam - yikallim	to talk (to s.o.)
(bi-)kam	how much/many?
ka-mā	as adjt.
kāmil	whole
kam-mā	as many as; however much adjt.
kammal - yikammil	to finish; complete (s.th.)
kammīyih	amount f.
kammūn	cumin m.
kaššāf pl. *-āt*	torch m.
kātib pl. *kuttāb*	writer; scribe m.
kaṯīr	a lot; many
kawā - yikwī	to cauterise
kawdak	you're always!
kawkabān	Kawkaban [place in Yemen] f.
kayf	how
kayyas - yikayyis	to wash with a *kīs*
kibrīt	matches coll. m.
kidmih pl. *kidam*	a roll of soldiers' bread f.
kīkih	cake f.
kīlū	kilo m.
kīs pl. *akyās*	wash bag, mit m.
kisir - yuksar	to break
kiṯir - yikṯar	to be many
kitlī pl. *katālī*	tea-kettle m.
kūfīyih pl. *kawāfī*	coloured head cloth f.
kull	each; every; all

kulūnīyih	cologne f.
kurih	ball f.
kūt pl. *akwāt*	jacket m.
kuṯrih	many; large number f.
kwayyis	good
lā	if
labbas - yilabbis	to dress (s.o., in s.th.)
laḏa^{c} *- yilḏa*^{c}	to strike (s.th.) lightly
ladah	clothes
laff - yiliff	to turn
laggam - yilaggim	to feed (s.o., s.th.)
lāḥaḍ - yilāḥiḍ	to observe (s.th.)
laḥḥag - yilaḥḥig	to chase (s.o.)
lāḥigih	catch f.
lā^{c}*ib* pl. *-īn*	player m.
lākin	but
lammā	when adjt.
law	if
law-mā	when; until adjt.
lawn pl. *alwān*	colour m.
law samaḥt	please [lit: if you allow]
lawz	almonds coll. m.
laxbaṭ	to mix up
layl pl. *layālī*	night m.
laylat al-gubūl	wedding night f.
laylat al-ḥilfih	wedding night f.
lī	to me
li'ann / lann	because
li^{c}*bat al-lazrār*	the button game f.
li^{c}*bat az-zanb*	date-stone game f.
li^{c}*bih* pl. *al*^{c}*āb*	game f.
libis - yilbas	to put on, wear (s.th.)
lībiyā	Libya f.
libs	clothes m.
ligī - yilgā	to find (s.th.)
li^{c}*ib - yil*^{c}*ab*	to play (s.th.)
liji' - yilja' (lā)	to resort (to)
lilmā	why
līm	lime juice m.
limi'	why
lisān pl. *alsinih*	tongue m.
liṯmih pl. *liṯam*	tight black covering to cover mouth and nose f.
lubnān	Lebanon m.
lugf pl. *algāf*	mouth m.
lūkandih pl. *-āt*	small, cheap hotel; rest-house f.
ma^{c}	with
mā	what; isn't it?
mā'	water m.
ma^{c}*ārif*	acquaintances
mablaġ pl. *mabāliġ*	amount m.
mablūl	wet
mabnī	built m.

mabsam pl. *mabāsim*	lip m.
madā^{c}*ah* pl. *madāyi*^{c}	waterpipe f.
madagg pl. *-āt*	pestle m.
madallih pl. *-āt*	large water jar f.
madd - yimudd	to stretch out
maddad - yimaddid	to spread (s.th.)
māddih	material; substance f.
māḏī	past m.
madīnih pl. *mudun*	town f.
madrasih pl. *madāris*	school f.
mafāriš	furnishings
mafraj pl. *mafārij*	room with a view in which *gāt* chews are held m.
mafrūš	furnished
maftūḥ	open
magaṣṣ pl. *-āt*	scissors m.
magbirih pl. *magābir*	graveyard f.
maglā pl. *magālī*	stone cooking pot m.
maġrafih pl. *maġārif*	scoop f.
magramih pl. *magārim*	large colourful cloth to cover hair and face f.
maġrib	sunset m.
maġsal pl. *maġāsil*	modern-style sink m.
magṭaṣ pl. *magāṭiṣ*	bath; Jewish ritual bath m.
ma^{c}*had* pl. *ma*^{c}*āhid*	institute m.
maḥallī	local
maḥaṭṭuh pl. *-āt*	station f.
mahr	bride price m.
maḥwaḍ pl. *maḥāwiḍ*	trough m.
majmū^{c}*ah*	group f.
makān pl. *amkinih*	main sitting room m.
makarūnih	macaroni m.
m'akkad	certain
maklaf pl. *makālif*	woman f.
maktab pl. *makātib*	office m.
maktab al-barīd	post-office m.
maktabih pl. *makātib*	library; bookshop f.
maktūb pl. *makātīb*	letter m.
makwih pl. *makāwī*	cauterisation f.
mal^{c}*ab* pl. *malā*^{c}*ib*	playground m.
malābis	clothes
mal^{c}*agih* pl. *malā*^{c}*ig*	spoon f.
mal^{c}*agih* ^{c}*ūdī*	wooden spoon f.
malak - yimlik (lā)	to conduct the *milkih* (for s.o.)
malān	full
malāriyā	malaria m.
mallā - yimillī	to fill (s.th.)
malūj	large, flat bread coll. m.
malūjih	a large, flat bread m.
mamdūd	stretched
ma^{c}*mūl*	made
man	who; someone
ma^{c}*nā* pl. *ma*^{c}*ānī*	meaning m.
manāxih	Manakha [place in Yemen] f.
maraḍ pl. *amrāḍ*	sickness; illness m.
marag	broth m.

maraysī	sugar m.
mārib	Marib [place in Yemen] f.
marīḍ pl. *-īn / amrāḍ*	patient; sick person m.
marih pl. *niswān / nisā*	woman f.
markaz pl. *marākiz*	centre (e.g. of a *nāḥiyih*) m.
markūz	supported
m^{c}arraf	well-known
marrih pl. *-āt*	time f.
marrih	very
masā	evening m.
mā šā' allāh	goodness!
masāfih pl. *-āt*	distance f.
masār pl. *-āt*	head scarf m.
masār nāzilī	head scarf worn under *masār ṭālu^{c}ī* m.
masār ṭālu^{c}ī	head scarf worn over *masār nāzilī* m.
mašbūk	interlinked
mašġūl	busy
masḥalih pl. *masāḥil*	verticle draining surface f.
masjid pl. *masājid*	mosque m.
māšī	no; otherwise, or else
maṣmaṣ	to suck
maṣnū^c	made
maṣr	Egypt f.
maṣrī	Egyptian
masra^c	early; soon
massā - yimassī	to play *yā masā*
māt - yimūt (^{c}alā)	to die (on s.o.)
matā	when
maṯal pl. *amṯāl*	proverb m.
maṯalan	for example
maṭ^{c}am pl. *maṭā^{c}um*	restaurant m.
maṭār pl. *-āt*	airport m.
maṭbax pl. *maṭābux*	modern-style kitchen m.
maṭḥūn	ground adj.
ma tjīš	you m.s. are not coming
matkā pl. *matākī*	cushion support; arm rest m.
maṭraguh pl. *maṭārug*	hammer f.
mawḍū^c pl. *mawāḍī^c*	matter m.
maw^{c}id pl. *mawā^{c}id*	appointment m.
mawjūd	present; available
mawsim pl. *mawāsim*	season m. [the wedding season is after festivals]
mawt pl. *amwāt*	death; funeral m.
maxbazih pl. *maxābiz*	padded bread applicator used to make *xubz* as opposed to *malūj* f.
maxḍūb	beaten
maxṣūṣ (bi)	specially for; specialised in
maxzūg	having a hole
m^{c}ayyafih	having morning sickness f.
mayyit	deceased m.
mā zāl	it is still
mazḥagih pl. *mazāḥig*	stone for crushing herbs, vegetables or salt f.
mazkūm	having a cold
ma^{c}zūm	invited
ma^{c}zūmih pl. *ma^{c}āzīm*	guest f.

mġallaf	covered; wrapped
mi^{c}ayyan / m^{c}ayyin	particular; certain
mīdān pl. *mayādīn*	square m.
mīdān at-taḥrīr	Liberation Square m.
midawwir	rounded
migbār	burial m.
miġsālih pl. *maġāsil*	laundry f.
migšāmih pl. *magāšim*	*gušmī* patch f.
mihrih	price f.
mijabbir pl. *-īn*	traditional bone setter m.
mijābirih	consoling; mourning f.
miksir	broken down
mi^{c}lāmih pl. *ma^{c}ālim*	traditional school f.
milḥ	salt m.
milkih	wedding ceremony f.
min	from
min ajl	in order to; so that
minayn	whence; from where
min jadīd	again [lit: from new]
min nāḥiyih	on the one hand
min šān	so that
miš	not
mišī - yimšī	to walk; to go
misiḥ - yimsaḥ	to wipe (s.th.)
misik - yimsak	to grab (s.th.)
miškilih pl. *mašākil*	problem f.
mišrab pl. *mašārib*	mouthpiece m.
mistadīr	round
mistaraḥ pl. *-āt*	traditional bathroom m.
mistaṭīl	long
mišwār pl. *mašāwir*	errand; s.th. to do m.
miṯgilih	heavily pregnant
miṯl	like prep.
mitr pl. *amtār*	metre m.
mitwājid	very common
mitzawwij	married
mixaddir	narcotic; doped-up
mixbāzih pl. *maxābiz*	bakery f.
miyih pl. *-āt*	hundred f.
mizhir	in flower; blooming
mizmār pl. *mazāmīr*	pipe m. [played at weddings]
mlawwaḥ	large thin flaky bread often eaten with fish m.
mlawwan	coloured
msajjilih pl. *-āt*	tape recorder f.
mšakkal	drink of mixed fresh fruit juices m.
mṣallaḥ	made
mšamma^{c}	plastic sheet m.
mtadd - yimtadd	to lie down; stretch out
mtiḥān pl. *-āt*	exam m.
mtilī - yimtilī	to fill up; become full
mu^{c}aḏḏal	having neck-ache
mu^{c}allim pl. *-īn*	teacher m.
mubāširih	immediately
mudarris pl. *-īn*	teacher m.

mudīr pl. *mudarā*	manager m.
mugābil	fee; money paid to teacher/school m.
muġannī pl. *-īn*	singer m.
mugawwit pl. *-īn*	*gāt* trader m.
muġtsal	washing slab m.
muḥaddid	determined; certain
muḥāfaḏuh pl. *-āt*	governorate f.
muhtamm (bi)	concerned (with)
mujtama^{c} *[-īn]*	gathered, collected [oft. in plural]
mukawwan / mikawwan	made up of
mumarriḍ pl.*-īn*	nurse m.
mumkin	[it is] possible
munfalliṭ	left; isolated
murabba^{c} pl. *-āt*	square m.
murā^{c}*ī (lā)*	waiting (for s.o.)
murr	myrhh m.
murtāḥ	well off
muruḍ - yimraḍ	to become ill
mushil	laxative m.
mustašfā pl. *-āt*	hospital m.
mustawṣaf pl. *-āt*	clinic m.
muṭabbag	thin pastry pocket fried with egg, onion and tomato inside m.
muṭallaguh pl. *-āt*	divorcee f.
muṭhār pl. *-āt*	traditional bathroom m.
mūṭūr pl. *-āt*	motorbike m.
muwaḏḏaf pl. *-īn*	employee m.
muxaṣṣaṣ	specialised
muxlāṣ	silver m
muxtaṣṣ	experienced
mwaḏḏaf	employed
mwaggaṣ	trimmed [stone]
mwajjilih pl. *-āt*	widow f.
mxalfa^{c}	worn; trimmed [stone]
nabbā - yinabbī	to tell; inform (s.o.)
naḏḏaf - yinaḏḏuf	to clean (s.th.)
nafar pl. *anfār*	person m.
naffaḍ - yinaffiḍ	to dust
nafs	[the] same
nafsī	I really want to
nagaḏ - yingiḏ	to rescue (s.o.)
naggaš - yinaggiš	to tatoo (s.o., with antimony)
nagš	cosmetic painting m.
naḥḥās	copper; brass m.
nāhī	yes, okay; good
nāḥiyih pl. *nawāḥī*	district f.
nā'ib pl. *nuwwāb*	deputy m.
naks	smoke m.
nār pl. *nīrān*	fire f.
našad - yinšid	to sing songs [at funerals/births]
našīd pl. *anāšīd*	song m.
naššād pl. *-īn*	singer m.
naw^{c} pl. *anwā*^{c}	type; kind; thing m.
nazal - yinzil	to go down; get out

nāzil — below; downstairs
nazzal - yinazzil — to lower (s.th.)
nḍug — throw m.s.!
nīb pl. *anyāb* — canine tooth m.
nifās — childbirth; childbirth sickness m.
niks / nuks pl. *-āt* — pants m.
nīnī pl. *nawānī* — baby m.
nisbih pl. *nisab* — relation f.
(*bi-nisbih lā* — in relation to)
nisī - yinsā — to forget
niskafey — Nescafé
nišrab — we drink
nšaġal - yinšaġil (bi-) — to be occupied (with s.th.)
ntahā - yintahī — to be finished
nūbih pl. *nuwab* — round, defensive tower f.
nūrih — slaked lime f.
nuṣṣ — half m.
nušṭuh — activity f.

radā^{c} — Rada [place in Yemen] f.
radd - yiridd — to return (s.th.)
raḍī - yirḍā — to want
rāg - yirīg / yirāg — to pour (s.th.)
ragabih pl. *-āt* — neck f.
rāgid — sleeping
ragm pl. *argām [at-tilifūn]* — [telephone] number m.
rāḥ - yirūḥ — to go
raḥ - yiriḥ (li) — to go
raḥḥam - yiraḥḥam — to have pity
rajja^{c} *- yirijji*^{c} — to give back, return (s.th.)
rajjāl pl. *rijāl* — man m.
ramā - yirmī — to throw (s.th.)
ramaḍān — Ramadan m.
ramzī — token adj.
*rās / ra'***s** pl. *ru'ūs* — head m.
rāsal - yirāsil — to correspond (with s.o.)
raṣduh pl. *-āt* — main, asphalted road f.
rasmī — official
raṭab — bread layered with fat and baked in *tannūr* oven m.
rawānī — sweet cake
rawwā - yirawwī — to show (s.o., s.th.)
rayya^{c} *- yirayya*^{c} — to wait for
ridā' pl. *-āt* — cape of the *širšaf* m.
rīf pl. *aryāf* — countryside m.
rīḥān pl. *rayāḥīn* — parsley m.
riji^{c} *- yirja*^{c} — to return
rijim - yurjum / yirjim — to throw (s.th.)
rijl pl. *arjul* — leg f.; peddle [of bicycle] m.
rikib - yirkab — to ride (s.th.)
rikin - yirkan — to think
risālih pl. *rasā'il / rasāyil* — letter f.
rtāḥ - yirtāḥ (bi) — to be happy (with s.o.)
rtkaz - yirtkaz — to be set up; on top
rubbamā — maybe

rukbih pl. *rukab*	knee f.
ruzz	rice coll. m.
rxīṣ / raxīṣ	cheap
šā-	[future particle]
sāᶜah pl. *-āt*	watch; hour f.
sa'al - yis'al	to ask (s.o., s.th.)
saᶜālih	a cough f.
sabab pl. *asbāb*	reason m.
ṣabāḥ	morning m.
sabar - yisbur	[in neg.] can't be, do
ṣabbaḥkum	lit: he made you wake up
sabbar - yisabbir	to prepare (s.th.)
ṣabbar - yiṣabbir	[God] to grant forbearance
sabbūrih	blackboard f.
sābir	good
ṣaᶜduh	Saᶜda [place in Yemen] f.
šaḏarawān pl. *-āt*	fountain m.
sadr	hot room in Turk. bath m.
šāf - yišūf	to see (s.th.)
šafā - yišfī	to make (s.o.) well
safar	travel; journey m.
sāfar - yisāfir	to travel
ṣaff pl. *ṣufūf*	line m.
ṣaffā / ṣfā - yuṣaffī / yuṣfī	to bathe intr.; to wash trns.
šaffaṭ - yišaffiṭ	to make *šafūṭ*
ṣafīf pl. *ṣufwaf*	shelf m.
safīnih pl. *safāyin*	ship f.
safīr pl. *sufarā*	ambassador m.
šafūṭ	dish of sour pancake and yoghurt m.
šagā - yišgā	to work
šagā	work; wage m.
šaġal - yišġal	to bother; trouble (s.o.)
saggā - yisaggī	to water; irrigate (s.th.)
šāgūs pl. *šawāgīs*	small rectangular or square window which opens fully for ventilation. Sometimes in the middle of a *gamarīyih* m.
šagwar	to smoke a cigarette
ṣāḥ - yiṣīḥ	to shout; cry out
šahay	tea m.
ṣaḥḥ	true; that's right
ṣaḥḥ - yiṣuḥḥ	to get well
ṣaḥḥah	health f.
sāḥil pl. *sawāḥil*	traditional sink; washing floor m.
ṣaḥn pl. *ṣuḥūn*	plate m.
šahr pl. *šuhūr*	month m.
šahrayn	two months
ṣāḥub pl. *aṣḥāb*	friend; mate m.
ṣāḥub al-bayt	houseowner; landlord m.
sā'il	liquid adj.
šajarih pl. *šijar / ašjār*	tree f.
sakab - yuskub	to pour (s.th.)
šakkam - yišakkim	to perform the *šikmih* (for s.o.)
šākimih pl. *-āt*	parturient; newly married woman on day of *šikmih*
sākin	living

sākit	silent; quiet
šakkam - yišakkim	to perform the *šikmih* (for s.o.)
šakl pl. *aškāl*	shape; form m.
šāl pl. *šīlān*	large light-coloured shawl worn over shoulders m.
ṣalā	towards, to
ṣalaḥ - yiṣlaḥ	to be right; to do
ṣalāh pl. *ṣalawāt*	prayer f.
salām	peace m.
salāmih	peace f.
ṣalaṭuh	salad f.
ṣalfā	to clean
šalīyih	confusion f.
šall - yišill	to take (s.th.)
ṣallā - yiṣallī (ᶜalā)	to pray (for s.o.)
sallam - yisallim (ᶜalā)	to greet (s.o.)
ṣalṣuh	sauce f.
saltih	hot dish of meat broth topped with fenugreek f.
ṣāluḥ	Salih [male name]
sᶜam	i.e., that is to say
sāᶜ-mā	like
samaḥ - yismaḥ	to allow
samḥ	straight
samīrih	Samira [female name]
sammā - yisammī	to call (s.o., s.th.)
samn	clarified butter m.
samn baladī	local clarified butter m.
samrā	brown f.
šams	sun m.
ṣanᶜā	Ṣanᶜā' f.
ṣanᶜānī	Ṣanᶜānī m.
ṣanᶜānī	Ṣanᶜānī [dialect] f.
sanih pl. *sinīn*	year f.
sannab - yisannib	to stand up
ṣanūnuh	tomato, fish, and potato dish f.
sār - yisīr	to go
šaᶜr	hair coll. m.
šaraḥ - yišraḥ	to explain (s.th.)
šāriᶜ pl. *šawāriᶜ*	street m.
šāriᶜah pl. *-āt*	bride's dresser woman f.
ṣarmīyuh pl. *-āt*	head covering f.
ṣarmīyuh abū xaṭṭ	face veil: rectangular black cotton bordered in red f.
ṣarrāf pl. *-īn*	money changer m.
ṣarrāfuh pl. *-āt*	money changers f.
šaršaf / širšaf pl. *šarāšif*	long black overall with skirt, cape and veil which covers clothes and hair m.
šarṭ	bridal sum m.
šarṭ pl. *šurūṭ*	condition m.
šāših pl. *-āt*	very thin black cloth to cover head f.
satar - yistir	to be able; can
šāṭur	clever
sawā	together; properly
sawā ('ann) ... aw	whether ... or
sawwāg pl. *-īn*	driver m.
sawwāḥ pl. *-īn*	tourist m.

ṣawwar - yiṣawwur — to [photo]copy (s.th.)
šaxṣ pl. *ašxāṣ* — person m.
sa^{c}*y* — effort; endeavour m.
šaybih pl. *šayabāt* — old man m.
ṣayd as-samak — fishing [game] m.
saydanā — [teacher in *mi*^{c}*lāmih*] m.
saykal pl. *-āt* — bicycle m.
ṣāyum — fasting
šayx pl. *šuyūx* — learned man m.
sayyab - yisayyib — to carry (s.th.)
ṣayyaḥ - yiṣayyuḥ — to sing; shout
sayyārat is^{c}*āf* — ambulance f.
sayyārih pl. *-āt* — car f.
ṣbaḥtū — lit: you m.pl. woke up
ṣbu^{c} pl. *aṣābu*^{c} — finger m.
sfinj — foam m.
šī / šay pl. *ašyā* — thing m.
šibām — Shibam [place in Yemen] f.
šibiḥ - yišbaḥ — to take hold of; grasp (s.th.)
sidr pl. *sudūr* — chest m.
sifārih pl. *-āt* — embassy f.
šigg — beside; next to
si^{c}*il - yis*^{c}*al* — to have a cough
šijnī pl. *ašjān* — branch m.
šiklīt — chocolate m.
šikmih — day bride's family invites groom's family after wedding f.
simi^{c} *- yisma*^{c} — to hear (s.th.)
simint — cement m.
sinnih pl. *sinān* — incisor tooth f.
si^{c}*r* pl. *as*^{c}*ār* — price m.
širib - yišrab — to drink (s.th.)
širkih — red meat f.
sirwāl pl. *sarāwīl* — loose trousers worn under *zinnih* m.
sitārih pl. *sitāyir* — coloured flat wrap worn outside over indoor clothes f.
šrub — sugar syrup m.
ṣṭabaḥt — I had breakfast
ṣṭaff - yiṣṭaff — to be in line
štaġal - yištaġil — to work
sta^{c}*mal - yista*^{c}*mil* — to use (s.th.)
štarā - yištarī — to buy (s.th.)
staṭā^{c} *- yistaṭī*^{c} — to be able
stawā - yistawī — to be ready
staxdam - yistaxdim — to use (s.th.)
šubbāk pl. *šabābīk* — latticed cooler which juts out on outer wall of house and is used to keep food cool. Can be made of wood or mud m.
ṣubḥ — morning m.
ṣubī pl. *ṣubyān* — boy, youth m.
ṣubūḥ — breakfast m.
ṣudā^{c} — headache m.
ṣudg — really!
sūg pl. *aswāg* — market m./f.
sūg al-bagar — cattle market
sūg al-bazz — cloth market
sūg aḏ-ḏahab — gold market

sūg al-gāt	*gāt* market
sūg al-gišr	coffee market
sūg al-ḥabb	grain market
sūg al-ḥadīd	iron market
sūg al-^{c}*inab*	grape market
sūg al-^{c}*irj*	donkey market
sūg al-milḥ	salt market [general name for whole market area]
sūg al-muxlāṣ	silver market
sūg an-naḥḥās	copper market
sūg aṭ-ṭīsān	market for metal plates
sūg at-titin	tobacco market
sūg az-zabīb	dried fruit market
šuġl	work m.
šuġlih	hard work f.
sukkar	sugar m.
šukr	thanks m.
ṣumāṭuh pl. *ṣamāyuṭ*	men's turban f.
sūna	sauna f.
ṣundūg pl. *ṣanādīg [al-barīd]*	post box [as in post-box number] m.
sūriyā	Syria f.
surūr	delight m.
suxār	black on side of cooking pot m.
šwayyih	a little
syāsih / siyāsih	politics f.
ta^{c}*b (*^{c}*alā)*	tiring (for s.o.)
ṭab^{c}*an*	of course
ṭabax - yuṭbux	to cook (s.th.)
ṭabbāx pl. *-īn*	cook m.
tabdīl	replacement m.
ṭabī^{c}*ah*	s.th. natural f.
ṭabīnuh pl. *ṭabāyun*	co-wife f.
ṭabīx	mixed vegetables m.
ṭābu^{c}	habit; custom m.
ṭābu^{c} pl. *ṭawābu*^{c}	stamp m.
taḏkirih pl. *taḏākir*	ticket f.
tadrīs	teaching m.
tadxīn	smoking m.
ṭaffā - yiṭuffī	to do without (s.th.)
tafruṭuh / tufruṭuh	women's party f.
^{c}*tagad - yi*^{c}*tagid*	to believe (s.th.)
taglīd pl. *tagālīd*	tradition m.
ṭāguh pl. *ṭīgān*	opening window f.
ṭaḥīn	flour m.
taḥt	below, beneath
tā^{c}*ib*	unwell; tired
tāj pl. *tījān*	wedding tiara m.
tājir pl. *tujjār*	trader; merchant m.
tajwīd	Qur'an reading m.
taks pl. *-iyāt*	taxi m.
tākul	you m.s. eat
ṭalab	call; demand m.
ṭalāg	divorce m.
t^{c}*ālaj - yit*^{c}*ālaj*	to be treated

ṯalājih pl. *-āt*	thermos f.
ṯalāṯīn	thirty
talgīḥ pl. *-āt*	vaccination m.
ṭall - yuṭull (ᶜalā)	to look down (on s.th.)
ṭallag - yiṭallug	to divorce (a woman)
tᶜallam - yitᶜallam	to learn
ṭālub pl. *ṭullāb*	student m.
ṭāluguh pl. *-āt*	recently divorced woman f.
tᶜāmal - yitᶜāmal (ᶜalā)	to deal (with s.o.)
tamām	okay?
ṯaman	price; fare m.
ṯamān pl. *ṯawāmin*	week m.
ṭamāṭīs	tomatoes coll. m.
tamm - yitimm	to finish (s.th.)
tanak pl. *atnāk*	water tank m.
ṭannan - yiṭannun	to be distracted
tannūr pl. *tanāwīr*	traditional oven f.
tannūr ġāz	modern round gas oven [same shape as above] f.
tannūr ḥaṭab	traditional round wood-burning oven f.
ṭaraḥ - yiṭraḥ (lā)	to give (s.th., to s.o.); to put
ṭarḥ	wedding present coll. m.
ṭarḥah pl. *ṭaraḥāt*	wedding present; floor; level f.
ṭarīguh	way f.
tᶜaššā - yitᶜaššā	to have supper
ṭāsuh pl. *ṭīsān*	bowl; tin or iron container; plate f.
ṭawālī	straight on; all the time
ṯawm	garlic coll. m.
ṯawmih	piece of garlic f.
ṯawrih pl. *-āt*	revolution f.
ṭayramānuh pl. *-āt*	small room at top of house; watch-out room f.
ṭayyāruh pl. *-āt*	plane f.
ṭayyub	good
tbaxṭaṭ	to write (s.th.)
tbaxxar - yitbaxxar	to recover
tġaddā - yitġaddā	to have lunch
tgahwā	to drink coffee
tgargaš	to wear a bonnet
tġassal - yitġassil	to wash o.s.
tgaṭṭaᶜ - yitgaṭṭaᶜ	to be cut up
tḥammam - yitḥammam	to bathe
tḥannā - yitḥannā	to henna o.s.
tiᶜib - yitᶜab	to become tired
tiᶜizz	Taizz [place in Yemen] f.
tijāh	before
tilāwih	recitation f.
tilifūn pl. *-āt*	telephone m.
tiliviziyūn pl. *-āt*	television m.
timṯāl pl. *tamāṯīl*	statue m.
tištī	you m.s. want
tištarī	you m.s. buy
titin	tobacco m.
tkā' - yitkī (ᶜalā)	to sit, lean (on s.th.)
tkallam - yitkallim (ᶜan)	to talk (about s.th.)
tkarbas	to squat

tkayyas - yitkayyas	to wash o.s. with a *kīs*
tlaṯṯam - yitlaṯṯam	to wear a *liṯmih*
tmaddad -yitmaddid	to be spread
tmaššaṭ - yitmaššaṭ	to comb o.s.
tnaggaš - yitnaggaš	to tatoo o.s.
traḥḥam - yitraḥḥam	to pay respects
trawwaḥ - yitrawwaḥ	to go home
tsā^{c}*ad - yitsā*^{c}*ad*	to help o.a.
tsa^{cc}*al - yitsa*^{cc}*al*	to cough
tšaršaf	to wear the *širšaf*
ttafag - yittafig	to agree
ṭufāyuh pl. *-āt*	ash-tray f.
ṭufl pl. *aṭfāl*	child m.
ṭūl	length m.
ṭūl al-wagt	the whole time
ṯulāṯī	triangular
ṭulu^{c} *- yiṭla*^{c}	to get up; start doing s.th.; work out at
ṭunnānuh	wonder; distraction f.
turāb	dust, soil m.
tuṣfī	cleaning m.
txaṣṣaṣ - yitxaṣṣaṣ (bi)	to specialise (in s.th.)
tzawwaj - yitzawwaj	to get married
^{c}*ūdī* pl. ^{c}*īdān*	twig m.
uḏn pl. *āḏān*	ear f.
ummī	my mother f.
^{c}*urgūb* pl. ^{c}*arāgīb*	heel m.
^{c}*uṣbuh* pl. ^{c}*uṣab*	brightly-coloured, wide hair band f.
uslūb pl. *asālīb*	method m.
usrih pl. *usar*	family f.
ustāḏ pl. *asātiḏih*	professor m.
^{c}*uṭr*	perfume m.
^{c}*uṭūr* pl. *-āt*	perfume m.
uxt pl. *xawāt*	sister f.
w(a)	and
wāfag - yiwāfig	to agree
waga^{c} *- yūga*^{c} *(lā)*	to happen (to s.o.)
wagal	hopscotch m.
waggaṣ - yiwaggaṣ	to trim [stone]
wagt pl. *awgāt*	time m.
waḥdahin	on their f. own
waḥdiš	on your f.s. own
wahhaf - yiwahhif	to fan [a fire]
wāhimih	pregnant
waja^{c}	pain m.
waja^{c} *- yūja*^{c}	to hurt (s.o.)
wald pl. *awlād*	boy m.
wālidih pl. *-āt*	parturient f.
wallā	or
w-allāhi	by God!
warag al-gumār	cards
waragat al-milkih	wedding contract f.
waragih	leaf f.

wasaṭ / wasṭ	middle m.
wāsi^{c}	wide, broad
waṣṣal - yiwaṣṣul (lā)	to take (s.th., to)
wāṭī	low
wa^{c}y	awareness m.
wazīr pl. *wuzarā*	minister m.
wihim - yawham	to become pregnant
wilād	time after birth during which women visit the new mother m.
wilādih	birth f.
wizārih pl. *-āt*	ministry f.
wizwiz (^{c}alā)	to make fun (of s.o.)
wuga^{c} - yūga^{c}	to become; turn out
wulid - yūlad	to give birth; to be born
wusādih pl. *wasāyid*	mattress f.
xaḍab	antimony m.
xabar	information m.
(yiddī lih xabar)	he (will) let him know
xābar - yixābir	to talk (to s.o.)
xabbāz pl. *-īn*	baker m.
xabīr pl. *xubrih*	mate, friend m.
xaddar - yixaddir	to be doped up
xadījih	Khadija
xalag - yuxlug	to create (s.th.)
xalāṣ	that's it!
xalaṭ - yuxluṭ	to mix (s.th.)
xālatī	my [maternal] aunt f.
xālih pl. *xālāt*	mat. aunt f.
xallā - yixallī	to leave (s.th.); let (s.o.)
xallaṣ - yixalliṣ	to take off (s.th.)
xallāṭ pl. *-āt*	electric mixer m.
xamsīn	fifty
xarā	faeces m.
xaraj - yuxruj	to go out
xārij	outside
xārijī	outside adj.
xarraj - yixarrij	to take (s.th./s.o.) out
xarṣ pl. *axrāṣ*	earring m.
xašab / xšab	wood m.
xašabih	piece of wood f.
xāsir pl. *-īn*	loser m.
xaṣm pl. *xuṣūm*	opponent m.
xāṣum pl. *-īn*	opponent m.
xaṭab - yuxṭub	to engage (a woman)
xāṭam	ring m.
xaṭṭāṭ pl. *-īn*	sign maker m.
xaṭṭāṭuh pl. *-āt*	sign maker's shop f.
xayrāt	a lot
xazan - yixzin	to hold [e.g. heat]
xazwag	to make a hole
xazzan - yixazzin	to chew (*gāt*)
xazzān	chewing m.
xibrih	experience f.
ximār	loose black face veil covering all but the eyes m.

xirag	rags f.
xirī - yixrā	to defaecate
xisārih	loss; payment; f.
xisir - yixsir	to spend (s.th.)
xizānih pl. *xazāyin*	cistern; tank f.
xtalaf - yixtalif (ᶜan)	to differ (from s.th.)
xubz	flat round bread coll. m.
xubzih	a flat round bread f.
xuṭbuh	engagement f.
xuṭī - yuxṭā	to walk
xuṭṭ / xaṭṭ pl. *xuṭūṭ*	[telephone] line; line m.
xuṭūbuh	engagement f.
xuzaymih	[graveyard in Sanᶜā] f.
xuzgī pl. *xizgān*	hole m.
yā	[vocative particle]
yābis	dry
yad pl. *aydī*	hand f.
yā 'immā / yimmā … aw	either … or
y-allāh	come on!
yamanī	Yemeni m.
yamanī	Yemeni [dialect] f.
yamnih	right
yaᶜnī	i.e., that is to say
yā sᶜam	i.e., that is to say
yasrih	left
yawm al-jumᶜah	Friday
yawm aṣ-ṣabāḥ(īyih)	the day after the wedding night m.
yawmīyih / yawmī	daily
yawm ṯānī	the next day
yibis - yības	to become dry
yimkin	perhaps
yisallimiš	may he give you f.s. peace
yitḥākā	he speaks
yūnānī	Greek m.
zabaj - yizbij	to jest, joke
zabal	weariness; badness m.
zabīb	raisins coll. m.
zaff - yizaff	to accompany (a bride)
zaffāfih pl. *-āt*	woman who sings at weddings and makes the bride dance f.
zaggīnī … zaggaytak	pass to me and I'll pass to you! [name of a game]
zaġīr/zġīr	small; young
zaḥag - yizḥag	to crush (s.th.)
zaḥāwug	mixture of pulverised green chilli and tomato m.
zaᶜlān (ᶜalā)	sad; worried (about s.o.)
zalaṭ	money m.
zamān	time m.
zamīl pl. *zumalā*	colleague; friend m.
zamīlih pl. *-āt*	friend f.
zambih pl. *zamb*	date stone f.
zār - yuzūr	to visit
zaraᶜ - yizraᶜ	to cultivate
zārat + noun	some …

zārathīn	sometimes
zawāj pl. *-āt*	wedding m.
zawj pl. *azwāj*	husband m.
zawjīyih pl. *-āt*	pair f.
zawwaj - yizawwij	to get married
zawwaj fawgahā	he married [a wife] in addition to her
zāyid	increase
zayy	like prep.
zayyid - yizayyid	to increase (s.th.)
zayy-mā	as; like adjt.
zibādī	yoghurt m.
zibdih	butter f.
zid	again; more
zifāf	wedding procession to take bride to bridegroom m.
zigim - yizgam	to take; grab (s.th.)
zinnih pl. *zinan*	fitted women's dress f.; also loose full-length robe worn by men under *kūt* f.
*ziri*ᶜ *- yizra*ᶜ	to be cultivated
zirr	cloves coll. m.
ziyādih	a lot
ziyārih pl. *-āt*	visit f.
zugāg pl. *azgāg*	alley; lane m.
zuġayrī	small
zugzugī pl. *zagāzig*	alley; lane m.
zujāj	glass m.
zukkām / *zukām*	cold; flu m.

BIBLIOGRAPHY

Behnstedt, P. 'Zur Dialektgeographie des Nord-Jemen' pp. 261-288 in eds. Kopp H. and G. Schweizer *Jemen-Studien* vol. I *Entwicklungsprozesse in der Arabischen Republik Jemen*, Wiesbaden, 1984

Behnstedt, P. *Die nordjemenitischen Dialekte* vol. I *Atlas*, Wiesbaden, 1985

Jastrow, O. 'Zur Phonologie und Phonetik des Ṣan^{c}ānischen' pp. 289-304 in eds. Kopp H. and G. Schweizer *Jemen-Studien* vol. I *Entwicklungsprozesse in der Arabischen Republik Jemen*, Wiesbaden, 1984

Naim-Sanbar, S. 'Les performatifs explicites et le "présent" d'allocution paroles yéménites' in *Langage et Société*, no. 66, pp. 41-61, 1993

Naim-Sanbar, S. 'Contribution a l'étude de l'accent yéménite: Le parler des femmes de l'ancienne génération' in *Zeitschrift Arabische Linguistik*, vol. 27, pp. 67-89, 1994

Piamenta, M. *Dictionary of Post-Classical Yemeni Arabic*, 2 parts, Leiden, 1990 and 1991

Rossi, E. *L'Arabo Parlato a Ṣan^{c}ā'*, Rome, 1939

Watson, J.C.E. *A Syntax of Ṣan^{c}ānī Arabic*, Wiesbaden, 1993

INDEX